Galileo Galilei

Other titles in the Inventors and Creators series include:

Galileo Galilei

P.M. Boekhoff and Stuart A. Kallen

KIDHAVEN
PRESS™

THOMSON

GALE

San Diego • Detroit • New York • San Francisco • Cleveland
New Haven, Conn. • Waterville, Maine • London • Munich

© 2004 by KidHaven Press. KidHaven Press is an imprint of The Gale Group, Inc., a division of Thomson Learning, Inc.

KidHaven™ and Thomson Learning™ are trademarks used herein under license.

For more information, contact
KidHaven Press
27500 Drake Rd.
Farmington Hills, MI 48331-3535
Or you can visit our Internet site at http://www.gale.com

LIBRARY OF CONGRESS CATALOGING-IN-PUBLICATION DATA

Boekhoff, P.M. (Patti Marlene), 1957–
  Galileo Galilei / by P.M. Boekhoff and Stuart A. Kallen.
    p. cm.—(Inventors and creators)
Summary: Discusses the early childhood, education, interests, and inventions of Galileo, as well as how his studies led to conflict with the Church and tradition. Includes bibliographical references and index.
  ISBN 0-7377-1891-9 (hardback : alk. paper)
  1. Galilei, Galileo, 1564–1642—Juvenile literature 2. Astronomers—Italy—Biography—Juvenile literature. 3. Physicists—Italy—Biography—Juvenile literature. [1. Galileo, 1564–1642. 2. Scientists.] I. Title. II. Series.
  QB36.G2B588 2004
  520'.92—dc22

                             2003016250

Printed in the United States of America

Contents

Chapter One

The Scientific Method

Galileo Galilei is one of the most famous astronomers the world has ever known, but he was so much more. Galileo was a teacher, mathematician, author, and philosopher who overcame strong opposition while changing the way the world looks at the stars and planets.

Galileo was born in Pisa, Italy, on February 15, 1564. He was the oldest of seven children. His mother, Giulia, was well educated, which was unusual for women at that time in Europe. His father, Vincenzo, was a music teacher and a lute player. Vincenzo taught Galileo to draw and paint and play the lute. His father also taught him to draw in **perspective,** using mathematical ideas to make realistic pictures. He decided he wanted to be a painter when he grew up. He also showed an early talent for invention by making little mechanical toys.

Galileo learned from his father to experiment with new ideas using mathematics. For example, in the 1500s, musicians followed strict mathematical rules for composing music. Musicians stuck to these rules, believing it was the only way to make music. Vincenzo argued that the rules were created when musical instruments were much simpler. He experimented on the strings of his newer instruments and created wonderful new melodies by breaking the old rules.

Galileo's father thought other musicians should try to write new kinds of music as well. He wrote a letter to his music teacher Zarlino, a master of ancient musical ideas. Zarlino would not listen to Vincenzo's modern ideas, but

Galileo was talented in many areas from an early age.

The frontispiece (shown here) of *Dialogs of Ancient and Modern Music,* a book written by Galileo's father Vincenzo.

Vincenzo published them anyway, in a book called *Dialogs of Ancient and Modern Music*. A **dialogue** is a conversation, and in his book Vincenzo compared the old and new ideas by presenting them as two sides of a conversation. Galileo learned from his father not to be afraid of presenting new ideas.

Questioning His Teachers

Galileo's father came from a noble family that had once been rich but had lost its wealth. Despite their poverty, Vincenzo paid expensive tutors to give Galileo the education of a nobleman. When Galileo was eleven years old his family moved to Florence, and he was sent to study at a Jesuit Catholic **monastery.** Galileo decided he wanted to be a monk, but his father wanted him to become a doctor so he could support his younger brother and sisters.

When Galileo was seventeen years old, his father sent him to the University of Pisa to study medicine. At the university, Galileo was taught to memorize ancient ideas, such as those of Greek philosopher Aristotle, and repeat them in front of the class. Students were not supposed to question these ideas or think of new ideas. Galileo noticed that when new facts showed that these ideas were wrong, the facts were simply ignored.

Galileo questioned so many accepted ideas, his teachers and the other students nicknamed him Wrangler, which means a person who quarrels. Galileo had been encouraged by his father to experiment and believe in his own **observations,** even when they were different from what books said.

The Law of the Pendulum

When Galileo was nineteen years old, he made an observation that led to an invention. He watched a chandelier swinging back and forth like a **pendulum**. He noticed that it kept a steady rhythm just like his own pulse. Galileo went back to his room and made a pendulum and timed it again and again. Galileo discovered the Law of the Pendulum—the time it takes a pendulum to swing back and forth depends upon the length of the string.

Galileo adjusted the length of the pendulum until it swung back and forth in exactly the same time as his pulse rate. Different pulse rates could be measured by changing the length of the pendulum. Galileo had invented a machine for doctors to use to measure the pulse rate of patients. Many doctors began to use it, and later scientists used it to invent more accurate clocks.

Galileo was supposed to be studying to become a doctor at Pisa, but he was really interested in math and science, so he studied them instead. A professor of medicine made thirty times as much money as a professor of math and science, however, so his father disapproved. Galileo asked his teacher Ostilio Ricci, a mathematician of a noble family called the Medicis, to convince his father to let him study math. Vincenzo allowed Galileo to study math, though he was still enrolled as a medical student.

Professor at Pisa

In 1585 Galileo left school without finishing and continued to study math at home. Soon Galileo began to teach math to local students, and he became known as a math

Galileo (on right) watches a chandelier swing back and forth.
This leads to the discovery of the Law of the Pendulum.

expert. With the help of his powerful friend the mathematician Guidobaldo del Monte, Galileo was hired as a professor at the University of Pisa at the age of twenty-five. In his classes Galileo taught his students to observe and do scientific experiments. This was very different from the way students were taught at the time.

By dropping different-sized objects off the Leaning Tower of Pisa, Galileo showed that objects of different weights fall at the same speed.

Galileo taught math at the University of Pisa from 1589 until 1592, when he was twenty-eight years old. During this time Galileo wrote a short book called *On Motion*, which was never published. The book was based on his experiments dropping objects of different weights from the Leaning Tower of Pisa. He discovered the Law of Falling Objects, that two balls of unequal weight fall at the same speed.

Most professors taught Aristotle's idea that an object twice as heavy will fall twice as fast. Galileo's experiments proved that Aristotle's ideas about falling objects were wrong. Soon Galileo's enemies multiplied, and they packed the auditorium to hiss and boo when he gave his lectures. By the end of his three-year teaching contract, Galileo wisely decided to leave the university.

During the year 1592, Galileo almost fell into poverty. But before the year was over, he was rescued yet again by powerful friends. They helped him get a job at the University of Padua, about one hundred miles from Florence. Galileo was so poor he could not afford a carriage ride. He had to walk from Florence to Padua to start his new job.

Professor at Padua

At the University of Padua, professors were allowed to explore new ideas. Galileo was very happy there. He soon published his new ideas and became widely known as a brilliant scientist. Galileo wrote about how and why things happened. His writings about machines and military structures were copied and sent to universities and royal courts all over Europe.

Galileo developed many new ideas while teaching at the University of Padua.

Galileo sold telescopes to wealthy merchants in Venice.

Galileo's Italy

Padua

Venice

Pisa

Florence

Mediterranean Sea

Rome

Galileo was born in Pisa in 1564.

In 1611, Galileo went to Rome to get the Catholic Church's support for his discoveries.

As a young teenager, Galileo studied to be a monk at a monastery in Florence.

In 1597 he invented an instrument called a military compass. Soldiers used it to figure out the path of weapon fire and the height of fortress walls. Engineers used it to help them build buildings. Wealthy people all wanted one as a status symbol. So Galileo let an instrument maker and his family move into his house and make three hundred of them. People came from all over Europe to have Galileo teach them how to use the new invention.

Galileo continued to compare his own observations to the scientific ideas in the books he read. He read the works of ancient writers such as Ptolemy, who believed that the Sun, the Moon, the planets, and the stars all revolved around Earth. He also read newer books by writers such as Nicolaus Copernicus, who believed that Earth and the planets revolved around the Sun. These two opposing views of the universe were the cause of great public wrangling in the universities, and Galileo soon stepped into the biggest argument of his life.

Chapter Two

The Starry Messenger

Galileo learned to experiment and use mathematics to test accepted ideas when he was very young. But some ideas were very difficult to test and prove in this way. Astronomers used very complicated mathematics to find out how the planets moved, and they argued about the position of Earth and the Sun.

Galileo began to believe in the controversial ideas of astronomer Nicolaus Copernicus, who argued that Earth travels around the Sun. These ideas were not approved by the church. The church thought that Earth stood at the center of the universe. Galileo knew that it would be foolish to argue about this unless he could prove it mathematically first.

Copernicus had waited until the end of his life, in 1543, to publish his theory. He did not want to be accused of **heresy,** questioning the truth of the Bible, a very serious crime against the Catholic Church. Galileo was a Catholic and a religious man. He did not want to defy Catholicism. If Galileo opposed the Catholic Church without proving his view was true, he knew he would be accused of heresy.

So Galileo taught his students at the university the old ideas along with the new. He shared a house near the university with some of his students and the instrument makers who helped him to build his inventions. Marina Gamba, who became the mother of his three children, lived a short walk away from his house. In 1600 his daughter Virginia was born, and his second daughter, Livia, was born in 1601. His son, Vincenzio, was born in

Astronomer Nicolaus Copernicus argued that the Earth travels around the Sun.

1606. The children lived with their mother while Galileo devoted his life to science.

The Telescope

In 1608 Galileo heard about an invention that would change science forever: the spyglass, later known as the telescope. Galileo set to work to improve upon the design and soon made the most powerful telescope in the world. Galileo used his math skills to design better shapes for telescope lenses, making objects in his telescopes appear larger than in other telescopes of the time. In a letter to a friend, Galileo wrote, "I give infinite thanks to God who has been pleased to make me the first Observer of Marvelous Things."[1]

Galileo showed his telescope to powerful merchants in Venice, who were amazed at the sights it allowed them to see. Soon many people wanted one of Galileo's telescopes. He hired a man to make them, and soon many people were looking through his new magnifying invention. Galileo continued to make his telescopes more and more powerful.

Galileo turned his most powerful telescope toward the heavens in January 1610. Suddenly, hundreds of stars he had never seen before magically appeared in the night sky. He saw that the Milky Way is made of stars, and he observed the difference between stars and planets. He noticed the great difference in the size of planets and stars and that the stars are much farther away from Earth.

Galileo saw that planets and other objects in space such as the Moon are not perfectly round and smooth as the followers of Aristotle thought. Through his telescopes

Galileo's Telescope

Galileo's first telescopes were a simple type called a refractor, like this one shown here. These types of telescopes are still in use today.

1 Light enters through the front of the telescope.

4 The eyepiece magnifies the focused image for the eye to see.

2 A convex lens bends the light rays toward the focal point.

3 The light rays focus at the focal point and form an image.

he saw steep, rugged mountains and valleys on the Moon, something like the ones on Earth. When Galileo turned his telescope to Jupiter, he discovered four moons revolving around it.

Galileo wrote to his brother-in-law: "Some of the nobles and senators, although of great age, mounted more than once to the top of the highest church tower in order to see sails and shipping that were so far off that it was two hours before they were seen, without my spyglass, steering full into the harbor."[2]

SIDEREVS
NVNCIVS
MAGNA, LONGEQVE ADMIRABILIA
Spectacula pandens, fufpiciendaque proponens
vnicuique, præfertim verò

PHILOSOPHIS, atǫ *ASTRONOMIS, quæ à*

GALILEO GALILEO
PATRITIO FLORENTINO
Patauini Gymnafij Publico Mathematico

PERSPICILLI
*Nuper à fe reperti beneficio funt obferuata in LVNÆ FACIE, FIXIS IN-
NVMERIS, LACTEO CIRCVLO, STELLIS NEBVLOSIS,
Apprime verò in*

QVATVOR PLANETIS
Circa IOVIS Stellam difparibus interuallis, atque periodis, celeri-
tate mirabili circumuolutis; quos, nemini in hanc vfque
diem cognitos, nouiffimè Author depræ-
hendit primus; atque

MEDICEA SIDERA
NVNCVPANDOS DECREVIT.

VENETIIS, Apud Thomam Baglionum. **M DC X.**

Superiorum Permiffu, & Priuilegio.

The frontispiece of *The Starry Messenger* (Sidereus Nuncius),
a book written by Galileo explaining what he saw through
his telescope.

The Starry Messenger

In March 1610 Galileo wrote a book called *The Starry Messenger*, revealing what he saw through his telescope. He included maps of the heavens and drawings of the mountains of the Moon that he made himself. Galileo hurried to publish his book immediately, so he could be the first to take credit for the discoveries. The pages of the book were full of corrections and additions made while it was being published, and the final edition included slips of paper with last-minute changes.

The Starry Messenger was an immediate success. Copies of the book traveled quickly throughout Europe. Galileo's telescope and the things he claimed to see with it shattered old beliefs. Many scientists had to wait for a telescope from Galileo before they could see what he saw. Many supporters of the old view of the heavens refused to look through Galileo's powerful telescope. They thought Galileo was trying to fool them.

Many of the people who read *The Starry Messenger* and looked through one of his powerful telescopes became inspired. Galileo sent gifts of a telescope and a copy of his new book to all the kings and princes of Europe. Galileo dedicated *The Starry Messenger* to the Medicis, the most powerful supporters of new ideas in science and art. They were also the rulers of Florence and Pisa, where he longed to return.

The Medicis named Galileo the chief philosopher and mathematician to the Medici court. Galileo would be able to live in Florence and be given more money than ever to continue his studies. He named the moons of Jupiter the Medicean Stars after his new **patron** and ruler, Cosimo Medici II. Galileo would not have to teach or make scientific instruments to support himself anymore. He could devote all his time to studying new ideas and writing about them.

Discoveries in Florence

Galileo reached Florence in September 1610. He hoped to find the peace and freedom there to continue his studies. He wanted to write a book about the structure of the universe, as well as three new books about motion. He wanted to write about machines, light and colors, sound and speech, the movement of animals, and the movement of the ocean.

In Florence, Galileo saw what looked like two moons wavering in a path around Saturn. His telescope was not powerful enough to see that he had discovered not two moons, but rings of small meteors around Saturn.

Looking at the night sky through his magical instrument, Galileo saw that the planet Venus seemed to go through the same kind of changes as the Moon. It changed from a round circle to a half circle to a crescent shape. He had noticed earlier that Earth blocked part of the Sun's rays on the Moon as it revolved around the Sun. He thought this proved that Venus was not a star revolving around Earth, as most people thought, but a planet that revolves around the Sun.

The university officials at Pisa would not allow anyone to teach such ideas or even talk about them. Galileo

Galileo named Jupiter's four
moons (inset) after his patron and
ruler Cosimo Medici II (above).

had made many enemies, and they began to spread rumors that he was a heretic who questioned the Bible. Being a religious man, and afraid of being labeled a heretic, Galileo went to Rome to gain the approval of the Catholic Church for his work. The Catholic Church, and its leader the pope, were the most important rulers of the time. Galileo had shown the wonders of the night sky to all the rulers of Europe, and now he wanted the pope himself to see them.

Chapter Three

The Catholic Scientist

Galileo believed strongly in his ideas, and he believed that he could teach others to believe in them, too. He thought that he had very strong evidence that his ideas were true. And he thought that the truths of science and religion could exist together peacefully.

Galileo believed that his ideas did not compete with the church or the Bible. He believed that truth could be found in nature and in the Bible at the same time. He did not think that religion was for teaching science or that science was for teaching religion. He thought they should be kept separate. He agreed with his friend Cardinal Baronius that the purpose of the Bible is to "teach us how one goes to heaven, not how heaven goes."[3]

Galileo wanted the pope's astronomers in Rome to approve of and support his discoveries. He thought that if he could gain the support of the highest rulers, his enemies would stop trying to hurt his reputation. He arrived in Rome in 1611 and was treated very well by high-ranking church officials and politicians. They were very pleased when he showed them what he had observed.

Galileo explains his ideas to a Catholic monk. Galileo believed that the truths of science and religion could coexist.

Galileo even gave one of his most powerful telescopes to the pope and spent several nights teaching him how to use it. The pope showed him great kindness, and many church officials, including the pope, began to believe in his ideas. Galileo even convinced some of the strongest believers in Aristotle to look at the night sky through the telescope.

Academy of the Lynx

While giving his talks in Rome, Galileo met and became friends with Prince Frederico Cesi, who had set up a club, or society, to support the growth of science. The group was called the Academy of the Lynx, or the Lincean Academy, named after the lynx because the animal has such good eyesight. The academy was the first scientific society in the world. It helped scientists to share ideas and test each others' experiments by careful observation.

Galileo joined Cesi's academy, and the two men began to write letters to each other. Through the Academy of the Lynx, Galileo's ideas became known to scientists throughout Europe. Galileo's fame attracted other great scientists to the academy, and the academy began to publish Galileo's ideas. Members of the Academy of the Lynx became Galileo's most powerful supporters.

Instruments used by Galileo in his daily work.

Back to Florence

When Galileo returned to Florence, he argued with some scientists and religious leaders who urged the church to investigate him for heresy. Meanwhile, in 1613, Galileo brought his two daughters to live in a convent near his house. His son remained with his mother. In March of that year, he received a letter from his friend Father Benedetto Castelli, saying that some professors in Florence told the Grand Duchess Christina of Lorraine that Galileo's teachings went against the Bible.

The grand duchess was the mother of Galileo's patron, Grand Duke Cosimo of Tuscany, so Galileo decided to explain his ideas to her. In a letter to the

Church officials at the Vatican in Rome order Galileo not to discuss his idea that the Earth travels around the Sun.

duchess, Galileo explained that his ideas did not disagree with the Bible and that the people who said they did were just jealous of him. He also pointed out that science and religion were two very different things. Copies of the letter were passed among Galileo's enemies. His enemies chose to use some of his words in ways that made him look bad, so Galileo decided to go back to Rome to explain his ideas in person.

But in Rome his enemies were already talking about calling a hearing of the **Inquisition** on his theories. The Inquisition had the power to accuse, judge, and execute people who were suspected of heresy. People who appeared before the Inquisition were considered guilty unless they could prove they were innocent, and that rarely happened. But Galileo felt certain that the church would support him when he proved to them that what he was saying was true. He felt that religion and science could work side by side in harmony.

Arguing with the Pope

Galileo went to Rome in December 1615. The grand duke of Florence sent letters of support to Rome to smooth the way for his visit. Church officials treated him with great respect during his three-month stay. Once again, Galileo gave talks about his ideas and showed people how to use a telescope. He gave a great show and attracted large crowds wherever he went.

But he also made fun of respected scholars, who became very angry and reported details of his activities to the Inquisition. For nearly two months, officials of the

Inquisition questioned scholars and other church officials about Galileo and his teachings.

When Galileo was called by the Inquisition to speak to Cardinal Bellarmine, he thought he would be allowed to explain his ideas. Instead, he was told that the pope had ordered him not to say or write that Earth travels around the Sun. Galileo was very disappointed because he had been planning to write a book about it.

Through his powerful friends, Galileo arranged to talk to the pope in person to try to convince him to change his mind. The pope treated him with kindness but would not change his mind. Galileo was discouraged, but he did not give up trying to convince the church that his ideas were true.

The Assayer

When he returned to Florence, Galileo's friends convinced him that life would be easier if he studied something else. Galileo began to study the ocean. He found that by observing the changing shadows on Jupiter's moons, sailors could figure out their longitude, or how far east or west they had traveled. He tried, without much success, to find a way to keep a telescope steady enough to see the shadows on Jupiter's moons from a ship that was being rolled and tossed by the sea. He also worked on theories about why the tides rise and fall.

Then, in 1618, three new comets appeared in the sky. Although Galileo was ill and did not observe the comets, he responded to their appearance by secretly helping his student Mario Guiducci to write and publish *A Discourse*

Cardinal Maffeo Barberini supported Galileo and encouraged him to write *The Assayer.*

on Comets. Galileo's friend Cardinal Maffeo Barberini showed support for these ideas. Feeling encouraged, Galileo wrote a book called *The Assayer.*

An assayer is a person who weighs metals, using mathematics to determine how much gold, lead, or other metals they contain. In *The Assayer,* Galileo claimed that the way to understand comets and other objects of nature is through mathematics. In his book, Galileo ridiculed the Jesuit priest Orazio Grassi for trying to explain comets by relying on Aristotle's ideas instead of weighing out the evidence himself.

But Galileo based his own theories about comets on those of Aristotle. He had not observed a comet himself since his childhood. Like Aristotle, he thought comets were only appearances, like the Sun's rays reflected on the sea or in the clouds, not real physical things. Comets are very real chunks of dirt and ice hurtling through space.

The Assayer, published by the Academy of the Lynx, was very funny, clever, and popular. Meanwhile, Galileo was overjoyed when his friend Cardinal Maffeo Barberini became the new pope. Galileo and his friends at the academy immediately wrote a long letter dedicating *The Assayer* to the new pope.

Barberini, or Pope Urban VIII as he was named, was very pleased and was proud to protect the Academy of the Lynx and Galileo's wonderful writing. In 1624 the pope even gave Galileo permission to write a book about the two conflicting schools of thought, Earth-centered versus the Sun-centered universe, in the form of a dialogue. Because a dialogue is a conversation, his ideas would be presented as possible beliefs—opinions—instead of facts.

This still did not change the decision of the church from 1616, however. Galileo was still not allowed to teach his ideas as truth. But Galileo had waited for twenty years to write his book, and he felt encouraged by his friend. Once again, he felt he had reason to hope that science and religion could go hand in hand. He returned to Florence in June to begin work on the *Dialog*.

Chapter Four

New Sciences

Galileo was encouraged by the support he gained in Rome. Although he still had many enemies, he felt that his friend the pope could protect him. He had waited many years to write about the Earth-centered versus Sun-centered universe, and now he felt he had permission.

Galileo began writing his book, *Dialog Concerning the Two Chief World Systems*, in 1624. He wrote it as a conversation between three characters. One person supports Aristotle's world system, one supports the views of Copernicus, and the third person is the one they are each trying to convince of their views. The dialogue allowed Galileo to write about many ideas without saying that any one idea was true.

Galileo finished writing his book in January 1630. Like all other books at the time, Galileo's had to be approved by the Catholic Church. So Galileo sent his manuscript to Rome, where the editors made sure it did not contain any heresy. The church mathematicians and the Inquisition approved the book with only small changes. Galileo dedicated the book to the pope, who offered his protection to Galileo. The pope himself directed the writing of the **preface,** and the book was printed on February 21, 1632.

When *Dialog Concerning the Two Chief World System*s was published, it was sold-out immediately. In Galileo's time, most books about important subjects were written in Latin and could be understood only by a small number of highly educated people. But Galileo wrote his *Dialog* in Italian, so more people were able to read it. And

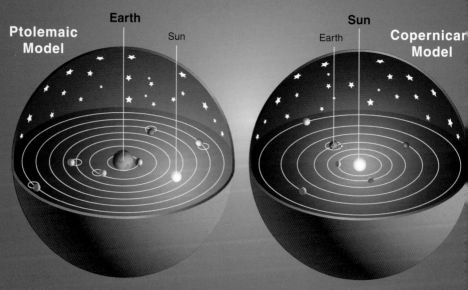

The Universe:
Ptolemaic Versus Copernican

Ptolemaic Model — Earth — Sun

Copernican Model — Sun — Earth

The Ptolemaic Model was based on Aristotle's view of the universe. It was a sphere of stars with the Earth at the center. The Sun, planets, and sphere of stars all revolved around the Earth.

In the mid 1500s, Nicolaus Copernicus proposed that the Sun, not the Earth, was the center of the solar system. The Copernican Model was accepted scienc until modern times.

his writing was funny and easy to understand, so the book became very popular.

A Very Popular Science Book

Galileo became very famous, and people everywhere were talking about the planets and the stars. Because such arguments usually were understood only by mathematicians and astronomers in the universities, they usually had very little effect on the ideas of ordinary people. Suddenly more people knew what the argument was about. Galileo's book encouraged more people to discover the world through their own experiences.

Galileo's book caused trouble for the teachers who taught the old view. Many of them opposed it. This caused trouble for the Catholic Church, which controlled the schools. And the pope already had trouble brewing with other challenges to his authority. Urban VIII began to see Galileo's book as yet another threat to his power. And he thought that Galileo had made fun of some of his ideas in the book. So, in 1632, Urban banned the book, but it was too late. The booksellers had no books left to return to the pope.

Suddenly, everybody tried to buy copies of the book to keep them out of the hands of the Inquisition, which would have destroyed them. The price of the book skyrocketed to ten or twelve times the original price. And it was already being translated into Latin and other languages to be distributed throughout Europe. Because his book was so popular, Galileo was in trouble. He was called to appear before the highest ruler of the land, the pope himself.

Galileo appears before the Inquisition in 1633.

The Sentence

In 1633 seventy-year-old Galileo made the two-hundred-mile trip to Rome for the last time. As he rested in the home of the Medicean **ambassador,** Galileo felt confident. He learned that he would be charged with tricking the church into granting him permission to publish the *Dialog*. He was confident he had done no wrong and could prove it. But as the trial began on April 12, Galileo's confidence turned to fear.

The Inquisition presented an unsigned note from Cardinal Bellarmine to Galileo. The note said Galileo was never allowed to talk about his ideas either as truth or as opinion. Galileo said he had never been told this. Finally,

Galileo was found guilty of heresy. After the trial, some judges visited him and told him if he confessed, it would go easier for him. Rather than face torture and possible death, Galileo agreed to confess to the crime of heresy.

Galileo was sentenced by the Inquisition to spend the rest of his life alone under house arrest, locked in his

Sister Maria Celeste (inset), Galileo's daughter Virginia, was happy her father's trials had ended and he could spend the rest of his life at home (below).

house under guard. He would not be allowed to speak or write about Earth moving around the Sun. Galileo was disappointed that, in the end, the church refused to see things his way. But he was happy to be allowed to go back home, and his daughters were happy that his trials had ended. His devoted daughter Virginia wrote: "Nor are your daughters alone in our rejoicing, but all these nuns, by their grace, give signs of true happiness, just as so many of them have sympathized with me in my suf-

Galileo discusses his ideas with his son.

fering."[4] Their rejoicing did not last for long, however. Three months after Galileo returned home, Virginia died at the age of thirty-three.

Two New Sciences

Living alone under house arrest, Galileo began to write about all of his observations of motion. His new book was called *Discourses on Two New Sciences*. A **discourse** is a long, formal expression of ideas about a subject. This book was more technical than his last book and harder to understand. In his *Discourses*, he explained some details of his past work, such as the math used to compute the speed at which objects fall and how friction causes objects to move more slowly. He formed the First Law of Motion, called **inertia,** which explains why a ball keeps rolling after it is pushed and why it eventually stops rolling.

Galileo was afraid his *Discourses* would never be published because he was not allowed to leave his house and no one was allowed to come see him. "It is easy to see," he wrote to a friend, "that every effort is being made to remove all memory of me from the world."[5]

But as Galileo grew older and more frail, a few people were allowed to visit him. In 1638 when Galileo was seventy-four years old, his friend Prince Matti de' Medici smuggled the manuscript of his *Discourses* out of the house. It was printed in Holland, a country that was not controlled by the Catholic Church. That year, blindness and illness forced Galileo to stop working on his experiments.

The Vatican (shown here) is the headquarters of the Catholic Church. The church pardoned Galileo in 1992.

Galileo died on January 8, 1642. He never saw his ideas accepted, but they are now considered basic to modern science. Three hundred fifty years later, on October 31, 1992, the leaders of the Catholic Church pardoned Galileo and admitted that his opinions about the motion of Earth were true.

Galileo's ideas lived on in his writings, and many of his students became great scientists. And Galileo's work eventually inspired Isaac Newton to continue to answer questions about motion. While he was alive, Galileo inspired others to actively observe and do experiments, an inspiration that continues to this day.

Notes

Chapter Two: *The Starry Messenger*

1. Quoted in Elma Ehrlich Levinger, *Galileo: First Observer of Marvelous Things*. New York: Julian Messner, 1952, p. 76.
2. Quoted in Levinger, *Galileo*, p. 77.

Chapter Three: The Catholic Scientist

3. Quoted in Stillman Drake, *Discoveries and Opinions of Galileo*. New York: Doubleday, 1957, p. 186.

Chapter Four: New Sciences

4. Quoted in Dava Sobel, *Letters to Father*. New York: Walker, 2001, p. 377.
5. Quoted in Bern Dibner and Stillman Drake, *A Letter from Galileo*. Norwalk, CT: Burndy Library, 1967, p. 55.

Glossary

ambassador: A person who lives in a separate country from the one he is a citizen of and represents his government in the second country.

dialogue: A conversation between two or more people.

discourse: A long, formal conversation about a subject.

heresy: A belief or idea different from beliefs or ideas considered to be absolutely true by the Roman Catholic Church.

inertia: The tendency of a body at rest to remain at rest or of a body in motion to stay in motion unless acted on by an outside force.

Inquisition: A movement within the Catholic Church that included courts, investigations, and torture set up to keep religious thought uniform. Those tried for heresy were often coerced into confessing guilt to avoid torture.

monastery: A place where a community of people, especially monks or nuns, promise to live within the rules of a religious life, often apart from social contact with others.

observation: The act of watching something carefully and making notes about it.

patron: An influential or wealthy person who supported and protected someone in exchange for certain services.

pendulum: A suspended object that swings freely back

and forth under the influence of gravity, often used in clocks.

perspective: A mathematical way of drawing objects on a flat surface so they seem to have depth.

preface: An opening statement introducing a book that explains its viewpoint or purpose, usually written by the author.

For Further Exploration

Mike Goldsmith, *Scientists Who Made History: Galileo Galilei.* New York: Raintree Steck-Vaughn, 2001. Galileo's life story and his key discoveries in astronomy, physics, and mathematics and how they still affect us today.

Jacqueline Mitton, *What's Their Story: Galileo.* New York: Oxford University Press, 1997. Galileo earned a place in history by observing the skies through a telescope and using his observations to sweep away old ideas about the universe.

Steve Parker, *Science Discoveries: Galileo and the Universe.* New York: HarperCollins, 1992. Tells the story of the life and discoveries of seventeenth-century astronomer, physicist, and mathematician Galileo Galilei.

Michael White, *Galileo Galilei: Inventor, Astronomer, and Rebel.* Woodbridge, CT: Blackbirch Press, 1999. This biography describes the life and work of Galileo in the context of Europe in the seventeenth century.

Index

Picture Credits

About the Authors

P.M. Boekhoff is an author of more than twenty-five nonfiction books for children. She has written about history, science, and the lives of creative people. In addition, P.M. Boekhoff is an artist who has created murals and theatrical scenic paintings and has illustrated many book covers. In her spare time, she paints, draws, writes poetry, and studies herbal medicine.

Stuart A. Kallen is the author of more than 150 nonfiction books for children and young adults. He has written on topics ranging from the theory of relativity to the history of rock and roll. In addition, Mr. Kallen has written award-winning children's videos and television scripts. In his spare time, Stuart A. Kallen is a singer/songwriter/guitarist in San Diego, California.

Refreshed and the cars filled with gas, the Redingtons continued their travel north on the rough, newly built Alcan Highway. The Alcan had already taken them through the northern reaches of the Rocky Mountains and rolling hills of spruce and birch forests in the interior of Canada and now into Alaska. This road was built during World War II to carry supplies from the contiguous United States to what was the Territory of Alaska. It was finished in 1942 and civilians had been using it for only a short time. The door to Alaska was now opened to the world. The Redingtons were not the only ones traveling north. Quite a number of war veterans also moved to the Last Frontier along this road of potholes and huge rocks.

Joe's preparedness for this trip turned out to be a blessing. There must have been some pretty heavy rains just before they got to one particular creek, because the bridge was totally washed out, and they couldn't ford it with their jeeps.

Joe and Ray stood on the bank of the swollen creek scratching their heads.

"Well, there's only one thing to do," Joe said.

Turning around, he began to dig in the back of his trailer. He hauled out his axe, some nails, and rope. Together he and Ray started to work, building a makeshift bridge. Vi made lunch for everyone while Joee and Tommy played. There were plenty of trees, so before very long Joe and Ray had their rough bridge built and were on their way again.

The Alcan wound through the Alaska Range and Wrangell Mountains, past majestic glaciers, towering, rugged mountains, crystal clear streams, and silt-filled glacial rivers. Then the road snaked through the Talkeetna Mountains to the north and the Chugach Mountains to the south. The Matanuska River poured out from the mouth of an ancient winding glacier. The river braided itself across the valley floor until it twisted and turned into the beautiful, wide Matanuska-Susitna Valley.

Everyone was so happy. Joee was happy because it was his fifth birthday. And Joe, Ray, and Vi because they had finally arrived at their new home. The day was June 2, 1948. They had been on the road now for twenty days.

The U.S. Agricultural Department had just opened up a new area near the old community of Knik for homesteading. Joe had $18 to his name. He couldn't afford the 160-acre homestead, so he bought as much land as he could afford—101 acres for $13. That left $5 to purchase fuel and food for the winter.

They drove out the old narrow wagon trail to Old Knik. Joe's land was thirteen miles south of the small railroad-stop community of Wasilla.

During the early 1900s Knik was the earliest, busiest, and largest trading port in Cook Inlet. From there a freighting trail led to Interior Alaska.

Vi picking high bush cranberries that were in abundance in the Knik area.

The trail came into existence after 1908, when gold had been discovered at Iditarod. In 1911 the Federal Government set up a mail run between Seward, an ice-free port, and Nome, using the same trail. As a result, Knik grew into a town of 500 in the summer and 1,000 in the winter.

"The first mail arrived in Knik from Iditarod after seventeen days on the trail," recorded Orville George Herning, who built a trading post in Knik in 1905.

And one of his last recordings of gold stated, "The Iditarod Gold Team came into Knik with 3,400 pounds of gold, hauled by forty-six dogs." In 1917 he moved his store to the growing railroad town of Wasilla, right near the railroad depot, which is still in the same spot today.

By 1948, when the Redingtons arrived, only about fifteen deteriorating buildings remained of the gold rush days in Knik and only a few families remained in the area. The majority of the small population lived near the train stop in Wasilla.

On the Redingtons second day in Knik, Joe shot a bear. Now they had meat. This bear must have been eating lots of berries and roots that spring because Joe said, "The meat was very sweet and tasty." In the fall when the bears are feeding on fish, the meat is not very good at all. So, with good food for their stomachs, they set about deciding where and how to build their two new homes.

Before long, some neighbors came to the Redington campsite and gave them a hundred pounds of potatoes and more dogs to breed. Then a family, who had just started homesteading near them, brought them a big box of food staples from Teeland's General Store in Wasilla. Helping your neighbor and being neighborly was a way of life in Alaska. Joe fit right in.

The mosquitoes almost carried them away that first summer. They had to wear head nets when they went out in the woods. Despite those pesky biting bugs, Joe had his first cabin entirely built in thirty days.

As Joe was building his house, he thought running water in the cabin sounded like a swell idea. So he built two rooms, more or less. One room was four feet higher than the other and sat directly over a cool, clear spring.

"I had a big spring," chuckled Joe, "and I run a six-inch pipe inside into a big wooden barrel, a fifty-five gallon barrel. Then I run a pipe out and had runnin' water right in the kitchen." Now this was living. The log house was crude, but it was a cabin all the same and would keep Cathy and their three children warm.

After Cathy arrived they called their place Raven's Roost.

Ray and Vi called their place Rainbow Ranch, because as Vi said, "We were always seein' rainbows and double rainbows from our house."

A month after Joe and Ray's arrival, their dad and a friend arrived. Everyone called Jim Redington, Granddaddy. Granddaddy had purchased forty acres of land adjacent to Joe's and soon began clearing his land by hand and building his own cabin. Now there were three new cabins in sunny Knik.

Much too quickly fall was upon them. The fireweed blossoms were nearly bloomed out and the rich magenta seedpods were bursting open filling the air with little white parachutes spreading the word—prepare for winter.

As the temperatures crept lower and lower and snow covered the ground, Joe discovered a problem in their cabin. "One real bad one," said Joe, shaking his head. "Well, you learn by mistakes."

What Joe hadn't taken into account when building the cabin was that with all that running water in the house and low temperatures outside, came moisture and lots of it. The house was way too damp.

"I had to have two barrel stoves in there to keep the place warm."

The cabin was nice and warm and dry, but with it came more work. He had two hungry stoves that were continually crying out for more wood. That meant double loads of wood that needed to be cut, hauled, and stacked. To do this heavy work, Joe needed a sled. So he built one.

Joe took this picture a few years later in Knik. Milton and Cora Hoffman, Vi's parents, are having a good time visiting with the grand kids, Raymie, Shelia, Tommy, Joee, and Timmy. Cora played the organ at the local church in Knik for years.

"I went to the army dump and I found an airplane seat. I attached a pair of skis to the bottom. The seat had legs that had bolts to hold it to the airplane, so it had places to put the bolts. So I bolted the seat right to the skis and pulled the skis up and put a little bed on it between the front of the skis and the back of the seat and had the ski runners runnin' out to the back. In an hour I had a sled made. That was the first sled I had. It didn't hardly look like a sled, but I had nothin' to go by and it worked. I used it for years."

He then hooked up his sheepdogs to his new sled and they pulled the birch and spruce logs to the house to be cut into firewood.

"They didn't work out too good, but we used 'em all winter haulin' logs and things. The sheepdogs' hair matted with all the deep snow."

Joe continually had to pull the packed snowballs off their fur and from between their toes. Even with that problem, Joe somehow managed to keep both stoves stoked and water running in the cabin all winter. But oh, the work! He was glad to have the dogs. They were a big help.

Besides the everyday work of living, the Redingtons played lots of card games. Vi also wrote many long letters to her parents, Milton and Cora Hoffman, that first year.

The following year Vi's dad came to Knik and then her mom. "Dad missed me," she said. "I wrote such glowin' letters about Alaska and the homestead and the land, that they just had to come up. I don't think Mom was that keen on the idea. She thought it was like goin' to the moon!" But she came anyway.

Now the whole family was living in Alaska.

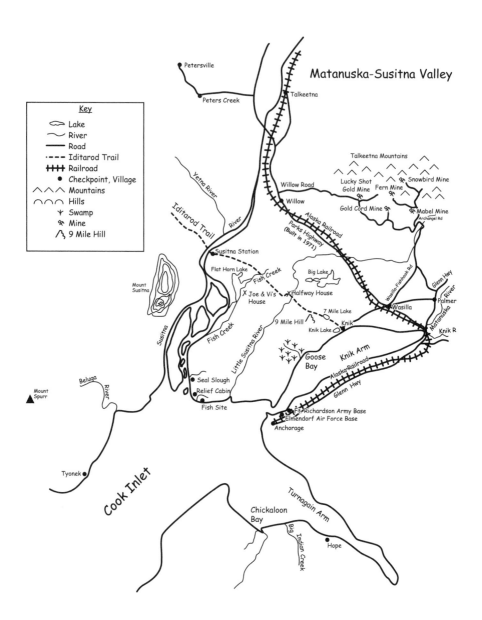

Key

⌒ Lake
〜 River
— Road
-·-·- Iditarod Trail
╫╫╫ Railroad
● Checkpoint, Village
︿︿︿ Mountains
◠◠◠ Hills
⅄ Swamp
⚒ Mine
⌂ 9 Mile Hill

Matanuska-Susitna Valley

Petersville

Talkeetna

Peters Creek

Talkeetna Mountains

Snowbird Mine

Lucky Shot
Gold Mine   Fern Mine

Willow Road

Yetna River

Willow   Gold Cord Mine   Mabel Mine
Archangel Rd

Iditarod Trail

River   Alaska Railroad

Parks Highway
(Built in 1971)

Susitna Station

Flat Horn Lake   Big Lake   Glenn Hwy

Fish Creek   Wasilla   Palmer

Mount
Susitna   X Joe & Vi's   X Halfway House
House   Wasilla-Fishhook Rd

7 Mile Lake   Matanuska River

9 Mile Hill   Knik   Knik R

Knik Lake

Susitna   Little Susitna River

Fish Creek   Goose   Knik Arm
Bay

Alaska Railroad

Beluga   Seal Slough
River   Relief Cabin   Glenn Hwy

Mount   Fish Site
Spurr
Ft. Richardson Army Base
Elmendorf Air Force Base
Anchorage

Tyonek

Cook Inlet

Turnagain Arm

Chickaloon
Bay
Big Indian Creek
Hope

CHAPTER 4

Alaska Sourdoughs

*A friend may well be reckoned
a masterpiece of nature.*

RALPH WALDO EMERSON

Joe was called a cheechako to some, for he was new to Alaska and had yet to experience its rugged challenges.

Lee Ellexson was just the opposite. He was an honest-to-goodness, true Alaska sourdough who had wrung a wealth of knowledge out of tough day-to-day living in this wild northern land. Lee was in his seventies when Joe met him in mid-October of his first year in Knik. Lee had a homestead on Knik Lake right close to where Joe lived. Lee and his wife ran the Happy River roadhouse in the early 1900s on the old Iditarod mail and freight trail and then the roadhouse in Knik. Lee was also the last mail carrier on the Iditarod Trail. It was Lee who opened the door for Joe to a whole new chapter of Alaska history.

During the long winter nights Joe and Cathy, Ray and Vi, and other neighbors would get together for a lively game of cards and lots of storytelling. Joe loved a good story and Lee had some dillies. Joe was all ears every time the two of them got together. He listened intently to Lee's stories of gold-mining, mushing dogs, carrying mail, and tales of survival in the cold depths of winter in early Alaska.

Joe was enthralled by the tough men and women who lived by the code of the North. This code was based on the simple Golden Rule, for without honesty and a brotherly helping hand, life in this untamed land could easily end in disaster.

When Lee told tales of the fiercely strong and tough Alaskan huskies, Joe was all ears. He eagerly stored every bit of learned wisdom Lee was passing on to him about the working dogs of the North. These ideas filled the storehouse of Joe's mind with dreams of possible adventures to come.

But for the time being, Joe had only one desire—that he, too, could mush his own dogs over this old freighting trail.

Lee told Joe that he carried mail and supplies by dog team from Knik to Rainy Pass beginning in October of each year. He would head out on a three-day trip that took him across frozen rivers, up and down the rugged Alaska Range foothills, and end at Rainy Pass. On his three-day return trip, he would carry out the miners' mail and the pokes of gold they had dug from Alaska's cold but wealthy land. He rested one day and then headed back to Rainy Pass. This he did until April when the break-up came. Spring in Alaska brought warm days and cold nights. Thick ice on the rivers and creeks weakened and began to break up. The trail thawed during the day, making pools of water and mud, then froze during the night, making an icy, often torturous trail. Travel by dog team became impossible. So Lee's dogs rested for five months. Come fall, Lee and his team were back on the Iditarod Trail, carrying gold, freight, and mail. His last mail run was in 1925.

Lee had seven aging malamutes, descendents of his original freighting team. "If I remember right," said Joe, "I think he told me his lead dog weighed 140 pounds. They were pretty old then," but not too old to still haul Lee trapping up the Little Susitna River, about halfway between Knik and the Susitna River, or to haul wood.

During one of Joe's visits, Lee told him about a cabin on the Little Susitna. He was using it now when he trapped. Lee called this log cabin the Halfway House. At one time it was a roadhouse. Travelers and gold seekers using the trail stopped to rest, get a good meal and warm place to stay, and then continue on their journey. Back in 1908 the Alaska Road Commission surveyed a trail they called the Seward to Nome Trail to carry mail and freight into the Interior and carry the gold out. Today it is called the Iditarod Trail. The roadhouses or relief cabins were built about twenty miles apart or as far as a man could walk on a good day.

Lee's invitation to go out to the Halfway House was one Joe simply couldn't refuse.

"You bet. When do we go?" asked Joe with a typical ring of enthusiasm in his voice.

Lee met Joe at Raven Roost with three of his veteran malamutes and his 12-foot double-ender toboggan, (a toboggan that can be pulled by dogs from either end). Turning a loaded sled around on the narrow trail was very difficult. With a double-ender it was much easier. The dogs could be unhitched from one end and rehitched to the other end of the sled and head back.

However, when they were getting ready to leave Joe's cabin and Lee was sitting on the toboggan to turn his dogs, they wouldn't turn. The malamutes decided they wanted to trot straight into Wasilla. Joe saw what was happening and without hesitation, jumped out in front of the team and turned them around. Just as quickly he scrambled onto the toboggan behind Lee and away they flew—one sourdough and one cheechako heading up the old trail that eventually led to the gold rush town of Iditarod.

This was Joe's first eighteen mile run with dogs on the almost forgotten trail. They mushed out to the Little Susitna Roadhouse and spent the night. The next day they headed back, bringing with them a load of logs roped to the toboggan. Joe and Lee rode atop them like they were riding a wooden horse. The narrow, overgrown trail had not been used for anything except for trapping in over twenty years, so they had to keep their legs tight against the logs or get pulled off by all the brush that seemed to grab out at them.

On the way back Joe asked how he could find more of this trail. Lee pointed out the blazed cuts on the trees and the ruts in the ground. The blaze, which was once a simple downward axe cut in the tree's bark, had grown over, leaving a deep, folded scar cut down the center of the tree with the two outside edges growing outward.

The old mail and freight trail traversed the tundra northward across the marsh, and deep grooves carved out by years and years of use were all that remained. Sleds, dogs, and human feet made the first ruts, much like the ruts made by the wagon wheels and horses and early settlers on the Oregon Trail which took the pioneers west. When the Iditarod Trail ceased to be used by dog teams carrying freight, the moose, bear, caribou, and all the little wild critters used the trail, keeping it alive. During Alaska's wet, soggy summers and deep-snow-covered winters, animals use the easiest path available for travel. Some animals will even defend that trail for their own use.

Folks said the Iditarod Trail was lost—lost in memory and lost from sight. But lost it was not. Not with Joe Redington Sr. around. Joe knew someday, somehow, he would find more and more of that old Iditarod Trail.

"Lady would hop behind a sled with her front paws on the handle bars!" She was quite the dog.

Blue-eyed Lady was the first leader Joe had for his dog team.

At the end of that unforgettable overnight trip, Joe knew that all he wanted to do was be on the trail with a team of huskies. This was the kind of lifestyle he had been dreaming about for so many years.

Joe's next undertaking was to learn how to mush a team of dogs. Sharon Fleckenstein, another longtime Alaska sourdough, lived right out of Wasilla. "His family came here in 1914 and homesteaded right up there in Wasilla. His dad was a U.S. marshal here in Alaska. I could tell you a lot of stories about Sharon."

Joe spent hours and hours talking, working, and learning from this colorful sourdough. Both men loved dogs. Both men were inventors. Both men had adventurous spirits. And they became fast friends.

"In 1948 when I was tryin' to learn how to mush dogs, there were only two or three people between here and Wasilla and he was one of 'em. It was Sharon who taught me how to run dogs." Sharon freighted supplies up into the Talkeetna Mountains to the gold mines.

"Sharon bought me a sled at Teeland's store. It was what you'd call the Yukon sled. We put some handlebars on it and that was the first real sled that I had."

Joe continued to use his homemade, funny-looking airplane-seat sled on short distances for many years. But the Yukon sled—now that sled became his first real dog sled.

Joe's team resting and looking back at Joe. Slewfoot, the black dog in the lower right, was one of Joe's first wheel dogs.

Then another longtime resident, Ilah Senske, gave Joe his first leader for his team. Ilah was one of the few women mail carriers in Alaska and had a dog team that she had used for hauling mail up to the Independence Mine area. Now she was the cook at Wasilla School. "She was a tough gal," said Joe. "She'd been here then twenty-five years or somethin'. She gave me a dog. Lady was her name. She was a wonderful lead dog." Joe ended up with Lady because Ilah was not at all happy with this dog. Lady got into her chicken coop and killed some of her chickens. So now Lady was with Joe at Knik Kennels.

Lady was a little, blue-eyed, reddish brown Siberian husky mix. Joe said, "Lady was an honest leader and boy, was she a fast learner. And she would do anythin' for me!"

In the early days, Joe said, "I had a different setup for my dogs. I had 'em all in a line. Made my own harnesses. It worked real good in the woods."

One time Joe and Sharon hooked up several dogs each and went up into the Talkeetna Mountains. The snow was very deep and Lady and the other dogs were really struggling, but Lady continued to plow forward. This was hard travel for the dogs. That's when Sharon decided he would try and make some snowshoes for the dogs. He had used snowshoes for horses a long time back and he said he didn't see why it wouldn't work for dogs.

"We made the snowshoes out of willow switches and made them round, about five or six inches across, and tied it together where it was rounded, and then we put webbin' across. Then we just hooked a bootie to it, so that when a dog picked up his foot the back part would drop just like snowshoes and the dog could walk on 'em."

One thing Joe learned from that trip was that Lady had a big heart and "remembered any trail we ever traveled!" What a good leader.

For Joe those early years in Knik were full of new learning adventures and the making of fast friends. Joe would talk with Lee and Sharon for hours putting away their wealth of knowledge for later use. Often Sharon's nephew, Frank Smith, would be there listening. Joe and Frank were closer in age and good friends, too. Frank said, "Younger fellows listened more than they talked. Joe and my interests were very similar. Dog teams and boats were the main transportation in western Alaska for most people back then."

Common interests, great stories of the early mining days and running sled dogs, discussions of better ways to live in this still mostly untamed great land, brought sourdoughs and cheechakos into a bond of friendship that lasted a lifetime.

Chapter 5

Launching out into Cook Inlet

*You gain strength, courage, and confidence
by every experience in which you really
stop to look fear in the face.*

Eleanor Roosevelt

The Redingtons now had their first Alaska winter under their belt. Spring was poking its nose around the corner and Joe had made a decision. Time to build a new cabin. This new cabin would have only one stove to stoke this time. And no running water. The first batch of mosquitoes made its grand and noisy entrance. Though their bite was weak, their size foretold the next wave of vicious and voracious mosquitoes. What the second wave lost in size, they sure made up in numbers. But as most Alaskans do, the Redingtons learned to overlook those noisome insects and tune in only to the work at hand. Joe learned that "if you don't make a fuss at them, they won't make a fuss at you."

Vi added with a smile, "When people fuss about mosquitoes now, I just kinda laugh."

Joe had a house to build.

Just up the hill from Joe lived Art Welch, who had a little sawmill. Joe walked over to Art's place to talk to him about his new plan.

He said of his first cabin, "I thought it would be great. You'd just dip in that barrel and get all the water you wanted. Fresh water runnin' into the place. Well, I'm learnin'. I just didn't know."

Raymie, Shelia, and Joee proudly standing in front the big, new, log house their dad built. They had their own bedroom on the second story.

Ray and Vi had their second son, Timmy, in 1949.
Granddaddy is taking care of Timmy and Tommy for
awhile with the help of his goat for entertainment.

"So, do you suppose I could get you to cut three-sided logs out of some spruce trees I felled this winter?"

A deal was made.

From these logs Joe built his second house. By the end of their second summer, he would have a new one-and-a-half-story log cabin.

Joe made another decision—he had to get a boat. He needed to catch fish to feed his growing dog team and to get lots of fish he had to have a boat. Lee Ellexson and others told him, "You don't want to try the Inlet without a 30-foot boat or bigger."

Unfortunately, Joe said, "I didn't question it any further." That was a mistake. Joe would be the first to admit that a lot of learning is done by trial and error, and this was no exception. He was to learn that asking as many questions as you can to get all the information you can is a number one rule, if you want to make life easier and even survive in this land.

He found an old 30-foot, flat-bottomed river boat and put an old 22-horsepower Johnson motor on it. The boat was only three feet wide. "The whole thing probably didn't cost me more than fifty bucks."

Then he met a fellow who wanted to go commercial fishing with him the following summer. This man and his wife and another couple needed to go into Anchorage and Joe said he'd take them in his boat. What Joe didn't know was how very rough the waters in Cook Inlet could be when the tide came in.

On a partly sunny day Joe and his party headed across Knik Arm to Ship Creek eighteen miles away. The trip would take about an hour and a half to two hours. However, as they were crossing the Knik Arm the weather took a turn for the worse and pretty soon they found themselves in a terrible storm. The waves were getting higher. On top of that Anchorage's notorious high tide was coming in. That meant that the sea waters were rushing up Cook Inlet, bringing in twenty-five to thirty foot tides.

Joe said in his quiet, understated way, "It got really rough."

Joe was fighting to keep his engine from drowning. His engine didn't have a cowling, or cover, and the spark plugs stuck right out in the open and were getting drenched and not firing. He threw his rain jacket over the engine hoping that would keep it running.

Meanwhile, water was pouring over the sides and filling the boat. He hollered at his passengers, "Start bailin' and bail fast!"

"We didn't have much to bail with either," said Joe. So they used anything they had that would hold water.

One of the ladies was getting pretty exhausted and stopped bailing.

Joe looked directly at her and said, "If you don't want to drown, you'd better keep bailin'." So she picked up her hat and continued bailing.

They had two or three miles to go to get to land and battled the high waters all the way. "They were bailin' for all they were worth. And finally we went to shore and the bottom fell out of the boat right when we hit the shore. So we got us a rock and drove a lot of the nails back in and waited until the storm got a lot better."

When the waters calmed down, they very carefully got in the repaired boat and set out for Anchorage again, following the shoreline. This time they made it just fine.

Joe told his passengers, "As soon as the weather improves, I'm heading back home."

One couple was so scared they told Joe they were taking the train back to Wasilla. "They didn't want no more boat. And he never went with me fishin'." The other couple decided to go back with Joe, but only after he assured them that they would only go back in very calm water.

"So I learned right there that you don't go out in this inlet without a good boat," declared Joe. "From then on I had a pretty decent boat."

Joe with his dogs in his boat and
Anchorage is in the background.
Joe's dogs were good travelers.

When Joe got back, he looked up Lee and bent his ear asking one question after another about the do's and don'ts of boating in Cook Inlet.

Several years later Joe was out in his boat by himself. His dogs were in Anchorage and he had to get back over there to take care of them. A storm came up in Cook Inlet and the waves were high. Joe started bailing with a 5-gallon can he had in the boat. He found himself steering the boat with his hip, since his hands were busy bailing. Suddenly, a huge wave swept over the side of the boat, taking Joe's bailing can and flinging it to the wind. No time to let fear clutter his thoughts. This was a time for clear-thinking action! Without a second thought Joe whipped around, grabbed his 5-gallon fuel can, pulled his knife out of his pocket, cut a hole around the top of the can, and started bailing again. "I don't think I lost thirty seconds. I lost five gallons of gas though." Then he added, "Things like that get you to where you'd know pretty well what you can do and can't do."

Joe was also learning you can't have enough pockets! He always had lots of pockets in his clothing. He kept his pocketknife readily available, as well as matches, a pair of small pliers, string or wire, and several other invaluable survival items. Each year he seemed to add at least one more "very important" piece of equipment to his survival gear.

CHAPTER 6

Working Sled Dogs

Coming together is a beginning; keeping together is progress; working together is success.

HENRY FORD

All too soon the fireweed had shed her white feathery seeds. Fresh snow, called termination dust by Alaskans, was covering the tops of the mountains, ending a short summer. The very distinct smell of high-bush cranberries filled the air. Temperatures dropped and snow soon covered the frozen ground.

Joe's new cabin looked south over the gray, silty glacial waters of Knik Arm to the majestic 5,000-foot peaks of the Chugach Mountains. Outside, the yard was dotted with about forty doghouses and most of the dogs were malamutes. Joe's Knik Kennel was growing!

One crisp winter day in 1949 Joe hooked up Lady and some of his other dogs to his sled and headed into Wasilla to get supplies. On the way his dog team met a jeep that was traveling down the narrow road at a pretty fast clip toward him. Joe couldn't turn his dogs fast enough, so the driver of the jeep headed for the snow-filled ditch. The driver slowly climbed out of his jeep to survey the damage. Thankfully, there was very little. Joe helped the man get his jeep out of the ditch and then the two men stood there talking.

That's how Joe met Lieutenant Caswell. A new friendship was begun and Joe's life was going to take an important turn.

Shelia is holding one of Lady's puppies. Lady
is in the wooden barrel doghouse.

Lieutenant Caswell told Joe why he was in such a big hurry. A large plane
flying out of Elmendorf Air Force Base near Anchorage had run out of fuel.
The pilot had been forced to land wheels up in Goose Bay Swamp, a few miles
south of Knik. Lieutenant Caswell had hoped to drive out to the downed
plane, but he couldn't get his jeep anywhere near it.

"Do you have any idea how I can get fuel out to them?" he asked.

Joe thought a moment and then said, "Sure. I could haul it by dog team."

By then Lieutenant Caswell was game for anything.

"Come about," Joe hollered to Lady and she turned the team around. The
two men headed out to the downed plane. Joe's team of eager sled dogs hauled
out several loads of fuel. Next they began to work on clearing a runway so
the plane could take off. After several more hours of hard work, a makeshift
runway was built and the plane was in the air.

At that point a very grateful Lieutenant Caswell turned to Joe and asked,
"Say, would you like to work for the air force, using your dogs to retrieve
downed planes in the bush?"

No thought was needed for that question. "You bet," was his quick reply.

So Joe's career with working sled dogs took a giant leap forward.

His team was growing also. Joe was given a little dark Alaskan husky pup
with a white face. He called him Lobo. Joe knew he was smart right at the

This is Joee's favorite picture of Joe and Lobo, Joe's faithful and very intelligent leader.

Friends of the Redingtons having fun with Joe's sled dog team. Lobo is the leader with the swing dogs, Dodger on the right and Nenana, Lobo's sister, on the left. Dodger is the husky they got at the Border coming into Alaska in 1948.

Joe, a passenger, and Bud Nesji running beside the team, coming back from some work at Hatcher Pass. Lobo is leading with Belle and Tanana as swing dogs.

Joe and his army reclamation crew at a crash site near Anchorage.

Joe at crash site. Usable parts were removed and then they used dynamite to destroy what remained of the downed plane. This guaranteed there would be no question that this was not a new crash site. Mount Spurr is in the background.

get-go. When he first got Lobo, he put him in his jeep and drove over to see Ray and Vi. He left Lobo in the jeep and told him, "You stay now, ya hear?"

Lobo just sat there obediently, that is, until the door of the house was shut. Joe wanted to see what Lobo would do. What he saw happening made him grin and he called Ray and Vi to come look out the window.

Lobo's intelligent eyes were darting everywhere. They could almost hear that little Siberian husky thinking, "Don't see anyone. Looks like the coast is clear. Now for the getaway."

Gradually, one step at a time, he began backing up. Finally he got to the rear of the jeep. Then over he went!

He didn't get far though. Joe was out the door.

"You get back here, Lobo!" And Lobo obeyed.

Joe and Lobo became fast and trusted friends. Lobo grew to be a huge Siberian husky and he was Joe's main leader.

From 1949 to 1956 his team of huskies would be criss-crossing Alaska hauling freight and people. In a way Joe was stepping back in time to the early 1900s—the time of extensive freighting across Alaska by sled dog teams and following the footsteps of the legendary Leonhard Seppala, who freighted mining supplies and raced his dogs in northern Alaska.

The Seppala legend was being reborn.

Joe wearing his warm fur clothing made by Margaret Saccheus from Elim and Old Edna Ekon of Unalakleet. This is one of Joe's first dogs named Roamer. Roamer was a quarter wolf.

CHAPTER 7

Building a Team

*I am of the opinion that dogs are still the most
dependable mode of travel in the Arctic.*

Muktuk Marston

"I learned to be prepared workin' for the air force. I always found I was a little bit short on what I had with me for keepin' warm and also for doin' what I had to do," Joe stated. He learned quickly to make sure he was well supplied for each mission.

Weather conditions around this great land were always changing, but one factor remained the same—when it was cold, it was cold. Sometimes the temperatures would drop to minus fifty degrees Fahrenheit. The only moving air was the foggy breath coming from Joe and his dog's mouths. With each exhale the little bit of moisture would instantly cling to the first thing it touched. The dogs' whiskered muzzles became frosty beards of ice. Joe's black eyebrows turned icy white and his furry parka ruff surrounding his face caught the tiny water particles and froze on each hollow hair.

Sometimes the wind was whipping and swirling snow in such a fierce manner that the snow crystals became tiny little needle-like pellets slamming into man and beast alike and zapping all the warmth right out of them. Visibility would be so low that the only thing to do was to hunker down and wait out the storm. At times like this the temperature might be forty below zero, but with a wind blowing twenty miles per hour the wind chill would bring the temperature down to a minus seventy-four degrees Fahrenheit.

The dogs would dig a hole in the snow and curl down inside out of the wind and cold. They made themselves into tight fur balls with their noses buried in their tails and were amazingly nice and cozy.

But Joe, with only man-made fabrics to protect him was freezing. The old expression "When in Rome, do as the Romans do," Joe took to heart. The Eskimos and Indians had survived in this cold land for thousands of years. So, he had some Eskimo and Indian women make him suitable clothing.

Before long, Joe was wearing clothing made by Nature herself, but sewn by man. He had tough seal-skin pants, a warm caribou coat with a protective ruff, and cozy boots made of reindeer leggings and oogruk seal-skin bottoms for walking on ice or in somewhat watery spring conditions. He made himself a beaver hat with flaps that came down low over his cheeks and forehead to protect his face. And he had big furry mittens that he could slip on his gloved hands. His thumbs were the only things that were hard to keep warm. Joe was now prepared to meet Alaska's bitter cold.

Joe built a tripod to hold the engine of a downed plane to repair what could be salvaged. A knowledge of knot tying was invaluable in this work. One special knot was a Spanish windlass.

Joe's job with Rescue and Reclamation took him around the territory for seven years, and later he contracted out for specific jobs. He was called whenever a plane went down. His job was to go out and rescue the survivors or bring back their remains and then recover the downed plane. Anything not of value had to be destroyed or buried. This was so that old wreckage sites would not be reported as new crash sites.

"When we turned it over a guy got hurt. Pat Bliss flew in there with fifty mile an hour winds and I got the guy on the airplane and then I ran ahead of him. He couldn't see to take off. I ran ahead of him and as soon as he caught up with me I dropped down and he took off. It only took 100 feet in fifty mile an hour winds."

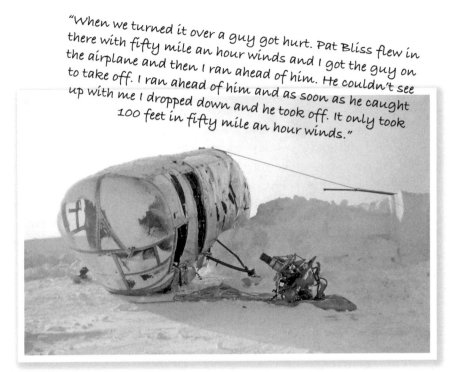

Joe and Otto Wurm, an old timer and miner who "ran the first cats and stuff in Nome", went out to Granite Mountain to reclaim a Beech 21 helicopter that went down. Joe took Lobo as his leader. They tied ropes to the helicopter and used come-a-longs and the dogs to pull it upright and took back the parts the military needed.

As vast as Alaska is, the road system was very, very small. The Alcan Highway connected Alaska to the rest of the United States through Canada. Crossing the border to Tok, the road divided going north to Fairbanks and south through Anchorage to Seward and Homer. Less than ten percent of Alaska's communities were on the road system. Flying or traveling by dog team was the only way into all the other communities in the Interior of Alaska in the winter. Boats could also be used during the summer months, but that was only a few months out of each year. Since airplanes could fly in both summer and winter months, the airplane population in Alaska grew by leaps and bounds. And with that, unfortunately, came many crashes.

Joe also freighted materials and supplies for the air force to White Alice sites, U.S. Air Force telecommunication sites, which dotted Alaska during the cold war. The cold war was that period of time after World War II when there continued to be a sharp conflict, but a standoff, between the Communist countries and the Western democracies. A line of communications and a radar system were being built across Alaska and Canada to relay early warnings of Communist activity onto the North American continent.

To get to these job sites, Joe flew or used his dogs.

When the air force changed their direction of operations, the 10th Rescue was deactivated. Joe took over that job as a civilian and was given a contract for the rest of his jobs. He also got some dogs from the Reclamation, 10th Rescue Division, to use in his team. They were Greenland Eskimo sled dogs. And they were a cantankerous, fighting bunch of dogs.

Joe said, "They were terrible fighters. These dogs would rather fight than eat."

For generations the Greenland sled dogs were bred for fierce toughness. Because of that, the military had them tied to iron posts and made concrete food bowls and galvanized dog houses for them. Joe had never seen a sled dog kennel quite like it.

Joe said, "One of the men on base told me, 'You'll probably have the same set up a little later.' But I told him, 'I don't think so.' So I brought 'em up here and my dad had his place fenced in. He had fence posts and barbed wire. So I tied 'em to the fence posts and they chewed the whole fence post off that night. Chewed it right off!"

"I couldn't believe it!" exclaimed Joe, shaking his head. He and his dad had a little discussion and then Joe said, "Well, there's nothin' to do but fix it better. I told my dad, 'I've got a stash of large tin cans at the house.'" Joe saved anything and everything that might be useful later on. They put the tin cans over the poles. All the while they were working, the dogs sat there and watched. Perhaps these tough canines were planning their next move, too.

"That should keep 'em," Joe declared.

The following morning he went to check on the dogs again. Granddaddy was just walking out of his cabin and together they walked to the dog lot wondering what they would find on this day.

They were speechless. All they could do was shake their heads in total disbelief.

"They completely eat them up to where I couldn't even find a piece of tin anywhere. So that is why they had concrete houses."

Joe had his work cut out for him trying to keep these new additions to his team in the dog lot and also to keep them from fighting. But he was not one to give up easily. He could be as determined as they were and figured out how to have them work for him rather than against him.

Joee, Raymie, and Joe are in seventh heaven playing with a bunch of their huskies.

In addition to the Greenland Eskimo sled dogs, Joe had the large malamutes. The malamutes were much gentler and had a lot of the bad traits bred out of them. These big, beautiful Eskimo dogs weighed between seventy-five and one hundred pounds. They had pointed ears, a short thick neck, and hair that was rather coarse. Their stocky build made them very good freighting dogs, able to pull extremely heavy loads. They would fight, too, but not as fiercely as the Greenland Eskimo sled dogs. Then Joe learned about another breed of dog.

Joe's job took him to Interior Alaska to many Athabascan Indian villages. At that time six or seven dogs were tied up behind every house. These dogs were much smaller. They were Alaskan huskies and they were working dogs. The Athabascans used them to haul wood, water, and supplies. They worked their traplines with dog teams, and these teams provided travel between villages in the winter. When Joe saw a husky he liked, he'd offer to buy it. It wasn't long before he began adding a whole different breed of dog to his dog lot, the small, tough Alaskan husky.

They didn't fight. They were very pleasant to run. And Joe said, "I had a real good feel for these dogs."

The best dogs Joe got were from along the Yukon River in villages like Galena or Ruby. He sometimes paid $25 for a dog, or $75 if the dog was a really good leader. Then he put it on an air force plane and sent it back to Anchorage.

Joe later said, "Lucky for me that I was able to do that."

He began identifying qualities in the dogs that he needed for his work such as good feet, good appetites, strength, and endurance. He kept notes in his journals of all his dogs. With each year Joe's dog lot grew and his working sled dog team grew stronger.

CHAPTER 8

Missions Accomplished

Life for me is always adventure after adventure.

COLONEL BERNT BALCHEN,
COMMANDER OF 10TH RESCUE SQUADRON

In the early spring of 1951 Joe was sent on a mission east of the Susitna River where a jet had gone down in a swamp. The pilot had already been rescued. Now the air force wanted to save the jet and fly it out somehow.

The size of his team would vary depending on the job to be done. "Sometimes I used nine dogs, sometimes twelve, sometimes twenty. It depended on the job."

Joe did have other men help on some of these missions. On this mission Joe, Lieutenant Caswell, and one corporal went with dog teams. Joe had Lobo, his huge Siberian leader, and Chinook and Kobuk as his wheel dogs. They had their hands full on this mission. The jet had gone down directly across Knik Arm from Elmendorf Air Force Base in the Susitna Flats. Fortunately, the snow-covered swamp provided a soft landing, so there was very little damage to the jet.

Joe sized up the situation and decided they needed to jack up the jet so that when the snow melted it would not sink down into the boggy swamp. They began cutting the stunted black spruce that grew in abundance around the swamp. The dogs hauled loads of logs to the downed jet. Slowly the jet was jacked up high off the ground. Joe knew when the ground thawed this platform of logs would sink into the wet muskeg. How far down they would go, he wasn't sure. So he had to build it high enough to be on the safe side.

Nature's clock was ticking into spring. Four to five minutes of sunlight was added to each day. Joe was aware of the effect longer daylight hours had on the frozen ground and rivers. He saw the snow melting. He knew that the frozen Susitna River would soon be creaking and groaning and cracking. He could smell spring in the air. Joe watched the weather closely and paid attention to the direction of the wind. If a chinook, an unseasonably warm wind, should blow, the ice in the Susitna River would take the hint and start to break up earlier than usual.

With noses to the grind stone and taking advantage of each longer day, they pushed themselves, and finished shoring up the jet in about three weeks. And none too soon either.

To get home with their laden dog teams, they had to cross the Susitna River. Joe knew the ice was getting ready to move. Time to get out of there.

As Joe and his crew headed out onto the thawing river, Joe watched his leader closely. Lobo walked tentatively out onto the ice, paused as if sensing the stability of river ice, then continued across. Within a day or two the whole Susitna River broke up and ice flowed freely into Cook Inlet.

Alaska was now officially into "spring breakup." The ground that had been frozen for eight months was thawing. Icy crystals formed in air pockets in the dirt. They began to melt, and mud said hello to Spring.

Later that summer when the ground dried up, Joe took his crew out again to build the runway. They used a boat this time, and they took a little Caterpillar bulldozer to help do the job. Reclamation also sent out a new engine and specially built skis. "The skis were twenty-two feet long and two feet wide, I believe," Joe explained. These were fitted to the aircraft. Then Joe and his men left. The job was just about complete. When winter set in and the ground froze again, the jet with skis was flown off the snow-covered swamp by Carl Benedict. Very impressed, Joe said, "He was quite a pilot!" The jet was flown back to Elmendorf Air Force Base and landed alongside the runway.

"That was the only jet I ever heard of on skis," Joe commented later.

This one mission took eight to nine months from start to finish.

Another job Joe had in 1951 was getting a helicopter off the side of a mountain. Helicopters were quite new to Alaska then. This particular helicopter had flown higher than it was capable of flying and crashed.

The Redingtons caught salmon, cut them, and hung them on racks to dry. All the kids are standing by the family fish rack on the beach at Knik. From left to right: Timmy, Tommy, Shelia, Raymie, and Joee.

"I spent thirty days over Christmas haulin' in a tail boom for a little helicopter. It was the only one in Alaska that had dual controls and they wanted it outta there right away."

Lobo, Chinook, Kobuk and a few other huskies hauled the tail boom up the mountain to the crash site with Joe pushing the sled from behind. Once at the crash site, he attached the tail boom to the helicopter. Now the helicopter was in operation again. The same pilot who had flown out the jet on skis also flew out this helicopter.

"He was one good pilot. No one else could fly that helicopter sittin' right on the side of the mountain like that. We were right at the height where you couldn't fly it any higher and he got it off of there."

Joe's reconnaissance missions not only took him across land and up mountains, but also across water. His navigational skills in the silty gray and often treacherous waters of Cook Inlet improved greatly while doing this work. Another jet had gone down northwest of the mouth of the Susitna River at a place called Flat Horn Lake.

He and three other reconnaissance men set out from Anchorage in boats to find and dismantle it. They crossed Cook Inlet then headed up the Susitna River and finally steered up the smaller Fish Creek which flowed from Flat Horn Lake. They searched all around the lake. Just about everywhere they looked they spotted moose browsing on the juicy sweet vegetation surrounding the lake. They spotted a total of seventeen moose on that trip and even surprised a bear, but saw neither hide nor hair of the downed jet.

As they floated back down the Susitna, Joe found himself dreaming up a new idea. His head was spinning. This little corner of Alaska was just what he was looking for—his El Dorado. Flat Horn Lake was remote, yet accessible by boat, plane, and dog team. The fish and game were plentiful. The land was beautiful and Mt. Susitna lay peacefully in the close distance. He continued to mull over all the advantages and disadvantages of living at Flat Horn Lake. It didn't take long before he knew just what he was going to do.

The minute Joe got back he told his family, "I've found the best place to live! And boy, is that good moose-huntin' country."

As soon as he could, he was going to look into buying some land in this area and he did. "It was a business site—Flat Horn Lake Lodge," Joe said. "I had twenty acres out there." This was going to be his new home. He could live off the land, raise his family here, have ample room for his dogs, still get in to work, and start a guiding business. This was the ideal homesite.

Missions accomplished with more to come. But now another grand adventure was just beginning.

Vi at Flat Horn Lake with her swede saw cutting wood.
They heated and cooked food with wood fires.

CHAPTER 9

Flat Horn Lake

It's all in a days work.

ANONYMOUS WRITER
FROM THE 18TH CENTURY

Joe's reclamation jobs took him away from home a lot and that was not easy for Cathy. With each passing year, Joe was becoming more and more settled into a lifestyle that suited his love for adventure and his vision to dream big. While this was great for Joe, it was not so great for Cathy. She didn't share his love of a rugged lifestyle and this put an additional strain on their already uneasy marriage.

Ray and Vi were also having their challenges. After Ray came back from the war, their life together was different. By now they had two boys, Tommy and Timmy. They were trying to make their marriage work, but they also faced some real challenges.

Sometimes marriages don't work out as planned. Both Redington families tried hard to make their marriages work, but no one was happy. Joe and Cathy agreed to end their marriage, even though they continued to be close friends. Ray and Vi ended their marriage. Ray moved away taking Tommy with him. Vi kept Timmy. They were all trying to do their highest sense of right, and then move forward.

So what happened next?

Joe loved dogs and Vi loved dogs. Joe liked the more rugged lifestyle and so did Vi. They were both game for adventure. Their kindred spirits simply drew them together. The postmistress in Wasilla, May Carter, married Joe and Vi on February 18, 1953. Frank Smith stood up with Joe and Cathy stood up with Vi. Their marriage lasted forty-six full, exciting, difficult, supportive, and loving years. They became an undaunted team.

Joe and Vi made plans to move out to Joe's twenty acres at Flat Horn Lake as soon as the snow melted and the ice left the rivers. In the meantime, Joe would continue working for the air force.

The sweet smells of spring brought promises of a new life together for Joe and Vi. Days were getting longer and the Redingtons, like so many other Alaskans, learned to take full advantage of this gift of nature. The sun would soon fill the land with almost twenty hours of blessed solar light, encouraging all plant life to grow for all it was worth. And now it was time to move to their new home at Flat Horn Lake, a stones throw from the Iditarod Trail, which Joe was beginning to use more and more.

They loaded up their boat with supplies and dogs, piled the boys in, and headed out for their first summer at Flat Horn. Their trip took them down Knik Arm, along the Susitna Flats shoreline bordering Cook Inlet, up the Susitna River to Fish Creek, and up Fish Creek into Flat Horn Lake. Everyone was so happy to pile out of that boat. It was one long trip!

They walked around the property a bit looking for the best place to set up a campsite for their new home. They decided on a lovely spot at the mouth of the Upper Fish Creek where it flowed into Flat Horn Lake and set up their 10-by-20-foot dark green army tent.

"We lived high on a hill," Vi said. "The creek was really wide in front of the tent and seemed like part of the lake."

The floor was packed dirt and Joe put a stove there with a chimney stack coming out the middle of the roof. They had everything they needed to be warm and cozy. Once the tent was set up they went about looking for a good place for Vi's garden. Joe, Vi, and the boys looked for a spot with few spruce, birch, or cottonwood trees to cut and started felling the trees. The once quiet woodland was now ringing with the sounds of a handsaw, the chopping of the axe, and children. Joe used his dogs to help haul the logs. Once the trees were cut, each stump had to be pulled out. Joe and Vi's saw, axe, and shovel really got a workout during those first few weeks.

When the boys weren't pulling up the brush by the roots, they were running around with their homemade spears playing games. Little Timmy, wearing his red cowboy hat, was having a ball.

Timmy and Joee are standing in the middle of their big clearing project at Flat Horn Lake.

The last step was to dig up the soil, one backbreaking shovelful at a time. To their surprise the ground was loamy—no glacial rock—and that made it a little easier. And they had a goal.

"We're not quittin' until this is done," stated Joe. And they didn't, even though the buzzing mosquitoes and the warm days made the cold lake look mighty inviting. Finally, Vi had her garden plot at Flat Horn. She would start planting her vegetable seeds next.

Seeds in, she moseyed over to the family campfire and sat down on a stump. "The world's pretty good," she murmured mostly to herself, as she watched Joe show Joee, Timmy, and Raymie how to make snares for catching rabbits and spruce hens.

Joe taught the boys to build a fish trap and anchor it in Fish Creek, where they caught whitefish. Later in the summer they caught salmon, which Vi canned. And there were burbot in the lake, although they called them ling cod. "The first time the boys caught one, I thought we had a monster!" Vi grimaced. "We never ate them. We gave them to the dogs." But in later years she found a good batter recipe to dip the fish in for frying.

When they got a moose or bear before the hard freeze of winter, "Vi would make jerky out of part of the moose and pickle bear hams like you would a hog, and can the rest," Joe stated matter-of-factly.

Their backyard was their grocery store. Nothing was passed over or wasted. Everything was put to good use. Why? Because the store was over forty miles away in the winter by dog team and much farther in the summer because they had to travel by water.

Later Joe reminisced, "We lived off the land. We had to buy milk and flour and things like that. Our eggs we got off the land, moose and bear we shot

Joee preparing dog food on their barrel stove at Flat Horn Lake. Some of their dogs are in the background.

Vi at Seal Slough with their dogs in camp and fish nets hanging.

right there. Vi raised all kinds of garden—everythin' you could think of. And then we had fish right there all winter. Fish under the ice. The last thing that ran through there in the fall was salmon. Beautiful pink silver salmon—real firm and hard. They'd come under the ice and still be runnin'. In those days we had no pike."

Early in the summer Joe and Vi visited with an old-timer from Susitna Station and an Eskimo hunter. These men were hunting seals at the mouth of the Susitna River for a three-dollar bounty the State of Alaska would pay them for each sealskin. At that time seals were in great abundance in Cook Inlet. They would get caught in the nets of the salmon fishermen, causing a great deal of trouble. So to accommodate the commercial fishing economy, the State thought the seal population needed to be sized down and put this bounty on seals. The seal hunters simply discarded the carcasses.

This was appalling to Joe and Vi. They had a great respect for all nature's creatures and hated to see this kind of waste.

What could be done?

"I thought maybe I could use them to help feed the dogs," Joe stated. He had read books by Vilhjalmur Stefansson, the Arctic explorer who drove dogs exploring arctic Alaska and Canada. Stefansson fed his dogs seal meat and had said it was very nutritious and was an abundant source of fat, which the dogs needed in that cold region.

Joe could do that, too. This would be a productive way to use the seal meat and feed all his dogs. Knik Kennels was growing. Feeding nearly sixty dogs took a lot of dog food. He wanted his dogs to be healthy, so he was always listening to old-timers, reading, figuring, and trying different diets. This fatty seal meat was just what his hard-working dogs really needed in the winter.

When he asked the seal hunters if he could have the carcasses, they didn't mind at all.

So Joe took his family and set up a seal camp just inside the mouth of the Susitna River away from all the silty glacial muck of the Cook Inlet. The rich seal meat was dried and added to the dog's diet. Joe would cut the meat into thin strips and dry it on spruce pole racks he had made. The blubber was rendered, melted down, for the oil.

He taught his sons how to dress or flesh out a seal. This was separating the sealskin from the body of the seal. Before long, young Joee had perfected this skill. Joe and Vi were both impressed with his steady hand. He was fast and could skin a seal and leave no flesh on the blubber or the skin at all. This was important, because the blubber had to be free from all flesh so the barrels of oil would not spoil from rotten meat.

On the larger seals the blubber was two inches thick. This was cut off, sliced into two-inch cubes, and put into baker barrels. The blubber would render itself down into a rich oil with small chunks in it. Most of the oil was used for the dogs, but some was put aside for family use. Vi would heat some of the blubber very slowly and can the sweet oil to use when she whipped up some of her wholesome home-cooked meals.

During the first part of July the sun was up most of the day, playing peeka-boo behind the tallest mountain peaks only in the wee hours of the morning. All the sunlight made for very full days. The Redingtons' meat racks were heavy with seal meat.

July 9, 1953, was one of those lovely, long summer days that was great for hanging freshly washed clothes out to dry in the warm sun, or in the Redingtons case, hanging the strips of seal meat to dry in the warm sun. Joe and Timmy had just come back in their boat from a trip to the fish cannery in Anchorage.

Joe, having been up most of the night, went inside their tent to take a little catnap.

Vi, Joee, Timmy, and Raymie were putting up seal meat to dry on the beach. Just before noon Vi looked down the Inlet at an odd sight. She got a funny feeling. Turning, she walked into the tent.

"You'd better come out and look. Somethin' is happenin'. There's a big dark cloud comin' our way," she said to Joe, gently waking him. Then she went over and turned on the radio.

Outside, the boys discovered tiny little black specks beginning to light on them. When they brushed it off their clothes, the stuff would smear across their hands and overalls. Looking up, they tried to see what this stuff was. Then they started blinking because, whatever it was, was falling into their eyes.

Everyone watched with squinting eyes as mean-looking clouds tumbled up Cook Inlet. These were no ordinary storm clouds. They were very dark and ominous and were enveloping all parts of the sky. Within a short time every-thing went from sunny bright, to gray, to black.

The Redingtons were not the only ones concerned. Just before the waves of darkness rolled over the camp Vi spotted movement near their tent. "A whole family of spruce hens ran in front of us." They were scurrying in front of the kids heading for cover under the wooden floor of the tent.

Then they heard the announcer on the radio say, "Oooh, the most won-derful thing. Mount Spurr has erupted!" The radio announcer's ignorance of what problems come with a volcano spewing forth tons of very fine ash, was, no doubt, very soon dispelled.

"It would eat a fish a day. We must of had it when the volcano erupted in 1953," said Joe.

Joe holding a baby eagle he found.

The air was so dense with the tiny black particles that the Redingtons had to cover their noses and mouths to breathe. Joe said, "It got totally black and you couldn't see your hand in front of you."

Joe, like a blind man feeling his way, slowly moved down to his boat on the beach to find his fuel. He poured some gas on wood in a five-gallon can and lit the gas on fire. "This was the middle of the afternoon," said Joe, thinking back on that day. "And you'd get just a few feet from the can and you couldn't see it. It was as dark as I ever seen it. The ash was real bad."

All they could do was wait it out.

Finally, the volcanic ash cloud passed and the sky began to clear. Breathing became easier. They stood in wonder as the tiny specks of "black snow" seemed suspended in the air around them. Four inches of very fine ash blanketed the ground. And if that wasn't enough—all around them were thousands upon thousands of "little ash whirlpools" swirling up and down the beach trying to fill in every crack and cranny with the innards of Mount Spurr. The air seemed determined to hold aloft these lightest of particles for as long as it could.

Several hours later the Redingtons surveyed their camp. "We had two hundred seals hangin' up. And we lost ever' bit of that." All the seal meat was totally ruined. Joe was not happy, but there was nothing he could do about it. He tried starting his boat motor, so they could head back to the homestead, but it wouldn't start because the fine ash was being sucked into the engine. So there was nothing to do about that either, except to stay put for a couple of days until the air settled.

The kids, on the other hand, had a blast romping around through the strange new ground cover. With each step a mini-eruption billowed up encircling their legs clear to their knees and thighs. The stuff was even floating on the water.

"The kids were all black!" Vi threw up her hands in disgust. Her little blackish imps were running around camp and there was simply nothing she could do but laugh.

After a couple of days, they were finally able to leave. Joe had quite a time getting the boat engine started, but once he got it running, they headed upriver to Flat Horn Lake and home. To their surprise and Vi's great relief, the ash cloud had completely missed Flat Horn. They had a clean, ash-free home, and a clean yard for the boys to play in.

Drying seal meat ended for that summer. But Joe and the boys would return the following summers, sometimes drying close to five hundred seal carcasses.

There was always something to do at the homestead. "The boys would haul the water with the dogs pullin' a cart," Vi recalled. "Later they had a trailer with a big barrel on the back." It was a lot of work to get up that big hill. But that was the boy's job, and they did it.

This was the same summer the boys had a special summer pet—a bald eagle. Joe came home with a baby bald eagle that he had found floundering on the ground. He did not see the nest or the mother. Joe knew it wouldn't survive without help, so he took the fuzzy gray eaglet home for the boys to feed and raise.

This baby eagle really wasn't very little. Its wing span was around two feet but would soon grow to be seven feet. The size didn't bother the boys. They just took special care with it. They would grab their fishing poles or spears and catch fish to feed the eagle. The day finally came when their summer pet's voracious appetite and the strength of his wings declared it was time for him to be on his own. His parting majestic flight took him up and over Flat Horn Lake into the wilds of the Matanuska-Susitna Valley.

The long summer days lasted through the starless summer nights. The vegetable plants matured quickly and before long Vi was busy canning all her food for the long winter ahead.

The sandy loam of Flat Horn Lake allowed the vegetables to grow, unhampered, to great size and in great abundance. "I loved livin' over there," smiled Vi. "The growin' season always seemed longer there and I could get out earlier than you could over here in Knik!"

Vi grew everything—plump potatoes, juicy carrots, large yellow rutabagas, leafy green lettuce, peas that went crazy on the vine, and huge heads of broccoli that kept growing and producing even after the snow fell.

Joe dug out a big hole in the sandy loam for their cellar and put a piece of plywood over the top. Into the cellar Vi stored Blazo boxes filled with layers of "gorgeous carrots" layered in sand to keep them moist and fresh a long time. Cabbages were pulled by the roots and hung from the sides of the cellar. She made sauerkraut only once. She was met with wrinkled noses after that meal.

"Well, that solves that," thought Vi. "I won't make any more sauerkraut. It is a lot of work anyway. I'll just stick with coleslaw."

And potatoes! Boy, did they have the potatoes. "We would plant a hundred pounds of potatoes. We would get about three thousand pounds of number ones and several hundred pounds of somethin' we'd cook up for the dogs," said Joe proudly. They lasted most of the winter. Joe added, "They would be a little bit wilted by then, but they had no sprouts and they were fine fer eatin'."

Her first small garden plot continued to grow a little more each year until it was about a half acre in size. From then on, every spring Joe or Joee rototilled the ground for Vi and she headed out with a big smile on her face to dig in the dirt and plant her outstanding garden.

Belle, a malemute-cross husky with
blue eyes, was Vi's first lead dog.

CHAPTER 10

Blazing the Iditarod: Not Lost

Two roads diverged in a wood, and I—
I took the one less traveled by,
And that has made all the difference.

ROBERT FROST

Bob Bacon was a neighbor on the other side of Flat Horn Lake. He also had dogs to get to and from his home. They were good friends and often got together to play cards and chat.

One day Bob mentioned to Joe that he was in need of a bed. Joe just happened to have an extra bed. At the same time, Joe was on the lookout for good sled dog pups and Bob had some. So he said, "I'll make ya a deal. My bed for that pup." They shook hands and the trade was sealed. Joe gave this new little puppy to Vi, and Vi named the seven-month-old husky Belle. They thought that was quite a deal—"one bed for one Belle." Winter was just around the corner, so their plan was to train Belle to be a leader for Vi's sled dog team. In the meantime, they loved and played with the pup.

On a beautiful clear August day, Joe and Vi were sitting by the campfire toasting marshmallows and chatting with Granddaddy, Joe's dad, who had come out to Flathorn Lake for a visit. Chickadees were chatting to each other, busily flitting from tree to tree storing food for the winter. The boys were gathering willow sticks and bringing them to their granddaddy and dad.

"This takes me back to the Depression," Granddaddy said, glancing over at Joe, as he twisted a stick around a tripod he had just made. "Remember our trips into Philadelphia to sell the baskets we made?"

"Yep, we'd make five or six dollars a week for our baskets," Joe reminisced. "And now you're teaching Joee."

Then, looking at Joee, Joe said, "This is how we'd eat during the Big Depression."

"During the Depression my dad and I made them baskets and we'd haul them to Philadelphia and places to sell them."

Joe standing proudly by the baskets
Joee made out of willow.

Suddenly everyone stopped. Their ears perked up. The boys pointed their fingers to the tops of the trees spreading over their camp and shouted, "Look!"

All eyes turned to see the noisy V-formation of geese float across the brilliant blue sky. Their call of departure filled the air. Canada geese, sandhill cranes, and ducks were beginning to gather on the lakes, in the marshes, and in the fields, preparing for their winter flight south.

Mother Nature, meanwhile, was having fun playing with her fall colors splashing the trees with brilliant golds and dabbing the forest floor and treeless mountain highlands with scarlets, reds, purples, and oranges. The mosquitoes were gone but the tiny, bothersome whitesocks and no-see-ums took over for the last gorge on humans and animals before the winter set in.

Immediately the conversation turned to the preparations they must make for winter. The Redingtons would leave most of their camping gear behind, because Joe and Vi and three-year-old Timmy would be coming back to spend the winter and get their new home established at Flat Horn Lake. But the older boys needed to be in school. Joee would be staying in Anchorage with Vi's parents and Raymie stayed with Cathy and Shelia in Wasilla. Once their camp was closed up, the whole clan piled into their boat and headed down Fish Creek to the Susitna River and back to Knik. Then they piled into their car and headed for Wasilla and the long drive into Anchorage.

After the snow fell, Joe, Vi, and Timmy loaded their dogs and supplies out to Knik and then followed part of the old Iditarod Trail by dog team to Flathorn Lake about thirty miles away.

Joe knew that being prepared was vital when living in this untamed country. He always tried to heed his inner voice of reason. He set up storage caches along the trails he set. Here he kept supplies to be used whenever they were needed. Their wood-burning stoves continually called for more wood. Their dog team was a big help with this job.

"We mushed dogs every day all over the country that winter," said Joe matter-of-factly. "Sometimes we'd visit the old-timers at Susitna Station, an old roadhouse along the Iditarod Trail."

Throughout the winter Joe and Vi had plenty of opportunity to rediscover the original mail trail, which was about three miles from their home.

Vi's Belle was learning to be a good lead dog—at least for Vi.

"She would do anythin' for Vi," said Joe with a grin.

"But not so much for Joe," added Vi.

Joe was quick to respond, "She didn't take commands well."

"She was an excellent lead dog," Vi argued, "but she needed her commands ahead of time. You gave the command right before you wanted it!"

All that being said, Vi loved her little blue-eyed leader.

"Anyway, we'd be out every day on the trail," continued Vi. "I would put Timmy in a sleeping bag on my sled and follow Joe—just in case my dogs would try to take off. Then Joe could stop them. I dumped Timmy over a bank one time. Didn't hurt anyone. It was a big corner right on a big hill. Joe stopped right away and ran down the hill. He gathered up Timmy and asked, 'You okay?' Timmy said, 'Yup.' The kids grew up on sleds."

"That was the best year we ever had, I think," Joe commented a number of times. Vi nodded her head in agreement.

Almost three months had passed and Christmas was nearing. Joe, Vi, and Timmy were so looking forward to spending Christmas with Vi's parents in Anchorage and seeing the kids. They decided to leave Flat Horn right around the winter solstice.

December 21 rolled around. With only about five and a half hours of daylight, they were up and ready to go to make full use of what little daylight

The Redington home at Flat Horn Lake in the winter of 1954.

they had. It seemed even less that day because the sky was overcast and snow was beginning to fall.

Vi happily began singing to Timmy, "Over the river and through the woods to Grandmother's house we go. The dogs know the way to carry the sled through the white and drifted snow!"

They hitched their dogs to two sleds, loaded them, and tacked a note to the front door of the tent leaving the date and telling the neighbors they were heading into Anchorage for Christmas to stay with Vi's folks. Then they were off, with Belle leading Vi's team and Lobo leading Joe's team. They hoped to travel about twelve miles that day.

In no time at all the lovely Christmas snowfall became a winter storm. The snow was falling so heavily, they couldn't see beyond the dogs. It was like Mother Nature's children were having a huge pillow fight upstairs and the pillows had burst wide open, letting fly buckets and buckets of downy flakes. And the skies showed no signs of let-up.

There was only one thing to do and that was stop at Joe's nearest cache on a hill by their trail. They unhitched the dogs and got them settled for the night. Then they took out the tent that was stored there and set up camp.

"Boy, oh boy, would you look at it snow!" Joe commented to Vi, as they shook the frozen crystals off their parkas and ducked into their small tent.

The next morning Joe crawled out of their cozy shelter. The whole woods were covered in a three-foot blanket of snow. And the dogs were nowhere to be seen.

Joe called them by name, "Lobo. Belle."

Lobo's barely visible nose poked above the surface of the newly fallen snow. Then Belle and the rest of the team reluctantly punched their noses through the snow. They were warm and toasty in their nests of snow and contented to stay right where they were. But Joe wanted to get moving. Christmas was only a few days away and they still had a long way to go.

Slowly the dogs stood up and tried to shake the snow off their bodies. But their heads were just barely above the top of the snow. Trying to walk in that winter surprise was almost impossible. The dogs were fairly swimming in the stuff.

Joe decided to leave one sled behind and hitched all the dogs to his sled.

Grinning, Joe looked at Timmy and said, "Looks like I'm going to be the lead dog for the rest of this trip."

He strapped on his snowshoes and began to trample down a trail for the dogs to follow. The brush along the trail was so heavily laden with snow that the branches hung right to the ground. Joe brushed off the snow, cut branches, and snowshoed out in front of his team. Vi drove the team with Timmy, who was all smiles, and stuffed inside a sleeping bag.

Normally, Lobo only worked for Joe, even though Vi fed him, but he sensed what was needed here and obeyed her commands. Besides, Joe was right out in front of him.

With each step Joe sank up to his knees. The leather webbing on the snowshoe prevented him from sinking all the way, but even so this was a lot of snow to stomp through. The going was very, very slow. The dogs floundered forward on Joe's heels. It took all of the few available daylight hours to slug only a couple of miles through the snow to the Halfway House on the Flat Horn Lake side of Little Susitna River.

The Halfway House was not in very good shape. Unfortunately, someone had ransacked the place. The door and window were gone. The floor was ripped up in places and someone had used the wood to build a fire right in the middle of the cabin. There was a little airtight stove, but it lacked the chimney.

Joe shook his head sadly. He remembered a conversation he had with an old gold miner. "Used to be miners out here would leave to the States for the winter and we'd have two or three thousand dollars that we'd leave in the dresser drawer and not think anything about it. No one would ever bother it and when we got back in the spring it was still there." The cabins might have been used by others going by, but there was a code of ethics most everyone lived by, so the places were always left in good condition, nothing was taken, and a stack of dry wood was left by the stove. This respect for other's cabins could save someone's life sometime, maybe even their own.

Joe and Vi often wondered what had happened that changed the way folks respected other people's property. It seemed the Code of the North was dying.

There was no time to waste talking about that. Joe had to get busy and make the cabin shipshape so they could get in out of the weather. He made a chimney from some Blazo cans they found scattered about the floor. The odd-looking square stovepipe wasn't much, but it did let them warm up the place a bit. Meanwhile, Vi got out a tarp and hung it over the door and window to keep the heat in and the snow and cold out.

Little Timmy was a real go-getter. Nothing seemed to daunt him and he loved the snow. This wintry day was just one more grand adventure to this little fellow.

Meanwhile, back in Anchorage Vi's parents, Milton and Cora, were getting a bit anxious. Joe and Vi and little Timmy were overdue. They were talking to a friend of the family who also happened to be on the Civil Air Patrol rescue team. He decided he would fly out to Flat Horn and see if he could find their trail. But it had snowed so much he couldn't see any trail. He did spot the sled Joe and Vi had abandoned, but it was empty. That caused him great concern. He continued to search the freshly snow-covered area.

Flying toward the Little Su he spotted Joe's team tied up at the Halfway House. He circled the cabin several times. Vi and Timmy were outside when the plane flew overhead. He didn't see Joe, so assumed that something had happened to him.

The CAP pilot dropped a K-ration box and a note that instructed Vi to walk in a circle if they were all right. So Vi and Timmy walked in a circle.

Actually, at that moment Joe was out hunting. He found only one set of tracks and followed them until he found the moose. The winter had been very hard on this small, skinny moose. But it was a moose nonetheless.

Vi said, "Joe probably got the only moose in the whole country."

For four years now Joe's job had been to rescue people and equipment from remote areas in Alaska. He knew how to take care of himself and his family. He knew the lay of the land. He knew where he was and where he was going. All that he really needed now was a little time. Their food situation was not so good, but again, Joe was a resourceful person.

When Joe returned, the hungry dogs were fed most of the moose meat because after all, these dogs were their only mode of transportation home. With what was left, Vi cooked up a warm simple meal for her family and all was well.

Then it started to snow again.

As they sat down to eat, Joe turned on their radio. To their utter astonishment, the airwaves going out across central Alaska were reporting that Joe Redington Sr. and his wife, Vi, and their little boy were "lost" and the Civil Air Patrol was out searching for them.

"What?" Joe exclaimed, looking at Vi. They were not lost just late.

"We knew exactly where we were, but we couldn't do much about it," Joe said later.

The snow clouds lifted briefly and a military C-47 transport plane flew over the Halfway House and to the amazed disbelief of Joe and Vi, the sky rained 40-pound boxes of C-rations plus dog food in gunny sacks. They had to run inside the cabin to avoid being hit by all the food the plane was air-dropping them.

"They almost killed us!" Vi exclaimed.

These supplies fell all over the woods! In fact, for the next year Joe was finding food boxes hung up in trees and all along the trail from this overly generous drop. He later stashed almost all of it in the caches he had built in the area.

Just about the time of the air drop, two neighbors who lived in the area found them at the Halfway House. They had heard the same radio message that Joe and Vi were missing and left to go looking for them. They brought out some supplies to tide the Redington's over until they could get back to Knik. Joe and Vi had a grocery store of supplies now.

The snow continued to fall.

A couple of days later the clouds lifted and a military helicopter landed to fly them all back to Anchorage. Joe said, "I'm not going. I've got the dogs to take care of."

Vi said, "I can't go because I have to help Joe get the dogs back."

They knew they had to send someone back, because it cost an awful lot of money to send out that helicopter.

So they decided to send Timmy back to his grandparents in Anchorage.

Getting him on the helicopter posed a little bit of a dilemma though. For some reason Timmy kept crying and wouldn't get on. That was so unlike him. They finally figured out that he didn't want to leave the raisins in the C-rations that were in the cabin. Vi ran back to the cabin, got the raisins, and gave them to Timmy.

Timmy, all smiles again, climbed aboard for his first helicopter ride. His grandparents picked him up and took him home.

With Timmy in Anchorage and the snowfall having spent itself, Joe and Vi hooked up the dogs and started breaking trail back into Knik. Their journey

Vi on the Iditarod Trail in 1954 with Lobo leading, Tanana the swing dog on the right, and Belle peaking her head over Tanana.

Joe and Vi stopped along the trail near Fish Creek to dry out their socks.

Time to take a break from their work locating the Iditarod Trail and have a nice hot cup of tea.

was not easy. Joe snowshoed through the deep snow ahead of the dogs bushwhacking willows and alders bent under the heavy snow with a Swede saw and axe most of the way. The job was long and tedious, but their high energy allowed them to keep plowing ahead.

Vi's parents kept the Christmas tree up until the whole family was together again around New Year's. They celebrated their belated Christmas and had a wonderful time.

When the media got wind that Joe and Vi were in town, they wanted to interview the "lost" Redingtons.

"We didn't want any part of that business!" Joe said with disgust. "We left town as fast as we could."

The rest of the winter Joe and Vi spent looking for the old trail to Iditarod. Lee Ellexson's descriptions of the trail were invaluable. The blazed trees Lee described were the easiest to see, if anything could be easy in all the snow. The swampy areas and lakes were the hardest. The trail would never go straight across the gullies. Joe and Vi had to wander around, zigzagging back and forth down gullies until they could see where the trail came out again. The same was true with lakes. The trail didn't go straight across the lakes because of the springs along the edges of the lakes that caused overflows. The trail tried to avoid those problem areas.

Joe's and Vi's eyes became more fine-tuned all the time. Together they began to pick out the remaining trees with blazed markings which designated the route of this old historic trail. There were lots of dead falls to climb over and cut out. The Iditarod was coming back to life.

Joe said proudly, "Vi could outwork most men!"

"We mushed dogs everyday. All over the country," said Vi. "We'd go to Susitna Station and visit some of the old timers. Cory, he couldn't hear at all. You'd have to get right up to his ear and holler in his ear. These old timers were still minin' from the old days."

They had fun telling stories and visiting about days gone by.

"Howard had a mink ranch back in the '20s," remembered Vi. He could get all the fish he needed to feed them from the river.

After their visiting, they would head back to Flat Horn.

They were having a great time that winter. Together they reopened the "lost" trail. They talked about what it must have been like back in the early 1900s and since both loved history and both had great imaginations, the work was not really work at all. This was an adventure.

And what a team they made!

Joe's truck loaded with his dogs and sled. He stopped in Wasilla
before heading up the Fishhook Road to Hatcher Pass and
the Fern Mine. Lady is in the middle of the sled dogs.

CHAPTER 11

Vi's Wild Ride

She's an eagle when she flies.

DOLLY PARTON

Spring was slow to work her way up into the Talkeetna Mountains, but around Flat Horn Lake the robins were calling in spring's arrival from the tops of the tallest trees. Pussy willows were puffed-out balls of yellow pollen just waiting to be pushed aside by budding green leaves. All sign of winter snows was gone from the valley floor, with only a few patches of mud remaining. Vi and Belle had one last sled dog trip to make.

Granddaddy had his cabin in Knik, but that winter he was the watchman for the Fern Mine. The Fern Mine was an old, hard-rock gold mine nestled back in the Talkeetna Mountains northeast of Knik. Joe decided it was time to go visit his dad and see how he was doing. He put his sled and some dogs in his truck and drove to Hatcher Pass. Then he hitched the dogs and headed up.

It felt like he was traveling back into winter. Snow still covered the ground and cold pockets of air hung in the valleys. The trail was well packed though, and with Lobo in the lead, they had a quick easy trip. Granddaddy had been up there by himself for several months and was getting a bit lonesome. He was mighty glad to see Joe.

Granddaddy could smell spring blowing across the crusty old snow and really had a hankering to leave. So he said to Joe, "I would sure like to head back down to Sunny Knik here soon."

"Okay, Dad. I'll come back next week and haul out all of your stuff," Joe replied.

When Joe got back to Knik he and Vi talked out a plan. "I'll take my team with Lobo."

"And I can test out Belle," Vi grinned enthusiastically.

"Very good."

This would also be Vi's first trip up to Fern Mine, Vi's first experience wearing snowshoes, and her first long-distance run with dogs. She had used the dogs a lot to haul wood and water, but had never gone on a long trip with them.

Vi started to get the supplies ready for the trip.

"We don't need to take sleepin' bags or supplies because Dad's got plenty of that up at the mine. It's only gonna be a couple, three hours and we'll be up there," Joe told Vi.

So they loaded the dogs and sleds in their Ford truck and took off. They drove up to the Little Susitna Roadhouse, where they were greeted by a thin covering of new spring snow. The mountains seemed reluctant to let spring melt the winter snows.

Joe and Vi unloaded their sleds at the roadhouse, hitched the dogs to their sleds, and headed up the mountain for the two- to three- hour dog team run to Fern Mine.

Ha! That was just not to be. Unbeknownst to them, Mother Nature decided more spring snow was needed in the mountains. Before long, huge snowflakes began to furiously fall. The higher up they went the deeper the snow became. This was not what they were expecting, but they continued up the hill.

Joe recalled years later, "Ya didn't get the weather reports like ya do now."

Progress was very slow. Joe and Vi looked at each other, shook their heads, and kept right on going. Granddaddy was expecting them and he would be worried if they didn't show. They really didn't have a choice.

The trail was getting more difficult all the time. The dogs were now struggling to break through the almost three feet of newly fallen snow . They were almost swimming in the white stuff. Finally, it was time to help the dogs more than just pushing the sled. Joe and Vi stopped their teams and pulled out their snowshoes.

"We're going to have to break trail for the dogs, " Joe told Vi.

Tromping in snowshoes is no easy task. Snowshoes are like a long flat, oval foot basket about five feet long. In those days they were made of a thin strip of wood bent and rounded at the toe, around a foot wide in the center, and tapering to a pointed tail in the back. Then rawhide webbing was woven between the sides. Leather straps were tied in the middle to attach to the toe of a boot. This allowed the heel to be free, so walking was easier.

Vi was a small lady with short legs, but she wasn't going to let that stop her. She tied her foot in the middle of each snowshoe. That meant she had to walk with her legs a bit bowed out in order not to walk on the other snowshoe. As if that weren't hard enough to try and get used to, she also had to lift her knees almost straight up to lift the snowshoes out of the hole they made in the deep fresh snow. If she didn't do that, the toe of the snowshoe would catch in the hole and she would find herself flying face forward into the snow. And that is exactly what happened.

"Oh, for Pete's sake!" she said as she struggled to get up.

But getting up in three feet of snow was no easy task either. Her arms sank into the snow and she ended up with another face plant into the fresh fluff.

"Good grief!"

The humor of it all got Joe and Vi to laughing so hard that the close, steep mountains echoed their fits of laughter. They would never make it to Granddaddy's at this rate.

"Well," recalled Joe, "six hours later or eight hours later we get to the Little V cabin." They were only about halfway to the Fern Mine. The temperature by then was below zero, the dogs were played out, and the night was pitch-black. Joe and Vi had pretty well exhausted themselves by then.

So there they were—snow up to their thighs, two small dog teams, no gear, and no food. That was not a situation Joe ever wanted to be in.

They unhitched the dogs and tied them up by the cabin. Then they stomped inside the cabin, thankful to be out of the cold, and yet it was still below freezing inside the Little V.

In the cabin they found a crust of bread on the table left from the summer before, maybe five lumps of coal, no firewood, and two old mattresses. They built a little tiny fire from the coal, which lasted only about thirty minutes, but that was enough to warm them up just a tad. They split the crust of bread and laughed at the predicament in which they found themselves.

"Next time, no matter what, we're takin' some supplies," they agreed.

The dogs had to go hungry that night, which Joe and Vi didn't like, but there wasn't anything they could do about it. The dogs had already dug out holes in the deep snow, built their little insulated nests, and were curled up in tight, furry balls with their noses stuck in their tails so they could breathe warm air and were sound asleep.

And Joe and Vi?

By the next morning they were wishing they could have had such a comfortable night's rest.

With the meager dinner fare in their bellies, they looked around for a place to lay their bone-weary bodies and get warm.

"Well," Joe said, lifting his eyebrows a bit and wearing a slight grin, "there are those mattresses over there. Let's try sleepin' under them."

So they lay on one and pulled the other mattress on top.

Even as tired as they were, they both started to giggle.

Later Vi said, "You can't imagine how heavy a mattress is until yer under it!"

After fifteen minutes it got so heavy they couldn't stand it. They threw it off until they got too chilly. Then they pulled it back over them until it became unbearably heavy and off it went again. They spent the entire night heaving that mattress on and off the bed. The one good thing about that night was that with all the exercise, they were able to keep their bodies a little bit warm.

The next morning they hooked the dogs up for the rest of the trip up to the Fern Mine. Again they had to break trail for the dogs, snowshoeing in front of them. Vi's short little legs were starting to get the rhythm of walking in these wide, basket-like shoes.

Most of the day was spent slugging through the deep snows uphill to Granddaddy's cabin. They arrived just before dark. The temperature had dropped considerably and the dogs were coated with frozen snow chunks. Ice crystals matted to their fur and balls of ice had formed on the bottom of their feet. Vi's breath had turned her loose blonde hair to frozen silver-white strands. Joe's eyebrows were crusted icy strips of white above each eye. "We're bringin' the dogs inside tonight," said Joe. And all of them thawed out by Granddaddy's warm fire.

Granddaddy rustled up some warm tea, then set about fixing a more substantial meal for his tired crew. Exhausted they were, but more than that, they were happy—happy to be in out of the freezing weather and all together.

"It was a terrible trip," Joe stated honestly.

That night all had a restful, warm, sweet sleep.

Joe was learning something about Alaska. If something is easy the first time, it's no guarantee it will be easy the next time. Nature is not very predictable. And you never go anywhere unprepared. Always have the basic survival supplies, such as matches, knife, a piece of canvas or ground cloth, sleeping bag, an axe, and a little something to eat.

Vi with Granddaddy in her sled and Belle leading the sled dog team down Fern Mine Road along Archangel Creek.

"Live and learn," Joe said.

The next day they loaded all Granddaddy's gear and equipment onto Joe's sled. Vi took Granddaddy on her sled. This would be Vi's first trip down out of the mountains with a dog team.

She told herself, "I can do this. I got myself up here. I can get us down. And Belle is leadin'."

With a "Mush" to Belle they took off down the hill.

The first part of the trail was pretty steep, so she rode the brake. Then it leveled out a bit. They made very good time even though the trail was soft. Then they got to the steeper road. This road was totally different. It had been plowed, so it was hard packed, icy, and slicker than grease. Vi came down off the Fern Mine trail onto Independence Mine Road wide open. Belle, the novice leader, tried desperately to stay in front of the other dogs and keep the gang line taut.

Those poor dogs' toenails were futilely gripping at the ice as they tried with all their might to stay upright and ahead of the sled. Vi was doing her best to keep some kind of control, but there was no control. She was riding her brake as hard as she could, but it was almost useless. Parts of that narrow, windy road were like elevators. Both riders left their stomachs floating at the top of each one of those drops in the road.

"I went down to the spring to get it," said Raymie. "I put it on my shoulder, then dropped it in the only sandy spot, but still it split wide open. It created some excitement."

Vi's folks brought watermelon over by plane when they came to visit. Though broken, they ate what they could anyway. You can't waste good watermelon!

"Holy cow!" said Vi. "It was like playing crack the whip around those sharp corners." The sled was at the end of the line and was getting whipped all over the place. "I didn't know when we were going to get killed, but I knew we were going to get it."

Granddaddy helplessly sat in the basket, eyes as big as saucers, and scared to death. Vi was hanging on for dear life. And Joe was right on their tail.

In no time they were at the Little Susitna Roadhouse and their waiting truck. Somehow they made it all in one piece.

Not much was said as they loaded up the truck and got inside; although each one in their own quiet way was thanking their lucky stars. Now to get the truck started and head home.

Joe turned the key. Nothing. He turned it again. Nothing.

As if to add insult to injury, that old truck wouldn't start. So out they piled, hooked the dogs up to the truck and had the huskies pull the cranky vehicle partway down the mountain until the engine decided it would lend a hand and start.

After that adventure you can bet everyone was glad to get home.

And as for Vi, this was just the beginning. She and Joe would be mushing side by side on many more wild and adventurous rides together.

CHAPTER 12

Subsistence Lifestyle

If one advances confidently in the direction
of his dreams, and endeavors to live the life
which he has imagined, he will meet with
a success unexpected in common hours.

DAVID HENRY THOREAU

In Alaska, what the summer loses in actual number of summer days, it makes up for in number of daylight hours. The stars faded with the light to return at the end of August. Sometimes Joe or Vi picked up a book and started reading at midnight without the use of a lantern.

"Vi loves books," Joe said with an admiring grin. "She does a lot of readin'. It's very seldom I start to tell her somethin' and oh, I already read that." Joe read a lot, too. There was always a lot to learn.

After a few hours of dusk, the robins started singing in full force and the sun popped its bright head above the horizon and another day began.

The Redingtons, like so many other Alaskans, learned to take full advantage of this gift of nature. Summer was the time to fill up their pantry and cellar with the groceries Mother Nature provided for them. To do this, they were up and down the river just about every day to their fish camp, or they hunted, or they grew it. Nothing was passed over or wasted and everything was put to good use. "We don't believe in wastin' nothin'. The most garbage we had was those C-ration cans." Joe chuckled. Those lasted for years. "Never had bears in the garbage."

But they always knew when a bear was in the area. The dogs let them know.

"They have a different bark for some things," said Vi. "When people come out, they all get excited like they're a happy bunch. A moose is out there, they're warnin' them to get out. If a bear comes in, there is not a sound unless you have some off-breed dog."

Joe continued, "With pure bred huskies, the bears don't seem to bother them. We've had bears go clear through the dog lot to find a little something to eat."

Vi interrupted. "And if it gets pretty close in the lot, the dogs will go in their house. They are all quiet. There won't be a sound," she giggled.

"The malamutes are the funniest," she continued. "They'd get in their house. We watched our big malamute one day and a bear was right in the lot and he'd be sound asleep lookin' out of his house just layin' there with his head hangin' out 'sound asleep' with one eye open. Then he'd close it again." He was very much aware that the bear was there, but he wasn't going to let him know it.

"They would repeat the same thing when the bear would leave. They'd growl a little and whoop a little bit and then when the bear gets out a bit, they'd start barkin'," Joe added, knowing that the dogs were thinking they were safe now.

When Joe was gone, Granddaddy was there to help. Vi's eyes filled with love. "He was always there for all of us. Granddaddy was as honest a person as I ever knew."

On one occasion when Joe was gone, Granddaddy and Vi were out cooking dog food. "We had a big barrel full of dog food out there and here was this big black bear puttin' his big paws over it and he was really eatin' outta the barrel."

Looking at Vi, Granddaddy said, "Why don't you shoot him?"

"Naw, he's not hurtin' anythin'. He's just gettin' some supper." When the bear was finished, he ambled on. There was a sense of harmony with nature at Flat Horn for the Redingtons.

Vi loved the bird life that came back each year. She was particularly drawn to the swans. One pair of majestic, snowy-white swans nested in the slough behind the house for many years. They'd proudly parade their little ones along the shore line for all the Redingtons to view. Flat Horn Lake also attracted the uniquely-painted harlequin ducks, the curious black and white loons and their unmistakable yodeling laugh, and the beautiful, green-headed mallards.

Spring also brought their supply of eggs for the year.

As soon as the ice left Flat Horn Lake and Fish Creek, Joe and Vi loaded up their boys and headed out to a place they called Egg Island in the Susitna

Vi, Timmy, and Raymie on one of their boats on Fish Creek with four little puppies, of course. Just about everyday in the summer the Redingtons were up and down the creek to Susitna River or Cook Inlet.

Vi put two white chicken eggs in a pan with three seagull eggs to show the difference in the eggs.

River. Hundreds of sea gulls nested there and laid their large, greenish-brown, spotted eggs. The boys thought they looked almost like Easter eggs, only they were about the size of a goose egg.

On their first trip down river each spring, they'd check the grassy island, then every day after that until they found the first egg.

"There were thousands of gulls layin' eggs and we'd go through there and gather up eggs. We could keep them layin' there for a long time," said Vi.

Each day they went back. Only nests containing a single egg were collected. If there were two eggs in the nest, they knew they hadn't collected from that nest. They passed it by because they were older eggs with chicks growing inside. Only the eggs just laid were gathered. The gulls would keep laying eggs all spring, so there was no depletion of the gull population. This practice of gathering eggs was accepted at that time, but today it is not, except in certain circumstances.

The eggs were gently laid in large buckets and taken home. Vi boiled water and carefully dipped each egg quickly into the water with something called water glass. This sealed the shell. (The first time Joe had ever seen this stuff was when it was used by a vet to seal a cast on a dog's broken leg. Joe and Vi thought if it worked on the cast, it should work on the egg shells, too. And it did.) Then they stored the eggs in their cool cellar. Once a month Vi went down and turned all the eggs.

The Redingtons much preferred gull eggs to "boat eggs", which came up on the barge from Seattle. Boat eggs weren't very fresh, but they weren't spoiled either. They just had a unique taste, and some were very runny.

One time an old-timer friend of theirs was given some fresh chicken eggs by a neighbor. What a treat. But after eating them for breakfast, he was very puzzled. They didn't have any flavor.

Vi said, "I reckoned he had plain and simply gotten used to eatin' rotten eggs."

The Redingtons weren't the only ones who appreciated these gull eggs. Dr. Jim Scott, the vet for Joe's dogs, said, "I ate the best-tasting cake I've ever eaten at Joe's place and it was made with gull eggs!" That was Vi's delicious chocolate cake.

Joe would take his boat across the Inlet to Anchorage to pick up Dr. Scott and bring him back to Flat Horn Lake to look at his dogs. "On the boat ride over we would be bucking the tides, which made it a long, slow trip with lots of time to talk. Joe wanted to learn all he could about nutrition, about what was best to feed the dogs, and how best to care for them. He always wanted to learn more."

Dr. Scott was impressed with the attention Joe gave his dogs and the time, effort, and thought he put into their care. "Everything in Joe's dog lot was set to take care of the dogs in the best way possible. The lot was clean and that makes for healthy dogs. Joe takes wonderful care of his dogs."

Then Dr. Scott added, "He knew that the dogs needed to be cared for the same throughout the year, if you want good, healthy dogs."

All that Joe was learning he was passing on to his sons. Joe made sure his boys learned how to hunt and fish. He showed them how to make traps and then sent them out to trap. "I never trapped a thing. Joee did. The kids were pretty good about survival in the woods," Joe said proudly of his sons.

"The kids would go out in a little boat and put out a little net and catch suckers, whitefish, and different kinds of fish. They'd fish for dog food and cook them up the next day—Joee, Raymie, and Tim would."

The boys fished and Vi canned the fish, mostly silver salmon because they came right up into their lake. Then if they got a moose or bear before the hard freeze of winter, Joe and Vi canned the meat. The family worked as a team, hunting, fishing, picking berries, taking care of the dogs, and relaxing together.

Joe was getting to know this part of the territory of Alaska quite well by now. He had survived the first five years in pretty good shape. He was learning to work with just about anything nature had to dish out and find a way to work with her. His cheechako days were now becoming a part of his past.

Joe had found his niche. Alaska was his home for good. He didn't think about becoming an Alaska sourdough, like his friends Lee and Sharon. But each adventure, each test in the northern environment initiated him into that unique category of men who could do just about anything. Each mile he mushed behind a dog team was putting him into the legend books with Leonhard Seppala, the man about whom he had heard and read so much. Being a true Alaska sourdough could only be achieved through the day-to-day honest living in a somewhat primitive land where man and dog depend on each other for survival.

Working for Rescue and Reclamation was mostly a winter job, so Joe decided he would get his guide's license. The Matanuska-Susitna Valley trails wove through the woods, over swamps, and across mountain tundra hillsides. The meandering rivers and clear lakes held lots of great fishing holes. Moose, bear, and caribou crisscrossed the country. He knew where and when to find them. This would be a good source of income for his family and it would keep him right where he wanted to be—in the heart of the Alaska wilderness, which he loved so much.

When Alaska was a territory, Joe said, "You had to be here five years before you could get a guidin' license here, so I didn't get mine until 1954." Then he added. "I didn't have the intention of guidin' when I came up here, but I did a lot of huntin'."

Because of Joe's work with a dog team on the military base and Joe's gregarious nature, everybody knew Joe. So it wasn't surprising that Joe's first client heard of him through a general on the base. This man was a United States senator. He had hunted all over the world.

Joe and the senator from Utah were flown in a Beaver bush plane to the Lake Louise area northeast of Knik. "We were looking for caribou and caribou were so plentiful in the fall," he said.

Caribou were continually on the move following centuries-old migration routes. At times they moved in single-file lines, gouging narrow ruts into the cushiony tundra carpet. At other times they just browsed all over the hillsides looking for food. The juicy green plants of summer were just about gone now, so they searched for the spongy gray-green lichen called caribou moss for their meals. Sometimes, using binoculars, Joe saw a lone bull caribou way far away on the top of a hill, but he was too far away for them to hunt.

On the third day, as they were sitting up on a little knoll, a herd ambled by not paying any attention to the two hunters. Joe said, "This looks as good as we've seen."

No sooner had he gotten the words out of his mouth, when he heard a rumbling noise behind him. He spun around to see what it was. Right before their unbelieving eyes lumbered a huge grizzly. Nose pointed up the hill, and barely thirty feet away. The grizzly slowly worked his way up the hill toward them! Where he came from Joe had no idea. The underbrush was very thick in this area, but he wasn't even warned by their moving upper branches.

"I didn't have a shell in my gun because I was walkin' behind. I had it in the magazine. And while I'm gettin' one in there, he shot, and hit the bear and turned the bear kinda sideways, but he's still tryin' to get us, still movin' up," Joe recalled. That grizzly was not losing any time. In seconds he would be on them.

The senator's aim was good, but it wasn't enough to stop the bear. The grizzly stepped sideways but kept coming. The senator shot again. Still the grizzly roared up the hill. The bear took six bullets and then veered off into the alder bushes.

This was not good. Joe never wanted to leave a wounded animal.

But heading into the alders after the wounded grizzly was not a good situation either.

"We don't dare go into the bushes. We've got ta wait awhile."

Nothing moved. There was no sound. Still they waited and then with both guns loaded, they very cautiously went down the hill in search of the bear. They found him not too far away—dead.

The senator went home with a 9-foot grizzly, a caribou, and a moose.

Joe never advertised for guiding work. He got his jobs by word of mouth. He guided mostly up the Susitna and Yentna rivers for fish, moose, bear, and caribou.

They usually had their clients fly into Flat Horn and they'd take them out from there.

"I took a lot of schoolteachers in. One time, I think I took five of them into Lake Creek fer a few days fishin'. In those days fishin' was great! There wouldn't be nobody there. I've got pictures of 'em. Usually Joee and I took 'em. And Vi held down the homestead."

One time he took a group to the Lake Creek and Skwentna area to get a moose, but they were unsuccessful. When he got home Vi said, "There's been a bull moose in the dog lot every night."

"Okay, I'll go look fer him tonight." Joe took a dog and went out and got his moose within a hundred yards of his dog lot.

Joe had moose meat for his family that winter. Vi had eggs stored and the vegetable garden was producing well. Joee, Raymie, and Timmy had fish and other game for the family and dogs.

And Dr. Scott said, "Joe's lifestyle was truly subsistence."

CHAPTER 13

Always a Way

Nothing is impossible to a willing heart.

JOHN HEYWOOD

If the military needed Joe to go out on a job during the winter while he was at Flat Horn, he mushed his dogs into Knik and then got in his Jeep and drove another ninety miles up and down hills over a narrow, potholey, snow-covered, gravel road winding around the long Knik Arm to Elmendorf Air Force Base. That took a long time. The military wanted Joe to be more accessible. So he and Vi moved into Anchorage. By then they had about fifty-six dogs in Knik Kennels. The dogs were kept on base and lived like kings with two GIs helping Joe and Vi to take care of them and keep the dog lot clean.

"That was great," Joe said. "But it didn't last."

There was a turnover in personnel at Elmendorf and the newly appointed full colonel didn't much take to the idea of having a dog team on base. This was going to be a modern air force Joe was informed.

His superiors told him, "Nowhere in the air force is there a job description for a dog musher. We are a modern air force. So we're going to have to do something about your job."

Joe stood there not saying a word, but wondering where this conversation would lead.

Then they asked him, "You've operated a crane, haven't you?"

Well, he thought to himself, I've driven a number of different vehicles and can fly airplanes. I reckon I know enough to figure out how to operate a little ole crane.

Joe looked at his superior and confidently replied, "Oh yeah." And that took care of that.

With his simple reply, Joe's official job description was changed from dog musher to crane operator.

"Then I went on a different deal with the air force." His first assignment was to move all his dogs off base. So the "crane" operator bought a house six miles out of Anchorage on the Seward Highway.

Finally the day came to test Joe's yet unproven skill as a crane operator. A master sergeant on base came up to Joe and asked, "Aren't you a crane operator?"

"I've never seen a crane," replied Joe honestly.

"Well, come on. Let's see what you can do."

Joe's reputation of being able to do just about anything was growing. He was a man of few words, but his deeds certainly spoke volumes.

The job was to move a house—lock, stock, and barrel—from the base to Knik. The problem was to get it lifted in one piece and onto a flatbed truck. They drove out to the site to see what they could do. Joe got in the crane and carefully experimented awhile trying this and that gear. It wasn't long before he had taught himself how to work that big crane.

Once he was confident in operating it, he said, "Let's get started."

The two men rigged up the house with ropes and cables and loaded the house onto the truck without a mishap. The master sergeant gratefully thanked Joe and drove his house to his homestead.

"That's the only time I operated a crane for 'em in three years," Joe said years later, "I sure couldn't get away with that today."

By now Joe had three types of dogs in his kennel. The malamute was a breed of freight dog that could haul heavy loads. These dogs had a heavy bone structure and were over a hundred pounds. Their coarse hair protected them from the cold. The smaller Siberian huskies were tough and had lots of stamina and speed, good for traveling long-distances. The legendary musher, Leonhard Seppala, had a team of Siberian huskies that carried him through a fierce Arctic storm to get diphtheria serum to the people in Nome in 1925. Finally, the Alaskan husky, which is a mixed breed. They had a good attitude and lots of endurance and were used by the Athabascans in Interior Alaska. They were faster, more even-tempered, and intelligent.

A good musher knows his dogs. Joe knew his. He had been loving and

Kobuk was Chinook's brother. They were malamutes.
Kobuk was a wheel dog and a leader.

observing dogs since boyhood. He was constantly alert to each dog's temperament, personality, movements, and how each dog related to the other dogs in the team. Every day he was learning something new, something that would help him take better care of them, something that would help make the dogs better working dogs in the harness. He knew the character of each one of his dogs. So when there was the slightest tip of the ear, Joe knew there was probably something not quite right, perhaps the harness might be rubbing or a foot might be a little tender.

Joe bought his first ready-made sled at Teeland's store in Wasilla. It came with all the gear—harnesses and neck collars. The collars used on the dogs back then were something like a hard, heavy, leather horse collar, but they were smaller.

"I bought Chinook from one of Earl Norris' handlers." Earl Norris was a longtime Alaskan and dog musher. He named the pup Chinook. Chinook was strong and grew into a big dog. Joe and Vi's boys loved to ride on Chinook like a horse, he was so big. Joe also got his brother, Kobuk. Both grew to be Joe's wheel dogs, but Chinook was a natural. Joe trained Kobuk to be a leader as well.

Just as people have different ways of walking or running, so do dogs. Some dogs run with their heads down and some with their heads up. Chinook ran with his head up. He wanted to be aware of everything going on around him.

99

Unfortunately, that made the heavy leather collar rub the hair off the back of his neck and a sore developed. Joe built a large pen to put him in while his neck healed rather than keeping him collared and chained in the dog lot.

"Chinook was the most unhappy dog you ever seen," Joe said. "He was just dyin' to get outta that pen and back on the chain even with a bad neck."

Joe watched Chinook's actions closely. Then he looked at the other dogs by their doghouses. As he studied them, he saw that the dogs weren't just running around the poles. They were actually "workin' on that chain." They were pulling as hard as they could away from the pole, just as if they were pulling a sled. They were exercising. Then he looked at Chinook sadly pacing around in circles. He couldn't pull. He couldn't exercise. The poor dog just couldn't do anything constructive.

Joe decided right then and there—working dogs should not be kept in a pen.

Just as soon as Chinook's neck finally healed up a bit, Joe put him back on his chain. Now Joe had his happy Chinook back again, and he learned something very important about sled dogs that simple observers of dogs don't realize. These dogs needed to be pulling! He also decided that those heavy leather collars were just too harsh on his dogs' necks and shoulders. He needed something better. So Joe made his own harnesses.

Chinook grew into a beautiful, 126-pound malamute that was not only very strong but also very intelligent. "He always did more than his share of the work and got along good with all the dogs," said Joe admiringly. Chinook was born to be a wheel dog, one of the two dogs that run directly in front of the sled. Their strength got the sled moving. And if they were good wheel dogs, they kept the sled on the trail. Joe could tell that Chinook knew the importance of his job just because of how hard he worked. And he would do anything for Joe. Joe used him as a freight dog and sometimes in short sprint races. Surprisingly, "He was really fast for such a big dog. He was just one heck of a good dog!"

If the trees and rivers, the muskeg and hummocks, the mountains and hills, the gullies and ravines could only talk, oh, the stories they could tell. The Iditarod Trail has stories of its own. Most will never be heard, some will be told, and there will be more in the making.

Now Joe was adding his own stories to this much used and little remembered trail.

October brought snows to the valley. Before long their dog teams had carved into the deep snow a narrow, winding trail that wound through the quiet spruce and birch forest and across the frozen lakes and swamps. And

"The Iditarod went where it was easiest for a trail," stated Joe.

Kiana and Belle are leading Joe's eighteen sled dog
team of Siberian, malamute, and Alaskan huskies on the
Iditarod Trail. Chinook is right in front of the sled.

with the snows came a rule of the trail—the musher with the most dogs got
the right of way. The other musher had to get his team off the trail. In pretty
quick time Joe and Vi were mushing eighteen dogs or better.

When two dog teams met head-on, a musher would holler, "How many
dogs do you got?"

"Eighteen, " Joe would call back, hoping he had the most dogs.

This time he held the trail. But there were times when he got caught short
and had to pile his dogs off the trail into the deep snow. Sometimes the dogs
didn't like it and as a team passed on the trail a dog fight followed. The mushers would run up and pull the dogs apart, let the team on the trail pass, and
then untangle the dogs out of the snowbank. That was no easy task when Joe
had hundreds of pounds of supplies on the sled.

Joe and Vi were mushing constantly to and from Knik either to visit
Granddaddy, to pick up clients for their guiding service, or to get supplies.
They loved to learn as much as they could about the trail. They were always
asking questions and having long conversations with the old-timers who used
the trail. Their stories sounded like tales right out of Jack London's stories. Joe
found himself living the tales of London's fictional Malamute Kid and experi-
encing the cold winters and heavy snows, using every ounce of wit and strength
to get from one place to another, or wrestling with the fighting dogs often used
in a dog team back then and training them into working as one machine.

So it's not surprising that Joe let his dog kennel grow. He and Vi wanted to have the most dogs so they could avoid being outnumbered and having to give up the packed trail and heading for the soft snow.

But the dogfights that might occur with passing teams or digging out of waist-high snow was nothing compared to the horrible, and sometimes terrifying Nine Mile Hill.

Nine Mile Hill was a monstrous, windy, and steep obstacle between Knik and Flat Horn Lake. Going out to the homestead they sweated bullets as they labored up its switchback trail, only to be met at the top by a massive birch tree blocking the trail. Then there was the wild ride down the backside of that steep trail.

Traveling back to Knik they had the tough push up to the top and then muster up all the courage they had to head down that steep obstacle course. The trail twisted and turned around trees only to dish out its final jab with a sudden drop in the pitch of the trail.

"Man, was it steep near the bottom!" Vi said.

The dogs' ears were flat to their heads as they headed down the hill. They ran as fast as their legs could carry them. Joe and Vi were fruitlessly crushing their brakes into the packed trail to keep the sleds from running over the top of their dogs while trying to keep the sleds upright. The hill seemed to have fun manhandling them.

Joe was complaining to one of the old sourdoughs about Nine Mile Hill and the ancient birch tree. He was quickly and firmly admonished by the old man with a "Don't ever cut that tree!"

Joe found out why later.

He had a particularly heavy load of supplies and going down Nine Mile Hill was not something he was looking forward to. As he stood there surveying the situation and trying to figure out a strategy for descending that treacherous slope, his eye fell to studying that massive tree.

"Well, let's see if you can help me out," he mumbled.

Joe hitched a rope around that granddaddy of a tree, and then attached it to his team. Standing at the top he slowly let the rope slide through his hands controlling the speed of his team and lowering the load clear to the bottom of the hill.

"Now that is pretty slick," he thought. Joe had just discovered the secret of the early freighters. Then he walked down Nine Mile Hill smiling and all in one piece. Not a bruise on his body this time.

Nope, he would not cut down that tree!

CHAPTER 14

Lobo and Chinook

My experiences have showed me that one doesn't achieve the best results with force and rough handling. Good dogs who know their master understand what he demands and is always willing to do their best.

LEONHARD SEPPALA

Joe's dogs showed love and respect for him. When training puppies he said, "Trainin' dogs takes time and patience. I used 'No' an awful lot. You've got to have discipline. You have to be firm." But he was quick to point out, "There is one thing you never do. You never kick a dog." Joe's love and firmness just naturally commanded respect from his dogs. They learned the joy of obedience and the freedom it brings.

Lobo, Joe's main leader in the '50s and '60s was no exception. There was great mutual love, respect, and trust between the two of them. Lobo showed this in many ways. If Joe got off his sled for any reason, Lobo would sense it, turn the team around and go back to Joe. "Lobo was one heck of a lead dog," Joe said with great pride.

Chinook, Joe's best wheel dog, always did more than his share of the work and got along well with all the dogs. On one particular mission Chinook shone as Joe's wheel dog.

Across Cook Inlet stood a very distinct long mountain called Mount Susitna. Many Alaskans called the mountain Sleeping Lady because that is what it looked like. According to Dena'ina legend, a young Indian girl fell asleep waiting for her beloved warrior to return home from battle. He was killed and she sleeps there yet, still waiting. To pilots, before the use of modern-day flight instruments, Mount Susitna was an obstacle to be weary of on cloudy or bad-weather days. Planes have flown right into her sides.

In the early spring of 1955 there was a tragic crash on Mount Susitna. A navy Neptune bomber flew into the side of the mountain with eleven men on board. There were no survivors. Dog team was the only means to get the bodies off the mountain. Joe was sent on this mission.

Mount Susitna is a very steep, stormy, and at times treacherous mountain. But Joe had a very tough freighting team with Lobo in the lead and Chinook and Kobuk as wheel dogs. Unlike the racing dogs of today, his freighting team didn't jump up and down to start pulling. Instead, they would get right down to the ground, put their bodies into low gear, and start to pull.

"They can move an awful heavy load," Joe stated.

Bad weather and the deep snow that spring made the work very difficult. Joe's team strained and pulled against their harnesses. The dogs were fairly swimming in the snow. Joe was using his snowshoes to help break trail. Lobo led the team close behind him. Even with that, their first two attempts up the 4,396-foot mountain were unsuccessful.

Could they get up such a steeply inclined mountain in this deep snow?

Joe walked up to Lobo talking to him and giving him encouraging, love pats. Then he went down the line talking to each of his dogs softly and telling them they had to get up to that downed plane. When he got to Chinook he said, "Chinook, you can get us there, boy!"

Finally, on the third try with Lobo's leadership and Chinook's determination and brute strength, they pulled that toboggan up the steep slope to the crash site. What they found was a sad sight. Wreckage was all over the side of the mountain. It took a long time to find the bodies.

"We had to dig them outta the snow. Some had twelve feet of snow over 'em. Three other men were helpin'."

Once the dead were all accounted for, they took them off the mountain. Lobo kept the towline taut and Chinook worked hard to keep the toboggan on the hard-won trail. The slightest unsteady movement would send the toboggan off into the deep snow.

"I never used neck runners on 'em. Chinook would jump right over the line and jerk that toboggan back on the trail before it would go in the ditch," said Joe. "They'd get good. They learned quick—better than havin' to pull it out of the snowbank."

Once the bodies were off the mountain, they attacked the problem of the

Lobo and the rest of Joe's team charging up
the steep slope of Mount Susitna.

wreckage. The men took only a few important parts of the Neptune down the mountain with them this time. The added weight of the airplane parts made an even greater challenge.

The heavily loaded toboggan picked up speed as they moved down the mountain and pressed against the legs of Chinook and Kobuk. The wheel dogs worked harder to keep ahead of the load. Joe was digging in with his break, but it wasn't helping much. Lobo felt himself moving freely down the slope and pulled harder to keep the gang line taut, but the toboggan continued gaining on all of them.

"Slow down! Slow down!" Joe yelled, as he pulled back and dug in.

Lobo knew he had to do something. A big clump of bushes came into view and as Lobo passed, he leaped sideways, pulling the whole team into the bushes and bringing the runaway toboggan to a screeching halt!

Lobo's intelligent insights as Joe's leader, Chinook's and Kobuk's strength of mind and body is what made Joe's freighting sled dog team so invaluable in this line of work.

"I was forty-five days getting' everythin' out."

By then it was May and there was still too much snow. "We hauled no wreckage out." Joe would have to go back during the summer when all the snow had melted to complete the job.

"Afterward we flew Chinook off Mount Susitna into Anchorage to a dog show."

Little Keith is a happy camper with the seal pup that spent the summer at Flat Horn Lake and one of Joe's puppies in his playpen.

Vi met the plane and picked up Joe and Chinook. Both took a hurried bath. Then Vi took her Siberian husky, Belle, and Joe took Chinook and they drove to the dog show. Joe and Vi ran around the circle for the judges to rate the dogs. Then they waited. As they left the building both Joe and Vi were laughing and so pleased.—"Chinook won Best of Breed!"

To Joe and Vi, Chinook was best of breed in more ways than just looks! Joe said, "Some of our little kids would ride on his back, he was so big!" Chinook was loved so much. "He was the best malamute I ever seen," said Joe. Chinook was one very special, devoted wheel dog.

The longer spring days soon melted the snow enough so that Joe and two GIs could head back to Mount Susitna to complete the job with the Neptune bomber. This time they took a boat up to Alexander Creek and walked about five miles up to the mountain site. They carried two packs of TNT and caps and depth charges and whatever else they needed to bury the aircraft. All their gear needed to be relayed up the mountain to the crash site. The grass was thick and the tall alder bushes were almost impossible at times to get through. And if that wasn't bad enough the bears were thick on Mount Susitna in the summer.

Vi and Keith in Vi's white Eskimo parka made by Margaret Saccheus. The laundry was done, so it was time for a walk down to Flat Horn Lake.

Joee and their little seal friend out in Flat Horn Lake.

When they set down one load to go back to get another one, they would come back to find a bear tearing open a sack of gear. They found they could go only short distances to insure the bears didn't ruin everything. Joe would shout and holler and wave his hands to shoo them away. Usually the bears were more scared of Joe and his men than the men were of the bears. But the men had their guns handy if they needed them. They finally got to the crash site, blew up the wreckage, and then buried it.

In 1956 the use of helicopters came into full swing and the military didn't need Joe and his dogs for reclamation work any longer. Only occasionally would he get a contract to do some work for them now. Joe was one of Alaska's last sled dog freighters, if not the last one. From 1948 to the early 1960s Joe was a sled dog freighter, following the footsteps of Lee Ellexson, Sharon Fleckenstein, and Leonhard Seppala.

After a couple of years in Anchorage with summers spent at Flat Horn Lake, Joe and Vi decided a change was needed. The town was getting too big for them and the neighbors had a hard time with all the dogs.

One bright sunny morning, as Joe was out checking on the dogs and water-ing them, he heard a sound that made him smile. He looked up. The geese were honking in the arrival of spring. Joe started thinking about Flat Horn Lake.

Time to move. The first part of June Joe packed up his family, loaded Lobo, Chinook, Kobuk and some other dogs in his boat, and headed across Knik Arm to Flat Horn Lake again. This time they had a new addition to their family. Little Keith was about three weeks old when they moved back.

They set up another wall tent. Vi put Keith's bed right in front of the window in the sleeping tent. It was in plain view of the cook tent. They also had a playpen in the yard for him. This way Vi could work in the garden or around the house and he would always be in her line of sight.

One time they found a little orphaned seal at the mouth of the Susitna River. They brought it home and took care of it. When Joe or Vi put the seal in the playpen, there was a squeal of delight as Keith snuggled and loved the furry seal pup. The older boys would take their rafts out into the lake and swim with the seal. When the boys walked back up the hill, the seal waddled up the hill after them just like a dog.

The friendly sea critter stayed with them all summer. The dogs did not bother him. Everyone was part of this family. He freely explored Flat Horn Lake. As the summer wore on he ventured out a little farther from the homestead until Mother Nature finally called in the fall and it swam out of the lake, down Fish Creek to the Susitna River, and out into Cook Inlet.

They were sad to see their sleek summer friend go. He was protected by this family and was now able to live his life in the wild on his own.

CHAPTER 15

Sled Dog Racing at Flat Horn

To fill the hour—that is happiness.

RALPH WALDO EMERSON

There was a lot of trial and error in the life of Joe and Vi, but both had grit and determination. Both believed that you learn by doing. If you don't do, you don't learn. Nothing was impossible to them. Difficult maybe, but if something needed to be done there was always a way to do it. In this fashion they raised their four boys—Joee, Timmy, Raymie, and Keith. If something needed to be done, Joe's attitude was "Let's get with it." The whole family learned to be self-sufficient and skilled in this manner.

"He was tough, but a good teacher. He has been a lot of places and done a lot of things," Timmy said years later.

Joe taught the boys how to use the dogs to haul their firewood. Loading and tying the logs to the toboggan was an art they learned well by trial and error. But Joe said they really learned.

"If your knots aren't tight, the logs will slip, makin' the load uneven and then you'll have trouble on the trail," Joe might comment after a mishap.

Weaving their dogs through the woods and around the corners, the boys had to take care or they would find their team wrapped around an unmoving birch tree. When the winter snows were deep, the spruce boughs kept snow

Raymie and Vi doing laundry at Flat Horn Lake in the summer.

Joee being homeschooled by Vi.

from piling around the trunks of the trees, thus making a great sinkhole at the base. At times like this it seemed as if the trees just loved to pull the boys' loaded toboggan into their deep winter caverns. The boys learned. This trial-and-error method was tough, but effective. And they were quick learners. They had to be. Their lives and livelihood depended on their learning the lessons of the wilderness and respecting all the changes in nature.

By now Joe had several tents at Flathorn Lake. The main tent was a 16-by-32-foot army tent. The boys had a separate tent.

Joe never was one to sleep much. Mostly he catnapped. And he was always the first one up in the morning. He would go to the boys' tent and hollered out in his soft but strong voice, "Get up and get with it."

Joe always had something for the boys to do. First came the chores and then they could play.

In no time the boys were up and dressed and outside. Their first chore of the day was to haul water. They'd hook up three dogs, put the five- gallon GI cans and dipper in the sled, and head down to the lake for water. In the winter they took their axe with them to chop the ice out of the waterhole. Then they scooped out the slush ice to get to the fresh lake water. "Laundry day required a lot of water," Joee recalled. And getting water was not an easy chore, but the dogs were a great help. The hill up from the lake was pretty steep. One part of the trail was particularly tricky and if they weren't careful going around the corner, the sled would tip and all the water would go flying from the cans.

Before they ate breakfast they cooked the dog food for the 190-odd dogs they now had. Vi would fix sourdough pancakes every morning. She got her sourdough starter from an old-timer, Bob Mathison, across Cook Inlet at Chickaloon. He had had it for over seventy years.

Raymie said, "She made the best hotcakes."

"Sure was good stuff," added Joe.

With good food in everyone's stomachs, they headed out to tend to the dogs. Every day the dog lot needed to be cleaned and the dogs fed. Then they ran them or sometimes they went hunting or used them to haul wood for the three stoves they kept going all the time in the winter.

When the chores were done, the boys had their schoolwork to do. Vi home schooled the boys at Flat Horn. Alaska did not have a program at that time, so she ordered materials from the Calvert School in Maryland. Vi would also borrow books to help with the boys' assignments.

"Dad taught us how to make a fish trap," said Joee, "making a box of chicken wire with a funnel with wings on the side for the fish to go in, but not get out."

Vi's team is in front of Joe's team. They're between Flat Horn Lake and Knik. They were always on the trail freighting supplies back and forth or visiting folks. Belle is Vi's swing dog on the right. Lobo, Joe's leader, is standing beside Vi's loaded sled.

Vi putting Keith on gentle Chinook.

Raymie is at Big Lake at an Aurora Dog Mushers event. He is preparing for a three sled dog race with Lobo leading.

In the winter the boys set these funnel-shaped fish traps under the ice. "We did a lot of fishin' for ling cod or brown suckers or white fish," Raymie remembered. "At night we'd go down to the trap and shine our flashlights into the hole and see if we caught anythin'." They would spear or dip net the fish out. And then head back home proudly sporting their catch of the day.

After a full day caring for the dogs, hauling wood and water, doing schoolwork, fishing or trapping, and some times dog racing, the entire Redington clan piled into the house for Vi's savory moose stew using the vegetables she had harvested in the fall, or a huge moose roast.

Raymie made a statement that was important to both Joe and Vi. "Every night our entire family would sit down together and eat."

Life didn't seem to slow down that much in the winter. Joe and Vi would be out using the Iditarod Trail extensively during the '50s and '60s. Vi, like Joe, was freighting 500 to 600 pounds of supplies to Flat Horn from Knik.

They were on the trail constantly. The more they use the trail, the more it became a part of them. Each year they were learning a little bit more about the history of this old trail.

Vi said, "We thought if something wasn't done to protect this historic trail in Alaska, it would be lost forever. It was as important a trail as the Oregon Trail had been that brought settlers west."

So in addition to all the daily chores and fun races, Joe and Vi had a faint vision that seemed to grow more clearly over the next twenty years or so. They started writing letters to Alaska's territorial governors and others informing them about this trail. They became champions for this life-linking trail long before anyone saw what they saw. They were tenacious.

Joee with dogteam at Flat Horn.

Raymie in the Junior Fur Rendezvous Race in Anchorage.

Timmy is driving his one sled dog
team on Flat Horn Lake.

"We opened up the trail from Knik to Susitna," said Vi. "We talked with old-timers that had used the trail. Most were gone. Joe finally found it. The trail was cut deep in the marshes. We were always interested in the history of the trails, dogs, and bringing dogs back to Alaska."

February and March were exciting times for the Redingtons. All ears would be pinned to the radio listening to the dog races. The Fur Rendezvous was the first major dog race of the year in Anchorage. It was held the third week in February. The third weekend in March began the last major race, the Great North American Sled Dog Championship held in Fairbanks. As soon as each day's race was finished, Joee remembered saying to Vi, "Get the stop watch and time us!"

Then the boys would put on their warm winter clothing. Before going out the door they drew names for the best dogs in the kennel. Then out the door they flew, hooked up their dogs, and raced around the trails they'd made through the woods and down on the lake. Vi stood by the house with the timer.

"Dad had plenty of things for us to do, but we'd find some time to play, too," Joee said.

Competition ran high in this family and the boys became good dog mushers. Young Joee raced in the Junior Fur Rendezvous for the first time in 1956. Vi was the only one left at the finish line. "She was waitin' in our old Plymouth station wagon," remembered Joee. "I won the Red Lantern." The Red Lantern was given to the last musher to finish the race. Ten years later instead of bringing up the rear, Joee would be the number one dog musher in the three-day, seventy-five mile Fur Rendezvous Race. He proudly had the number one team in Alaska!

Joee winning the 1966 Fur Rendezvous Race with two leaders, Happy and Wendy, that the army bought from Joe Redington Sr. Joee was racing dogs as part of his Public Relations work with the U. S. Army.

Joee used Joe's leader, Roamer, in the 1965 Fur Rendezvous Race and came in third place.

"Roamer," said Joe, "was one of the best dogs I ever had—an exceptional leader." He was born to lead. "When he was just a little teeny pup, we'd find him over there a hundred feet away from his mother, roamin' around." He was all over the place. "So we named him Roamer."

When Joe and the boys were racing or training their dogs, they let the puppies run alongside the sled. Roamer loved that. This little puppy would be right up at the front of the team. Then he'd look back to see if he was doing the right thing. Joe took note of that and saw Roamer's potential. This dog was a natural leader.

"He was half Russian-Siberian husky, one-fourth Belgian black sheepdog, and one-fourth, what we call Indian dog, the ones we get off the Yukon." Joe would get dogs when he was doing his Rescue and Reclamation work.

Roamer had one blue eye and one brown eye. He was intelligent, determined, had a friendly personality, and he was a good eater with good compact feet. He just flowed when he ran.

Vi racing in the Fur Rendezvous in 1954 with Lobo
as her leader. She finished fifth out of five.

All those training runs around the Flat Horn homestead led Roamer to
bring in Joee's team to place first in several big races and many smaller races.

Joe raced some, too, but he wasn't the sprint racer like Joee.

And then one day with Joe's typical impish grin he turned to Vi and said,
"I'm going to enter you in a race." Vi was in a couple of Fur Rendezvous races,
but she was quick to add, "I never really trained."

She was using Joe's dogs in her first race early in the 1950s. "Joe gave me Lobo
as a leader, but he wouldn't run for anyone but Joe. We didn't know that. Lobo
would do just fine and then he would look back and see me and start walkin'."

Then she'd say to Lobo, "Well, for Pete's sake, Lobo! Aren't you going to run?"

Finally Natalie Norris came along and helped to coax Lobo forward in the
race. "I'd have done alright if I could have gotten Lobo to move." Vi came in
seventh out of seven.

Vi ended her little story by adding, "I like the Siberians better."

The next race she entered was better. "Some of the dogs were mine and
some were Joe's. I was doin' pretty good but the trail was real icy." The sled hit
a bump on a right-hand turn and flipped over, tossing Vi head over teakettle
into the snowbank. She stopped, but the dogs kept right on going. She had to
run a quarter of a mile down the trail until she finally caught up with them.
She came in fifth this time. Fifth out of five!

Keith racing at Tudor Track when he was around seven
or eight years old. He is mushing Joee's lead dog, Snag.

"This is when we were racing at Big
Lake," said Joee, "when the Aurora Dog
Mushers more or less first started."

Timmy, Joee, Raymie, Joe, Keith with all their trophies.

Vi did win one race, though. Joe ran short sprint races at a drag strip in Palmer. One year he entered Vi. She went around the track and when she finished, she said to Joe, "Boy, they are slow today."

"What do you mean?" Joe responded. "You won the race!"

"That was the one race they didn't have a trophy," she said with her winning smile and a shrug, "so I don't have any proof that I ever won a race."

"I loved runnin' dogs," said Vi. But she wasn't much for racing. Vi decided she'd just stick with the old Iditarod Trail mushing.

Joe's green PA12 on the Susitna River with Mount Susitna behind it.

CHAPTER 16

Flying

*There is no sport equal to that which
aviators enjoy while being carried through
the air on great white wings.*

WILBUR WRIGHT

Joe loved to fly!

"I stayed away from planes for quite a while because I used to be pretty reckless," Joe said. "I wouldn't have hesitated to try and land on Mount McKinley, I mean when I was younger. I've always known my limitations. There wasn't nothin' I didn't think I could do with one of 'em. So I just used boats and dogs mostly. But in 1954 I decided we needed to have an airplane because we was movin' back to Flat Horn Lake."

Frank Smith, his friend who lived across the swamp from Granddaddy, also had a plane that he parked on the beach. Frank got his pilot's license when he was sixteen and loved to fly. Joe could see many advantages to having a plane.

Joe bought his plane before he had his license. He needed it to fly supplies and dogs to and from the homestead at Flat Horn Lake or Anchorage. In the early days of flight a lot of people were flying without a license. Joe wanted to be legal, though, so whenever he could get someone to instruct him he took lessons. Sometimes he had three instructors going at a time so he could log enough time and training.

Vi said, "He would grab whoever he could get."

Joe flew mostly in good weather. He studied the land to know the hills and creeks and swamps and dips. He thought it was important to know it like the back of his hand.

That knowledge of the land came in very handy one day. He had to get back to the homestead at Flat Horn. The visibility was very poor. "I couldn't see a thing." Actually, the weather was really awful.

He decided he would just have to follow the Iditarod Trail home. "I knew every little rise. Pretty well knew where I was all the time. That's Fish Creek. That's Goose Creek. That's Nine Mile Hill." He watched for each little rise and dip. When Flat Horn Lake appeared right below him, he gently set the plane down all safe and sound. There were times, though, when he did take some treetops out as he flew over.

But Joe was the first to say, "The safest way to fly in Alaska, if you can't see anythin'—don't go."

"I finally got a good set of instruments, but I flew a lot when I didn't have no radio, just turn and bank and compass."

He flew his first 1,000 hours in Alaska and never landed on an airstrip. The rivers and lakes were his landing strips. The first time he landed on an airstrip was at Skwentna.

"It was icy. No more of that. We're landin' on the river," Joe firmly stated to the three other passengers he had in the plane with him.

"I never was much for just flyin' around. I either had a reason for goin', to pick up fish or see somebody on business, and that seemed like all the time, or guidin' for somebody or flyin' for a guide."

There was one thing Joe never liked. He never wanted to call out the rescuers if he went down somewhere. He said, "If I'm alive, I'll get out."

Joe had his share of crashes, like so many other pilots in the Alaska bush or back country. But he was what you might call a hardy, inventive bush pilot.

Once he was moose hunting with Timmy. He went to land his plane on three feet of new snow. "As soon as I touched down, it kinda seemed like it picked up speed and right into the woods we went," Joe remembered. What he didn't realize was that the river had glaciered over and had new snow on top of the ice. That was a different kind of situation altogether.

The wings were in pretty bad shape. "I had to patch up the airplane to fly home." Joe carried his survival gear in his many pockets and if it wasn't in his pockets, it was in the plane. Properly prepared, he was able to meet the need of the moment as it arose.

He took out his pocketknife and he and Timmy went out in the woods and began gathering spruce boughs.

This is Joe' PA-11 with a sled tied to the wing.

"Spruce boughs will fill up the holes pretty good," said Joe. "You can make them stay pretty good. We had several holes. I've used them on several occasions. I've used them on wingtips. You can stuff them in there to where they bring the fabric right out. I only use them as stuffin' to get the aerodynamics. Don't want to do much maneuverin'. Just keep straight."

And that is what he did. He flew pretty much straight back to Flat Horn, no circling or banking, and landed safely on the lake.

The Fur Rendezvous Sled Dog Race in Anchorage was one Joe had raced with his dogs. On one occasion he had the opportunity to be the pilot for KYAK's radio announcer who was covering the three-day, seventy-five mile race.

The weather was not good flying weather during this race. It got so bad that all the planes covering the race headed in to the airport—helicopters and everything.

That is, all but Joe. He was still up in the air when the control tower at Merrill Field called him and said, "Joe, you're the only one in the air."

That was good news because now he could focus on following the mushers on the trail and not be concerned about the other planes that were covering the race, too.

"I finished flyin' the entire race. Never had to set down," Joe smiled quietly. "Everybody else set down. One time it was so bad I could only fly about a hundred feet above the trail. But with all the other planes out of the air, I didn't have to worry about flyin' into one."

When Joe stopped flying after twenty years, he had flown about 65,000 hours.

"Yep," lamented Joe years later, "I miss flyin'."

CHAPTER 17

Nelchina Rescue

Put your shoulder to the wheel.

AESOP FROM *HERCULES AND THE WAGONER*

The Redingtons didn't have a telephone at Flat Horn Lake, but they did have a radio phone. Twice a day at a set time, they would tune in to listen for messages or receive calls. One morning Joe was listening to the radio and drinking his cup of hot tea and honey, when he got a call from Earl Norris, a fellow mushing friend. "Do you want to make a little money?"

"What's the deal?" Joe asked.

"A Cessna 180 went down up at Little Nelchina," said Norris. "A weasel and a bombardier [a tracked machine] tried to get to the plane, but the mountainside was just too steep and there was too much snow. They couldn't reach the plane. Would you like to go?"

"Sure, I'll do it," replied Joe.

So he hooked up his team with Lobo in the lead and Chinook and Kobuk as his wheel dogs, loaded the sled with some gear, and headed into Knik to his truck.

The Iditarod Trail was not the easiest trail to drive dogs over. There were steep hills and turns that seemed to always grab at the sled or whip sled and team around hairpin turns. This trip out was no exception. Joe came to a steep bank and try as he might, he couldn't keep the sled on the trail. He took quite a tumble landing hard on one leg. Lobo held the team to the trail while Joe took inventory of the spill.

"I had a great big black spot and I crippled myself up a little, but I went on anyway." It would never occur to him not to go on. He said he'd come and he would, even with a badly bruised and very uncomfortable leg. That's just the way Joe did things.

Once in Knik he loaded up the dogs and his sled onto his truck and drove north into the Talkeetna Mountains.

Three men were waiting when Joe arrived. Norris, Bob Bacon, Joe's friend, and a writer who wanted to put together a story about this job.

Norris looked at the sun and said to Joe, "We have about four or five hours. It's only about eighteen miles back. We should be back before dark. I can pull a drag around Tudor track and it only takes me a couple of hours." Tudor Track is about twenty-five miles and used for dog races in Anchorage.

"Very good," Joe replied. "Let's get started."

Norris went up first with his Siberian dogs.

The Little Nelchina River is at the 3,000-foot elevation. The plane crash was further up the hillside. They had to cut down some trees and slash through thick brush. That made the going mighty slow. It was getting dark and they weren't even halfway there. Joe's two friends had to head back to Anchorage and that left Joe and the newspaperman.

"Well, I'm going up to the wreck," Joe stated and headed up the mountain. The newspaperman opted to stay with Joe. They continue slugging up the mountain until Joe said, "Let's call it a day."

They made camp for the night. Joe pulled out his tarp and built a shelter. Spring was in the air and a bit of warmth was beginning to fill the nights. Then he built a rip-snortin' fire to put a smile on the evening and they ate their dinner, visiting. Joe was a great storyteller and had a lot to fill the newsman's imagination. With the dogs bedded down for the night, warm food in their stomachs, good stories in their thoughts, they crawled in their shelter for a restful night in the fresh spring air.

The next morning they continued up the mountain, not reaching the crash site until the third day. Bacon joined them again and together the three men dismantled the plane.

They took the wings off the fuselage, the trim tabs off the tail, then pulled out the engine. Each part was loaded on their sleds and taken down.

Bacon took the trim tabs. Joe took the engine. That was where Chinook's strength and sharp wit were so important. They followed their trail going

Kobuk in training as a leader going back up the mountain near Little Nelchina River.

The brothers, Kobuk on the left and Chinook on the right, are gearing up for yet another pull. Chinook is really disgusted now.

down, which helped some but not much. The engine was very heavy and hard to keep on the trail. Chinook was a skilled wheel dog and jumped back and forth over the line to keep the sled from sliding off the trail. But there were times that even with his strength the sled was buried. The expression on Chinook's face was one of disgust every time the load sank in.

One time it was particularly bad. Nothing Chinook or Kobuk could do kept the engine on the trail. The weight of the engine caused it to be buried in a deep sinkhole.

Joe began digging around the buried sled while a disgusted Chinook looked on. Joe was up to his chest in the snow shoveling and shoveling. Then he got behind the sled and hollered out, "Mush."

Chinook, Kobuk, Lobo, and the other eight dogs pulled and tugged and yanked with all their might. Inch by inch the engine moved a little bit forward and up onto the trail.

"Hit it!" Joe's firm but soft voice commanded.

Chinook and Kobuk and Lobo gave one last powerful yank and the engine sat squarely on the trail again.

Everyone gave a sigh of relief.

Joe was proud of his dogs and loved to watch them work. Once a load got a little off center and before the dogs or Joe could respond, the sled slipped off the packed trail into the deep, soft snow again. Joe was not happy and, for that matter, neither was Chinook.

Joe always had his camera with him. He grabbed it out of his pocket quickly and snapped the picture that spoke for itself. The totally disgusted expression on that big, loving malamute seemed to say, "Well, I did my part. What happened to the rest of you? Now look what we have to do."

Joe and his team of huskies moving the wings off the mountain at Nelchina.

Joe is rough-locking, wrapping chains, around the spruce
pole runners to slow down the toboggan so it wouldn't run
over the dogs in their descent off the mountain.

At Joe's command Chinook's expression turned to one of determination. He had the job of pulling that heavy load out of the deep hole and by golly, that is just what he was going to do.

On command, Chinook put his shoulders into the harness and pulled with all his might until that freight sled was back on the trail. From then on he did anything it took to keep that sled on the trail. He jumped right over the line and jerked that sled back on the trail before it went off in the ditch—anything to keep it out of the deep snow. In fact the whole team knew that trick and they all worked together.

Joe could tell that Chinook really took pride in keeping the sled on the trail. He was reminded of Buck in Jack London's *Call of the Wild*. Buck took great pride in his work, pulling those heavy freight loads between Skagway and Dawson during the Klondike Gold Rush. Joe had his own Buck in Chinook.

At Joe's command, the team headed down the trail again to the road.

The next load was to bring down the wings. Joe made a twenty-two foot toboggan out of spruce tree logs and had the dogs haul it up to the crash site again. This time he put Kobuk as his leader. Kobuk was a determined leader, as well as a wheel dog.

Joe propped the wings up against each other like a pointed rooftop, tied them together, rough-locked the spruce logs, and headed down the snowy, well-pack trail to the Glenn Highway, where the truck was parked. Finally, the fuselage had to come out and the other smaller remaining parts. There was not one dent or tear in that plane by the time Joe finished getting it off the hillside.

The owner of the plane gave Norris $800. "He divided it into three lumps. I said, 'Wait a minute. I'd like to give this newspaperman $100. Then we divide it up." And that is what they did.

The job took days more than Norris had thought. Joe explained, "When you're doin' somethin' with dogs in those days, time don't mean anythin'. Somethin' you can do now in fifteen minutes might take ya a week back then."

Bob Bacon and Joe are standing by
a claim marker for a gold claim up in
Hatcher Pass in the Talkeetna Mountains.

Joe holding a chunk of quartz at
one of the mining cabins in Hatcher
Pass where he did assessment work
in 1949 and the early 1950s.

"This was at a mine past the Lucky Shot,
the last mine up there," said Vi. "That's
when the jeep incident happened."

From left to right: Milton and Cora, Vi's
parents, Timmy and Raymie, and Joe.

CHAPTER 18

From Mining to Fishing

It's the plugging away that will win you the day.

ROBERT W. SERVICE

"In 1948 and 1949 I did assessment work for Paddy Marion, an old timer here," said Joe, "He gave that mine to Vi when he retired and called it the Little V. But we never did much with it." The Talkeetna Mountains held gold under its rocky surface. The first notable discovery was made by Robert Hatcher in 1906 and when Joe moved to Knik, there was still mining going on.

"We had some mines up there at one time," continued Joe. "It was hard rock mining. Vi's father and I bought some from Paddy Marion up Craigie Creek."

One summer in the 1953 Joe took Vi, her mom, dad, Timmy, and Raymie up there. They all piled into Joe's gray, four-wheel drive jeep for the long ride.

As they crept along, dodging big rocks and potholes that would sink an entire tire, there was a loud "Crunch."

"For Pete's sake! What was that?" Vi said, looking over at Joe.

Joe stopped, got out, and discovered they had knocked the bottom out of their gas tank.

Never deterred, Joe set about looking for something he could use to fix the tank. He happened to have a five-gallon can of Blazo, a fuel used for gas lanterns. They had left it in the jeep from the last time they'd been up at the cabin. So Joe took the can and made a temporary gas tank out of it. He mounted it to the front of the jeep, hooked up some hoses, took a deep determined breath, and headed home.

"We've never been stranded," said Vi. "Joe always comes up with somethin'."

He said later, "I'm not sure how, but we actually got there."

Ingenuity, that's how. Joe simply was never daunted by circumstances. He was a thinker and he was always creatively determined to find solutions to any problem.

After a few summers working at different claims, Joe decided it was time to go fishing, and he said, "I never got back up there."

In the '50s and '60s June and July were the fishing months for the Redington family. Joee, Timmy, and Raymie became skilled fishermen. Joe made each boy his own eight foot boat equipped with a three-horsepower motor. One of the boy's jobs was to catch fish to feed the dogs. Joe knew that if the boys thought this was just work, they would probably protest. So he made a game of it to spur their interest.

"Dad made fishing for the dogs a competition. I guess that was smart on my dad's part," Joee said with a bit of pride in his voice.

He assigned each of the boys a special point on the lake or the creek to fish. They would each head out to see who could catch the most brown suckers or whitefish or burbot, which is a freshwater cod closely related to the marine ling cod.

"We fished with nets on the lake. We'd catch sixteen-inch trout," Timmy stated.

They worked hard to outfish each other. And the dogs always had plenty to eat. Before long they were out with Joe, commercial fishing. Joee had his own set net at the age of thirteen.

"I like set netting," Timmy stated, "but Mom hated it."

Joe often spotted large schools of small hooligan or smelt out in Cook Inlet. These fish are also called candlefish because they are very oily and can be burned like a candle when dried.

Joe got to thinking one day about all these hooligan. He knew folks would dipnet them as they were traveling upriver to spawn. He figured these five-inch fish would be a quick and easy snack for the growing number of dogs in his kennel.

Joe headed into Teeland's, the general store in Wasilla, to get supplies. He walked up to Walter Teeland, the owner, and asked in his soft, unassuming way, "I'll take all the toothpicks you got and some chicken wire."

Vi hanging hooligan on chicken wire with toothpicks. They had chicken wire stretched all around their place, all filled with drying hooligan.

Over the years Joe had become a well-known resident of the area and folks tried not to be too surprised at Joe's ideas or requests. But Walter just had to ask why in the world he needed so many toothpicks.

"I need to dry the hooligan we're goin' ta catch," was his simple reply.

A puzzled Walter watched Joe walk out of his store loaded down with thousands of toothpicks.

Joe loaded up his family in the boat with his supplies and a couple of hooligan nets on long handles, which were as big as a barrel drum, and headed down Fish Creek to the Susitna River to dipnet hooligan. They had a fish camp at the mouth of the Susitna River.

The surface of the water was a constant motion of tiny, tiny waves as huge schools of the little fish swam by the boat. There were billions of hooligan. Joe would have to be careful that he didn't dip too deep or he wouldn't be able to pull the net into the boat.

"I could fill a boat in just a few minutes."

Joe took them up to their fish camp, put them in tubs and went back and got another load.

Then he, Vi, and the boys set to work sticking tooth picks through the eyes of the hooligan and hung them through the holes in the chicken wire that was stretched out between sawhorses.

"It's up on stilts," said Joe. "Had to have it
like that there because of the high tides."
They painted it with dice because Joe
always said "fishin' is like gamblin'."

Joee and Joe at their fish camp at
the mouth of the Susitna River.

The other side of Fish Camp with Mount Susitna in the background.

"I think there was twenty-five thousand toothpicks and we put one hooligan for every toothpick," said Joe.

Unfortunately, once the fish were dried and they started giving the hooligan to the dogs for snacks, the dogs became sluggish and sick. Joe stopped feeding them the hooligan immediately, but it was a little too late for some of his dogs. With great sorrow in his heart, Joe said, "Chinook and Kobuk got bloat." He and Vi didn't know what to do and couldn't get them to the vet. Kobuk died in Joe's arms and Chinook in Vi's arms.

They were heartbroken. Joe had absolutely no idea something like this would happen. Later he learned this sometimes happens to big dogs and he learned what to do if it should happen again. But this was one hard lesson Joe wished he had learned another way. He figured the hooligan were probably just too rich in oil for his dog's diet. He would have to be more alert in the future. "Too much of a good thing," Joe lamented, "may not always be a good thing after all.

"One thing I've noticed. It's so easy to do things wrong. Anybody can do somethin' wrong. It's a lot more difficult to do it right. But somethin' that's the hardest to get is usually the best."

No more hooligan. Salmon would be the main fish for his dogs at Knik Kennels.

The Redingtons fished from Goose Bay on Knik Arm to beyond the mouth of the Susitna River in Cook Inlet. Joe had a boat and Vi had a boat. When the boys got old enough, they had their own boats, but when they were smaller, Joe took Joee and Timmy or else they would be at Vi's folks' house while they fished. Vi would take little Keith and put him in a playpen in the front of her boat. When he got bigger she couldn't take him out because he wouldn't stay in the playpen. They set their nets out from the shore in Cook Inlet and fished for salmon.

The Inlet was not very predictable and the stories Joe and Vi told about their adventures would make your hair curl. Vi never did care much for fishing. In fact, she said, "I hated it." But Joe and the boys loved it. And they needed the fish for cash and for dog food.

Navigating Cook Inlet was not always easy. Joe had to know the tides. Some of the highest tides in the world, next to the Bay of Fundy in the Atlantic Ocean, are in Alaska's Cook Inlet. He learned to keep his eye on the sky and the clouds. When he crossed the inlet, he looked at the clouds around Mount Susitna. If there were little clouds on the south end there would be a strong southeast wind blowing and he needed to beware. Or if all the seagulls were way high in the air, there was a big storm brewing. To find the mouth of the small rivers and streams, he learned to line his boat up with various points of land and head inland, but he always had to be watchful of the shifting, silty sandbars and the tides.

When the tide was out, the mud flats showed their shining, gooey faces. There were times when the tide went out and left them high and dry on the mud flats with a boatload of fish. They carried big burlap bags for just such occasions. They would wet the burlap and throw it over the fish until the tide came in again and raised the boat up, and they could get the fish to the cannery in Anchorage. Sometimes they sat there for hours waiting in the hot sun or windy weather. That northern sun can be very intense and Vi would come home with a face covered with freckles and brown as could be.

The mud flats can be very dangerous. All the glacial silt is washed down from the mountains and fills the rivers and inlets with sand so fine it floats in water. When the tide goes out there is still a lot of water between the silty sand particles and it acts like quicksand. Joe and Vi have had their rubber boots sucked right off their feet trying to get to solid ground or back to their grounded fishing boat. They learned to take great precautions and use wisdom when walking on the Inlet silt.

Vi was a little lady, standing not even five feet tall. Not too often was she on her boat by herself, but it happened that one day she was.

"I had to make a trip to Anchorage and pick up a helper," Joe explained. "See—the fish wasn't runnin' when I left and then they hit all at once. And when they did, they just filled the nets right up."

Straining and pulling with all her might, she managed to get part of the net in. "Oh, my word!" she groaned.

By then her long hair had come loose and was falling in her face. "Good grief," was all Vi could say. By now she was drenched. Silty salt spray soaked her to the bone. Salmon flopped and wiggled all over the bottom of the rapidly filling boat.

The *Nomad* with Joe and their friend, Jake Butler, finally showed up. Vi was at her wits end. Joe maneuvered the *Nomad* close to Vi's boat and Jake jumped on board to help her.

"I never was so glad to see you, Jake!"

"What a tough lady," smiled Joe admiringly. Then Joe gave Vi one of his lopsided grins, "It had a thousand fish in it."

After the commercial fishing which brought in some cash, the Redingtons would fish for themselves. Joe built a smokehouse to cure some of their salmon. Some they canned for the winter. The rest Vi and the boys cut and hung on spruce poles to dry for dog food.

"When the tide would go out," remembered Vi, "we'd have to sit there for hours."

At least she had the Sleeping Lady [Mount Susitna] to keep her company.

Joe got to know the waters and the land like the back of his hand. The state game wardens came over every summer to check with Joe about the fish in the Susitna River. His knowledge was of great assistance to the research they were doing in the area.

Jim Reardon worked for the Fish and Game and lives in Homer. He said, "Joe was an outdoorsman with all kinds of abilities and was known throughout the region." So Jim hired Joe to count salmon in the clear water creeks off the Susitna River. Joe needed a boat to do this, so Jim had a carpenter in Homer build him a river boat. Joe took the river boat with an outboard motor from Homer to Susitna. "I wouldn't have let anyone else do it, but knowing Joe and his reputation, I had no hesitation to have him take the boat from Homer.

"The Inlet is not a place for a thirty-foot riverboat with sides of eighteen inches," Jim said. "If it got rough, it would easily sink. He did a very fine job."

Joe ended up working part-time for the Fish and Game while they lived at Flat Horn. "We were settin' net for the Fish and Game," Joe remembered. "The biologists were studyin' the salmon."

The Alaska Fish and Game management wanted to know more about the kings. "Biologists would come over and I would have to show them how to put a net out, how to catch a fish, how to remove them out of the net."

They wanted to know why there was a depletion in the king salmon run. Joe took his fishing boat and caught the salmon as they went up different

The Fish and Game wanted to find out why the king salmon were declining and hired Joe to help them with their study. Joe is weighing a king along the Susitna River.

They measured and tagged king salmon on the Susitna River.

"We found out the first things that was ever known about the king salmon in this area," said Joe.

creeks along Cook Inlet. Then he and the Fish and Game biologists would put a tag near their fin so they could track them.

"We found out the first things that was ever known about the king salmon in this area," Joe said. "Where they laid their eggs, how far up the river they'd go, how many went out in the bay. Or the early ones that come in—whether they'd go up the Deshka River or the Yentna."

Joe was probably the first to count spawning salmon in the Susitna River. Joe said, "The king salmon was almost gone."

"Then later we tagged 'em to see where they was goin'. Some would go to Willow Creek, some would go up the Skwentna." Fish and Game gave all the fish to the Tyonek Indians.

"We got to know the people in Tyonek pretty good. We'd even take the *Nomad* and haul freight for them and stuff like that—Joee and I."

CHAPTER 19

The Mighty *Nomad*

*I am a great believer in luck, and I find the
harder I work the more I have of it.*

THOMAS JEFFERSON

The *Nomad* was Joe's pride and joy. This forty-foot wooden boat was built
in 1953 by Charlie and Bob Mathison. They had a place across Cook Inlet
on Big Indian Creek, which flowed into Chickaloon Bay. Years of experience taught them what was needed in a boat to withstand the rugged waters
of Cook Inlet. They built the sturdy boat with heavy beams that ran the
length of the keel making it a strong, powerful, boat that "could slowly plow
through some pretty rough waters." It had a tunnel stern which kept the
propellers up inside the flat-bottomed boat. This was great for fishing and
hauling freight in Cook Inlet because it could sit right on the mud flats and
not damage the props.

Raymie said, "These two men could do a lot of things. They were go-get-
ters and could move anythin'." The *Nomad* was built with the same toughness in mind.

Joe had learned just how important having good equipment was, so in
1955 he went to one of the best boat builders in the area and bought the
Nomad. He took it across Cook Inlet and all the way up Fish Creek to Flat
Horn Lake.

"One time I pulled two scows with thousands of fish in it to Anchorage." The *Nomad* was a very dependable boat for Joe. He used it not only for fishing, but also for hauling freight.

In the late 1950's a fellow hired Joe to haul a dismantled sixty-by-eighteen-foot building and other materials from Beluga River, which is south of the Susitna River, into Anchorage.

Joe was always very up front and honest in his business deals, so he told the man, "I don't carry no insurance, so be sure to insure each load so you'll be safe because it's a bad area, and it is a bad time of year for storms. We can do it, but it is risky and it's possible we could lose a load."

The man agreed to do just that.

Joe built a scow from one of the army's portable bridges, the ones they used to land troops on shores during the war. The frame was made of steel alloy. He put sides on it, turning that bridge into a scow the Redingtons called the *Stickleback*. "It didn't look much like a boat," stated Joee, "but it was sure sturdy and great to haul freight." They would use this to haul the building materials.

The *Stickleback*, a scow Joe built,
and the *Nomad* at Flat Horn Lake.

Joee helped his dad on this job. The day they set out to haul all the material was perfect. Cook Inlet was smooth and calm.

Joe used a one-inch, 400-foot nylon rope to pull the fifty-foot *Stickleback* behind the *Nomad*. Load after load of materials were hauled into Anchorage across Cook Inlet. One more load to go.

This last load took a while to load. "We had the scow loaded down good and heavy," said Joe. "Plus the *Nomad* was loaded, too."

As they headed across Cook Inlet with their last load, the weather began to change. The farther out they got the worse the weather became. The *Nomad*

The *Nomad* in Cook Inlet carrying a load of freight.

faced the full blast of winds that funneled down between the mountains surrounding Turnagain Arm. Within minutes the waves got so big, they broke the nylon rope that was pulling the scow.

Joe gasped. "This is the first time I've ever had that happen."

Now the battle was on!

The *Nomad's* engine was very powerful. Joe broke through each wave as they drove through the rough waters. But now he had to turn around and somehow get ahold of the scow again. Joee and the owner of the freight grabbed the long poles with hooks, but as they reached to hook the cargo ropes, a wave roared over them, taking the poles with it.

Now what? The fierce waves were pitching them all over the place.

Joe fought to keep the *Nomad* faced into each wave and he had to keep track of the loose 400-foot rope on the *Stickleback* all at the same time. One thing he didn't want to happen was to have that rope get sucked up and tangled in his props. And all the while, he was still keeping an eye on the scow. He had to get a rope on it quick.

"I don't know how in the world I'm going to do it, unless I get on top of it." Then Joe hollered above the roar of the storm to Joee, "There's only one thing to do. I've got to sit the *Nomad* right on top of that scow." The *Nomad's* flat bottom would allow that to happen.

"You get ready to jump and tie the rope to the cargo! Be careful!"

Joe skillfully maneuvered the *Nomad* around and rode the next big wave landing right smack on top of the *Stickleback*. Joee jumped off the *Nomad*, grabbed the scow's rope, then jumped back onto the *Nomad* and began securing the *Stickleback* to the *Nomad* again. The next big wave took the *Nomad* right off the load.

"That *Nomad* was one tough boat," Joe said.

They succeeded in getting the scow tied to the *Nomad* again. But the battle wasn't over. Joe surveyed the situation again. It wasn't very good at best.

"I'm great for going right for it—but there is a time to turn around and run. You've got to know when that is," stated Joe.

Water was coming in great waves over the *Nomad*. Joe looked at the tossing *Stickleback* and knew he was going to lose it again.

"Oh, we're not going to make it!"

The other fellow was petrified. He just knew they were going to die.

"Don't panic," Joe stated firmly. "You have a perfect right to be scared. But we are very safe with this boat. We are going to be all right. We may lose all the load, but we're going to be okay."

This helped some, but the poor fellow was still very much afraid.

"Now hang on and bail!" Joe yelled over the thundering waves.

Getting to Anchorage was out of the question now. Joe turned back and headed for the Beluga River again. As he got closer he could see a mountain of water roaring out of the Beluga River. The waves were huge.

That wasn't going to work. The *Nomad* could make it but not with the scow.

Turning to Joee, he said, "Well, okay. We know we're on the flats. Let's get out all of our anchors, tie 'em on the line, throw 'em out, and see if that won't hold."

So they took their three anchors—a 75-pounder and two 50-pound anchors and anchored the scow to the mud flats. Ordinarily that would hold the scow, but this was not an ordinary situation.

Once loose from the scow, Joe took the *Nomad* and went right through the towering waves into the mouth of the Beluga. With each surge of water the *Nomad* was lifted high enough so they could see the scow. Then before their very eyes the scow was lifted up and flipped over!

Joe kept the *Nomad* in the calmer Beluga River. Only when the tide was going out did he steer the *Nomad* over to the scow. Fortunately, the waves worked in Joe's favor. They were able to right the scow. Then, as the water level dropped with the outgoing tide, Joe set the *Nomad* on the mud flats right beside the empty *Stickleback*.

With the tide out there was a half mile or more of mud flats from the shore to the inlet waters. Lumber and barrels and other debris speckled the silty shoreline.

The owner of the cargo stood on deck shaking his head.

"What's wrong?" Joe asked.

"I didn't insure this last load."

"No insurance?"

"And now I don't have anything to pay you. I was thinking to sell that building to be able to pay you."

"Why didn't you get insurance?"

"Because everything was going so smoothly."

As the two men continued to talk, they struck up a deal. Joe would take all the building materials scattered up and down the flats as payment for the job. The three empty tanks he would haul into Anchorage in better weather.

This wrestle with Mother Nature proved again to Joe the importance of good equipment. He said, "I'm heck for strength. I like it to be heavy, but I want it to be strong. Even on my dog posts. I don't put any little thin posts in. If it's a seven-inch post, then I know it's goin' to hold."

Well, the mighty *Nomad* held Joe in good stead on this trip, that's for sure.

Joe and the boys hauled housing material up to the Susitna River and on to Flat Horn Lake in the *Nomad* for the next week or so. By the end of the summer Joe and his family had a new home.

"We built and raised our house around the tent," grinned Vi.

"It's like living in a mansion!" said Vi after they got it built. Their new home was seventy feet long with windows all along the length of the building. Joe built a room on top of the house that was Vi's den. She had a little desk and typewriter and she could look all around Flat Horn Lake. My, how she loved that little room. Joe and the boys painted the whole house green.

The tents had served them well. Now it was time to move on to a new chapter in their lives.

Vi had her own special place to write. She continued writing letters to people she thought might be able to help preserve the historical Iditarod Trail. If Joe heard of someone who might take up their cause, he told Vi and she sent off another letter. They would not see the results of their dream until more than twenty-five years had passed and uncounted hundreds of letters had been written.

One of the houses destroyed where the
land sloughed away in Anchorage.

CHAPTER 20

Earthquake Rocks Alaska

We learn geology the morning after the earthquake.

RALPH WALDO EMERSON

Light filigree snowflakes were falling from the late-afternoon March sky. Birds stopped singing. Vi did not see even one of her twenty-five chickadees—they were all gone. "The dogs never barked that day," said Timmy. Flat Horn Lake seemed strangely silent the whole day long. Then around dinner time, they heard a deep, ominous rumble. Without really knowing why, everyone sensed something was about to happen. Then it hit.

Earthquakes were common in this part of Alaska, but this one was different. The ground started to heave up and down like someone was shaking a huge carpet. No one could stand, not even the dogs—and they had four legs to balance them! "You could look across the lake and see the hillside waving," said Vi. The trees whipped back and forth touching the ground on each side with each upheaval of the ground. Ice on the lake cracked and mud was shooting up in the air like little geysers. The sound was deafening.

The day was March 27, 1964, and a tremendous earthquake rock'n'rolled and ripped through Central Alaska. The Good Friday quake hit at 5:36 p.m. registering 9.2 on the Richter scale and is the second largest earthquake recorded in the world.

"Here," said Joee, "is Bill Lydic and a friend who came by to visit on their Arctic Cat snowmachines. They lived at Susitna Station."

Their house was always chockful of everything imaginable. Homesteading for the Redingtons required that. Vi did not want to part with anything because she never knew when she or Joe or the boys would need it.

Joe said, "I could come in on a moments notice and say, 'Vi, I need a little can.' Vi would say, 'Oh, here you are.' and it would be just exactly what I wanted because she's got fifty of them setting there of different sizes and shapes."

When folks live miles from any store, their home quite often becomes their own multi-purpose store and at Flat Horn Lake, Vi was the shopkeeper that had everything.

"Right over the stove we had a bowl with a little turtle. It started to fall off the window sill at me," said Vi. "It was a white turtle and I grabbed that bowl and I couldn't do anythin' with it. I was tryin' to get outta the kitchen. I finally wobbled out of the place and rescued the kid's turtle."

"She comes out of there with a big smile on her face and says, 'Boy, wasn't that a dandy!'" recalled Joe.

The Redington's new home at
Flat Horn Lake made from the
materials that were lost when the
Stickleback was flipped in the storm.

"Scared everybody else to death," responded Vi. "I thought it was funny."

"Nothing fell though," grinned Joe. "The only thing that would have fallen was that turtle."

The earthquake lasted a good five minutes before it decided to stop shaking the dickens out of the earth's crust. The boys didn't know if a Russian missile had hit near their house or if an earthquake had hit. It just seemed to be too big to be an earthquake. Everyone took it in stride. No one got really excited, but they were very curious.

"I don't think anythin' broke. Nothin' could fall. It was congested. How could it. Everythin' just sorta leaned against one another," laughed Joe.

"Mud was shooting out of the lake," said Timmy. Then he grinned and said, "Mom likes earthquakes."

They turned on the radio to see what had happened, but there was no radio contact. It wasn't until the next day that they heard what was going on in the rest of Alaska.

Joe got in his plane and flew over Anchorage and saw how the land had sloughed away along the inlet, buildings had crumbled, and a fissure cut through downtown Anchorage and right up Fourth Avenue. The damage was terrible, but what caused the biggest problem was the tsunami that followed. Anchorage was not affected because it was at the end of the long Cook Inlet, but several communities and even towns in Oregon and California were. Unfortunately, 131 people died in this tremendous quake.

When Joe flew back to Flat Horn, he surveyed the area. He said, "We had a sawmill on an island. The whole island disappeared." They never saw any part of that sawmill again.

CHAPTER 21

1967 Centennial Sled Dog Race

Whether you think you can or think
you can't—you are right.

HENRY FORD

If Joe said he would do something, he made sure it got done. When he believed in what he was doing, he did everything in his power to make it happen. For Joe his word, his handshake, was a contract carved in stone. He said, "You get one shot at this life and you might as well make the most of it." So Joe always stood by his word.

Joe's true character would be tested again.

Joe and Vi and a number of other folks in the area loved dogs and dog mushing, so in the early 1960s they formed the Aurora Dog Mushers Club. Each dog-mushing club in the state sponsored short sprint races. And Joe drove or flew his boys to some of these sprint dog races. Each month these friends got together to talk about the best way to take care of their dogs, where to set sled dog trails, discuss upcoming sled dog races, and, of course, tell dog stories.

Tom Johnson, a local teacher, was one man who attended these meetings. He was a good friend of Joe's. He said, "Joe was a perfect meeting-goer. He was outspoken but very gentlemanly. He would always raise his hand and then speak. And the stories he could tell!"

At one meeting, Joe began, "I had fourteen dogs on a line and we ran across a snag. The tree went up through my bridle. The sled was stuck. And the dogs was jumpin' and pullin' at the harness wantin' to go. But I couldn't pull the sled backward to get it off the snag.

"I could turn the dogs around and go back the other way and let 'em jerk the sled around and then hope that I could get it righted and everythin'. Then go with the dogs and try it again and miss the snag this time. But maybe that ain't the best situation. That's when an axe will come in good. I always carry an axe. But here I am choppin' at the snag and all of a sudden the dogs are jerkin' on the line and I'm standin' here with the axe and there goes my sled. I had to run quite a ways to catch up with my team. My ice hook didn't stay. I shoulda taken the axe and dug a little hole so that I would make sure the sled would hold."

He told his listeners, "Get prepared before you cut off a snag. You will run across lots of those. If you're runnin' a dog team on a lot of these trails, there will be a time when you've got to do some thinkin'."

Joe always had lots of ideas—some worked and some didn't. But in Joe's mind there were no failures, just things that didn't work. Failure means you didn't learn something. He was always learning and improving his methods and techniques with dog training and feeding or sled building or boat building or whatever needed to be done. Joe would certainly agree with Thomas Edison, who said, "I know a thousand things that don't work." And just as Edison did succeed in the end with his light bulb, so Joe had his times of success. In fact, he was always on the trail to success. He was continually moving forward through the bumps and stumps and rough trails, but he was always moving forward.

Dog mushers helped support other dog mushers. Joe was a real doggy individual and always a champion for huskies, and he was all for helping others get involved with sled dog mushing.

"I met Joe in 1970 at an Aurora Dog Mushers meeting," said Gleo Huyck, another musher attending these meetings. "Joe would call and say, 'I've got a couple of dogs for you.' So I'd go home with seven or eight dogs and that's how I built my team."

The Aurora Dog Mushers sponsored a yearly sled dog race in February. Different communities around the state sponsored races at different times during the long winter months and mushers traveled to these races to compete. Sled dog racing in the winter in the '40s, '50s, and '60s in Alaska was as important as football games in the fall in the rest of the United States.

In the mid 1960s communities in Alaska, including Knik and Wasilla, were planning ways to commemorate Alaska's 100th birthday as a territory of the

United States. Alaska was purchased from Russia in 1867 for $7,200,000, which was about two cents an acre.

Dorothy Page, an avid historian, who had moved to Wasilla in the early 1960s, was chairman of the Wasilla-Knik Centennial Committee. She was also a fairly new member of the Aurora Dog Mushers Club. She had a great interest in the history of Alaska and had read about the Iditarod Trail. She thought a sled dog race on part of the old Iditarod Trail might be fun for the Centennial celebrations, but she couldn't find a musher who was interested. Then someone told her to talk to Joe Redington. He would be flying Timmy to the Junior Sled dog race at the Willow Winter Carnival. She knew Joe had rediscovered the trail and opened it for use in the early 1950s. She knew Joe used the trail to get to and from his home at Flat Horn Lake and of Joe and Vi's efforts to get it on the National Register. Joe Redington Sr. was the man she needed to see.

Dorothy made sure she was at the Willow race. Then she presented her idea to Joe. Joe didn't have to think very long before he responded with a quick, "That sounds like a good deal." After all, since 1948 he and Vi had been intrigued with the history of the Iditarod Trail and not too many years later began writing countless letters to get the trail recognized as a historic trail. A Centennial race on a section of the old trail they loved would surely help them in their quest to preserve the historic gold rush and mail route and get it recognized nationally.

"When do we start?" he asked.

And that was all it took.

Of all the mushers in the state of Alaska, there was only one man with a vested interest, knowledge of the trail, untold contacts, and the creative, hardworking drive it would take to put on a new sled dog race. That man was Joe Redington Sr.

The small community was a-buzz with discussion about the Centennial celebrations. Wheels started to grind. They had just over a year to make it happen.

"Mr. and Mrs. V.R. Wilkerson suggested Knik as a starting point," Vi said, "and talked to Mrs. Bjorn about the Roadhouse and preserving it for a museum." Vi had been saving a number of things for a museum and volunteered to keep the museum open once it got established.

Joe said the first thing he needed to do was get together with the Aurora Dog Mushers Club. There were so many dog races in February and March, that finding a day to hold the race would be a bit difficult. He needed to get permission from them to use their dog race date for this new Centennial Race.

He visited with Ed Carney, President of the Aurora Dog Mushers Club, and they talked over the idea. Joe had already given quite a bit of thought to this idea and shared it with Carney.

Carney said, "Let's bring it up at our next meeting."

The meeting was held, but there was not an easy, quick approval for the race. Some said, "This is too big a race for a small club of twenty-three to sponsor."

Some asked, "Where are we going to get all the money that is needed to sponsor the race?"

Others asked, "Who is going to set the trail?"

Still others said, "The Fur Rendezvous Race is very close to Aurora Dog Mushers Championship Race. Who will come to the Centennial Race with the Rendezvous having $7,000 as prize money?"

No one knew.

Somewhere in the mix of all the discussions about the Centennial Race, Joe reasoned, "Ten thousand dollars wouldn't be enough to draw people to come. So, how about setting the prize money at twenty-five thousand dollars? That will be bigger and better than we've ever had, but still under what they pay for golf matches Outside." *Outside* was a term used by Alaskans for the other contiguous forty-eight states.

Utter disbelief, and perhaps even fear, filled the thoughts of those who heard Joe's suggestion. It took a few minutes for what Joe proposed to sink in.

"Twenty-five thousand dollars?" several people mumbled, as their mouths fell open.

"Well," said Joe later, "I wanted a large enough purse to create a lot of interest. You have to have it big to attract the people." And boy, was Joe thinking big.

"Twenty-five thousand dollars!"

As the idea was tossed around, some mushers mumbled they'd sign up for a purse that big. But where would they find that kind of money? Joe, in his charismatic and enthusiastic manner, touched the spirit of sled dog racing in the hearts of those present, and they voted to go forward with the race.

Before long a special committee was appointed to plan the race. On the Centennial Race Committee were Joe and Vi Redington, Dorothy Page, Ed Carney, and Lee Twing. Joe was elected chairman. Even so, most of the people thought that sponsoring this race was way out of their league.

Just before one of the Aurora Dog Mushers meetings, Joe and Vi had themselves a little *sit-down talk* to discuss what to do about the $25,000 purse. They came up with a plan to donate an acre of their land at Flat Horn Lake. This acre would be divided into parcels of one square foot and be sold for $2.00 each. The legal deeds to the land would be a souvenir of the Alaska Purchase Centennial and would help provide the sorely needed money to support the Centennial Race.

The race committee presented Joe's idea at the meeting. Coming up with the $25,000 was a huge concern for the club members, so Joe and Vi's idea sounded good. The land was surveyed and then the mushers started selling the deeds. Vi was constantly at her typewriter and Joe was constantly talking to folks. Joe and Vi were coming back and forth to Knik so often that they decided to move into Knik. The upcoming race needed all their attention.

Joe and Vi moved into the little Bjorn cabin in Old Knik, just across from Knik Hall, the old pool room, dance hall, and roadhouse.

"Mel Bjorn, he owned the building, where the museum is now," Joe said. "It was in pretty bad shape. But Mel always wanted to see something good for the old building. That's why Jo [Mel's wife, Lois 'Jo' Bjorn] gave it to me. She said, 'I'm sure Mel would want you to have it,' so she gave me one acre of land and that building. I turned it over to the Aurora Mushers and they turned it over to the Borough."

Vi was part of a small group working to get the old buildings on the National Registry, so they would be preserved. The museum was her baby. She had been collecting historical items just for the museum. Joe was also busy. He contacted the Adult Correctional Camp in Sutton to see if the inmates might be able to help renovate the building. The work on the building was to begin the next summer. In the meantime, the dog mushers were going to use the Knik Hall as the headquarters for the Centennial Race, since they had decided that Knik would be the starting point.

The Centennial Race was to be held February 11 and 12, 1967, and had two 28-mile heats. The mushers would start at Knik and race to Big Lake on Saturday and back to Knik on Sunday for a total of fifty-six miles. The prize of $25,000 would be split between the top eighteen mushers. They also were going to honor Leonhard Seppala, known as one of the world's greatest dog mushers and a man Joe and Vi greatly admired.

The similarities between Seppala and his wife, Connie, and Joe and Vi were notable.

Leonhard Seppala was a hardy, hard-working Norwegian who came looking for gold during the gold rush era in Nome in 1900. There was no doubt that Seppala was a great dog musher. Seppala, like Joe, had his first dog team a year after he arrived in Alaska. He used dogs to work for him, just like Joe. He hauled freight and mail in and gold out from various gold camps in northern Alaska. Joe hauled freight, also.

Seppala was asked to train a team of Siberian huskies for the Arctic explorer, Roald Amundsen. Then World War I came along and Amundsen was not able to use the dogs. Instead, Seppala was allowed to keep them. From these dogs he developed a very strong team of huskies. Seppala was also a champion dog musher. He won forty-three silver trophies and bowls, and eight gold medals. For three years between 1915 and 1917, he won the All-Alaska Sweepstakes between Nome and Candle. Seppala lived in Alaska for forty-seven years, and the records show that he had mushed his dogs about 250,000 miles.

Seppala's wife, Connie, was a strong woman. Vi was a strong woman. Connie learned to trust in her husband's expertise and not worry much even though he was gone for long periods of time. Vi had developed the same trust in Joe and did not get worried when he didn't return when he said he would.

The Seppala's were now living in Seattle, but were going to come up for this Centennial sled dog race. Joe had never met Seppala, but had a friend, Ray Thompson, who knew him and had him set up this trip. Joe was really looking forward to their meeting. In Joe's mind, Seppala was a big part of the history of dog mushing in Alaska, and the Iditarod Trail was also part of dog-mushing history. It was only fitting that Seppala be a part of this race. Unfortunately, in January 1967, just before the Centennial race was to honor him, Seppala passed away. But Connie came, bringing his ashes with her. She wanted Joe to spread them near his property on the Iditarod Trail.

She told Joe, "You two would have really gotten along well. You remind me so much of him."

Seppala was small and wiry like Joe and their sense of determination would have made them kindred spirits. Connie gave Joe and Vi her favorite photo of Leonhard Seppala, which they hung proudly on their living room wall.

It's been said that Seppala represented all mushers and this Centennial race was patterned after the All-Alaska Sweepstakes he raced in Nome in the early 1900s. To honor Seppala's memory and his achievements, the race was to be called to the Iditarod Trail Seppala Memorial Centennial Race.

They had raised $12,000 from the sale of the land, but they needed more.

"We got to know the people at Tyonek pretty good," Joe said. "We'd even take the *Nomad* and haul freight in for 'em and stuff like that—Joee and I." One friend was the Tyonek Indian tribal chief.

"Bob Cummings was on KYAK [radio] and got with him in Fairbanks and told him I was having a little trouble." Other mushers went up to Fairbanks and wanted to know if the Tyonek chief could help out, too. Then he talked to Joe, "He said sure, I'll guarantee the money." The chief had returned to Anchorage when something tragic occurred. "See, he got killed in that fire in that hotel in Anchorage," said Joe sadly, shaking his head about the loss of his long time friend. Then he added, to explain the challenges that were to

The start and finish line at Knik Lake of the 1967 Alaska Centennial Race on nine miles of the Iditarod Trail between Knik and Big Lake.

follow, "And I lost my main support. And that's why we had to mortgage the place to secure the money."

Joe being Joe, a man of his word, was determined to find a way to make sure there would still be a race. Joe had a talk with the Tyonek elders and they agreed to lend the $15,000, but only with some collateral.

That is when Joe and Vi had another little *sit-down talk*. They believed in this Centennial sprint race, which ran along a nine-mile section of the Iditarod Trail. Somehow they sensed the importance of this event. For them there was only one thing to do—they would put up their homestead at Flat Horn Lake for collateral.

The purse was secured.

Now they had to find some folks to help lay out the new race trail. Joe knew Carney had a dozer and he would help. Dick Mackey, a friend and fellow musher, and Joe teamed up and put in many long days clearing brush and trees that had grown over parts of the trail. Nine Mile Hill, the steep hill with killer switch-backs, needed a lot of work. Many other people put in hours and hours to make this little race happen. In those days that's what folks did— they helped each other. Volunteerism wasn't the term used then as it is today. People simply got together and helped each other for the good of the cause.

The trail was set. And the race was on.

Sprint racers from across the state and from Outside showed up to race. Big name mushers like Herbie Nayokpuk from Shishmaref, George Attla from Huslia, Dr. Roland Lombard from Weyland, Massachusetts, and Earl Norris of Anchorage. Fifty-four mushers finished the fifty-six-mile race. Joe raced too, but because he had been so busy trying to put together the race, he didn't have time to train his dogs. His boys, who also raced, put together a team for him. It was not the best team, but he raced and had fun anyway. Dick Mackey raced, too. Isaac Okleasik of Teller, a true dog musher from his youth, was the winner taking home $7,000 in winnings. The rest of the winnings was split between the top twenty-five mushers. Joee was twelfth, Raymie was twentieth, Dick Mackey was thirty-fourth, and Joe was forty-seventh.

"Everyone who participated had a fine time." Joe was pleased.

"After the race ten of us," remembered Mackey, "me, Joe, Dick Tozier, Earl Norris and some others—got together and started the Iditarod Trail Blazers [a group dedicated to re-establishing the old Iditarod Trail]. We put up $100 each." This was put in a pot for the next race—maybe to Iditarod.

That summer reconstruction began on the Knik Hall to preserve the historical building and have a place for the museum. A local homesteader, Mel Behnke, worked as a correctional officer and supervised a crew of inmates from the camp in Sutton. "Another couple of months and that building would not have been salvageable. It was sinking into the ground. There was no foundation." And the roof was beginning to fall in on itself.

"We had to double the floor joists to get enough beef underneath to get it up in the air." He used come-alongs, chains, and collar ties as they jacked up the old, two-story building inch by inch. "It was creaking and struggling," Behnke said. But it managed to stay together under Behnke's expert supervision. Once they had a firm foundation, they tackled the sagging roof which was about to collapse. "How it lasted as long as it did, I'll never know."

It was completely rebuilt and took most of the summer of '67 to complete.

Behnke was also a pilot. "Sometimes I would fly my little J-3 plane over to work and land on Knik Lake near Joe's plane." Then he added, "Joe enjoyed going out overnight in the Interior. He would go out and siwash for a few days. And like most of us, he had a habit of taking everything but the kitchen sink."

Now the building was ready to become a museum in Knik. Vi couldn't have been happier.

When the next year rolled around, the race was cancelled because of lack of snow. In addition to that, Joe and Vi still owed the Tyonek Indians the $15,000 and the race committee was still trying to get out of debt. Joe and Vi were going to lose their property at Flat Horn, when the State of Alaska

Major renovation work was done on the old Knik Hall in 1967, supervised by Mel Behnke. Joe had been given the building and land around it. Today it is owned by the Matanuska-Susitna Borough. The building was saved and is now the Knik Museum housing the Musher's Hall of Fame.

Sled dogs going on a training run in the summer by Knik Hall. Knik Hall was the old pool room, dance hall, and roadhouse and now is the Knik Museum, which houses the Musher's Hall of Fame.

intervened and through a legislative act, the loan was paid off. How could they not support a very popular Alaska Centennial event and the extremely selfless motive of a man and his wife? Joe and Vi were speechless in gratitude.

Joe quit commercial fishing in 1968 and began working in Unalakleet in the summer at a fish plant.

"When I went into the villages in the '50s, there was a dog team behind every house," Joe recalled. Then Joe's work took him to Unalakleet and he saw a very big change had happened almost overnight. "When I went back in the '60s, the dogs were just about all gone. The snowmachine [also known as snowmobiles] had taken over. I came to Alaska to mush dogs and I didn't want to see the dogs disappear." This was when Joe began his quest to promote the Alaskan huskies. He felt compelled to preserve this magnificent breed of dogs and not have them die out or be replaced by modern-day snowmachines. It occurred to him that one way to champion the Alaskan huskies was to start a long-distance sled dog race. That's when he started talking in earnest about getting a race perhaps to Iditarod and back.

After fishing season finished, Joe flew home to Flat Horn Lake. Then tragedy struck. Their youngest son, Keith, died in an accident. Their sorrow was too great. Joe and Vi packed up and left Flat Horn Lake. Once they left, they never went back. Knik would now be their home for good. Life must go on and they knew that. Joe said, "We're not much for goin' back. Just going ahead with what we're doin'."

In 1969 they had a small race between Knik and Big Lake, but the snow conditions were not very good that year and there were only twelve mushers signed up. The support for this Centennial race had ended.

What didn't end, though, was the determination of Joe and Vi to continue to follow their dream and make the Iditarod Trail a living trail again. They continued working to get it on the National Trail Registry, and perhaps, they reasoned, dog racing was the way to do it. They didn't want to see the Iditarod Trail disappearing once more into the history books. They, also, had a few friends who were willing to help see this happen.

Once Joe set his mind on something, it was hard to get him off track. His determination and spirit was as strong as his old wheel dog, Chinook! Racing on the Iditarod Trail, he saw as a two-fold solution to a problem they wanted to solve: (1) bring back sled dogs to Alaska, and (2) get the Iditarod Trail recognized as a national historical trail.

"You've got to believe in it and you can do it. If you don't believe, it won't happen." This was Joe's thought for everything in life.

CHAPTER 22

A New Race is Born

Everyone has oceans to fly, if they have the
heart to do it. Is it reckless? Maybe. But
what do dreams know of boundaries?

AMELIA EARHART

"The Aurora Dog Mushers Club was the nucleus for brainstorming a long race," said Dan Seavey, a fellow musher and member.

Joe and a number of his mushing friends talked continually. "I would sit around with Joe and Vi in their little cabin, where they were living at the time," recalled Seavey, "and throw around ideas back and forth about a race to Iditarod." Then a hint of humor softly resounded in Seavey's voice, as he thought back to their very full, little cabin, "It was hard to find a place to sit, but we just wiggled in and found a place."

"In 1970 there was a little committee here that we had. We announced that we were goin' to have a race to Iditarod and back in 1973," Joe remembered. "We gave 'em three years to get ready for it. But no one had ever heard of Iditarod, even the local people. It was a dead issue. So we had to change that."

All the talking, planning, and dreaming of a new long distant race to Iditarod over a number of years wasn't taking hold. The little Centennial Race was a thing of the past. However, the old Trail Committee meetings were still happening. Ideas were exchanged, interest grew little by little. Concerns were addressed, and possibilities were dreamed.

Seavey called their discussions "kitchen table stuff." Seavey and Tom Johnson were fellow teachers from Seward. Then Tom moved to Palmer to teach, got involved with the Aurora Dog Mushers Club, met Joe, Mackey, and Gleo Hyuck, another teacher, and Dave Olson. Johnson got Seavey to be a part of the Aurora Dog Mushers. These men loved their dogs and the adventure of dog mushing.

But another new race was not what most mushers seemed to want. They looked at the financial challenges they had with the Centennial Race, plus all the work involved. Some skeptical reporters, mushers, and folks involved with the small Centennial Race said this new race to Iditarod was just another one of Joe's wild ideas—no substance, only trouble.

However, no matter what was said, Joe was not deterred. His enthusiasm was nourished by Vi and a few close friends. Vi was continually on the look out for any materials written about old Knik and the mail trail and Iditarod. They felt the more knowledgeable they became, the more this might help get the trail nationally recognized as an important trail in the United States. And interest more mushers in the process.

"We both wrote letters to get the Iditarod on the National Trail Registry," said Vi. "Joe would dictate and I would type out the letters."

The romance of the trail by sled dogs, the camaraderie on the trail, the adventure into the wilds of Alaska—Joe loved the idea. And once Joe got an idea and he knew it was feasible, he dogged it and just never gave up.

"I tried to get some money or interest and the first thing they'd ask is 'Where's Iditarod?' Nobody knew anythin' about it." But that didn't stop him from talking. He never passed up an opportunity to spread the word about this new idea of a long-distance race. The seed was planted and Joe's quest for a race on more than nine miles of the original trail was being fostered daily.

To Joe Redington, the idea of running dogs along the old Iditarod Trail burned in his thought day and night. Joe knew sled dogs. He knew the dogs could do it. He knew it was possible. For over twenty years he had been freighting with his dogs and racing his dogs. He knew how these Alaskan huskies loved to be on the trail—to be working in the harness. The mushers would be the ones the trail would really test. The mushers were the ones he had to convince.

All Joe needed was to find mushers who believed the same as he did. Mushers who were willing to try this unique long-distance race with him.

Johnson and Huyck, were two mushers who heard Joe's proposal at an Aurora Dog Mushers meeting.

"He and Vi would go to every dog mushers meeting," said Johnson. "Joe could have you spell-bound for hours telling stories about the things he did.

"But when Joe mentioned the idea of going to Iditarod, everyone thought, 'Ah, there goes Joe again with one of his dreams.' No one thought it was a good one at all. He got no encouragement from anyone. None."

The difficulties in finding the old trail beyond Susitna River to McGrath appeared almost insurmountable to most people. Vi had written Alaska's U.S. Senator Mike Gravel to see if there were surveying records left by the Alaska Road Commission, who had established the trail originally. That was a dead end. They talked to trappers along the trail who reported that little remained, if any, of the old trail markers.

In March 1971 the local paper carried a notice from the Iditarod Trail Committee, which was formed in 1967 for the Centennial Race, and the Aurora Dog Mushers. They planned an "overnight camping" excursion for dog mushers, cross-country skiers, or snowshoers. Interested folks were to contact Johnson. They hoped this would drum up interest in the trail and the race in 1973 and help to get the trail into the national trail system. But what took people by surprise was they billed it to be the "world's largest sled dog race" to Iditarod and back and the purse would be an unheard-of $50,000! Anyone reading this must have let out a belly laugh of total disbelief and thought, what a pipe dream. But what an incredible pipe dream to think about.

Four camps had been set up between Knik and the Susitna River to accommodate the prospective volunteers, but unfortunately, the weather turned cold, dipping to minus forty-degrees Fahrenheit. Only a few hardy souls, Joe and Vi with their nine dogs, Johnson with his seven dogs, Dr. Hal Bartko with a team of five dogs, and two cross-country skiers, Leo Hannon and his daughter Ellen, were undaunted by the weather and persevered to try and open up the trail.

"It was hectic," said Johnson. "I have great admiration for those early mushers with loads of up to 1,000 pounds." These mushers were pulling about two hundred pounds in their sleds. The sleds kept slipping off the wind-blown trail, so traveling was very slow. They only covered nine of the thirty-five miles they wanted to cover.

They tried the same thing a year later. "Bushwhacking willows and alders is long, tedious work," Vi remembered. "Then there is the zigzagging back and forth to find the trail when the indentations were very faint."

"Sometimes there would be areas where there was no blazed trees and we'd have to figure out where it came out over there. It was difficult to find," said

After trail blazing work was done by 110 soldiers and Joe and Dave Olson on the Iditarod Trail, they had a little church service. The sled dogs howled along with the singing. Then everyone celebrated with some short three-mile dog races.

Joe. "Dave Olson and I spent a lotta time out there. And Dick Mackey and I spent quite a bit of time out there."

Joe was also talking to the army and air force on numerous occasions to see if they could help. They had the manpower. He also reminded them that the Alaska Road Commission, which was part of the army in the early 1900s, had marked and mapped the Nome-to-Seward Mail Trail in 1908.

Finally he got a response from General Charles Gettys, who also liked dog mushing. They worked out a plan. In April 1972 the U.S. Army conducted cold weather maneuvers with hopes of finding and marking the old Iditarod Trail.

"We had the army out there. They had about 112 men out there searchin' for the trail," said Joe. These men were split into two groups—one group started in the Interior at Farewell Lake and worked south over Rainy Pass and the other group started at Knik and worked north. They met after two weeks at Shirley Lake.

The southern group was composed of fifty men and two civilians, Joe and Dave Olson with their two dog teams.

"It was not easy goin'." Joe had the army fly him back to Knik to get his Piper Cub because spotting the old trail was sometimes easier from the air.

Joe met an old friend of his at Skwentna, Joe Delia, who had a funny little story to tell him. Delia told him he was out on his trapline up the Skwentna River in a canyon, when he got quite the surprise—a soldier skied out of the bushes onto his trap line trail! Delia had the only useable trail out there at the time. Animals on the trail—yes, but a soldier? That was the last thing in the world Delia thought he would see in the middle of nowhere. They had a good laugh, then Delia got filled in on what was happening.

After two weeks of trail blazing, they had a little celebration.

"We had church out there an' all," Joe recalled. "They flew Chaplin William Hoehne out there to give a sermon that mornin'." They sang "The Old Rugged Cross" and "He's Got the Whole World in His Hands" with the dogs howling right along with all the soldiers. Then they had mini three-mile races splitting Joe and Dave's dog teams up between them. It was great fun after lots of hard work.

Later Joe and Mackey flew to Skwentna to see Joe and Norma Delia. They ended up using part of their trap line for the race trail. "We always tease and say we have a national trapline," Delia said a number of years later.

Sometime in October 1972 Johnson and Huyck were in Anchorage buying dog food and over cups of coffee, they again were discussing the trail work that was done and the possibility of actually getting a race to Iditarod, but the problem was there was no definitive action being taken to pull this race off in just a few short months.

"We really liked the idea and were all in favor of it," said Johnson. "Let's really get with it on this. He needs some support." So they called Joe from Anchorage and asked, "Do you really want to do this?"

"Yah!" came Joe's spirited absolute reply.

"All right, we'll do it. We'll help you."

They could almost see Joe's lop-sided grin when he said, "Sounds great."

Huyck asked, "Do you really think we can do it this year?"

"Well, it's October. We have until March to get ready. We can do this," answered Joe.

Johnson smiled, "As soon as he had our support, why he was BAM, let's go!"

Unfortunately, those who worked on the 1967 Centennial Race were not there to help or support Joe's idea until later. "When I guaranteed a purse of $50,000, we didn't have a dime. As soon as I guaranteed it, my committee quit."

That left four—Joe, Johnson, Huyck, and Vi—to start figuring out how to put together this race. Vi worked behind the scenes doing everything she could to support Joe's vision. Johnson and Huyck stuck with Joe's vision to make this race happen, even though they were not on the trail committee and they were teaching full-time.

Johnson said, "I thought that was the coolest idea I'd ever heard of. I loved it. That's why I stuck with him."

Until the mushers were on the trail to Nome, sleep was not going to be a part of these four dreamers' day. Together this team of four made up the heartbeat that brought the Iditarod Race to life.

First, they needed people, lots of people, who would volunteer their time and expertise to help with the mechanics of the race and to finish marking the trail. Johnson's wife, Kathy, suggested they get in contact with a businessman she knew, who was a "prime mover" of an organization in Anchorage. He had a lot of young, enthusiastic volunteers that might help pull off a race like this.

"He knew nothing about dogs or mushing, but he did know how to organize, and he knew what needed to be done," said Johnson. So they pursued Kathy's suggestions.

"We needed to incorporate to protect ourselves and the race. So we elected officers in Joe's truck as we crossed the Eklutna Flats," said Huyck, remembering their late-night trip home from one of their meetings in Anchorage. "Joe was president, Tom was vice-president, and I was secretary/treasurer."

Joe was a great promoter and knew many people. He also knew about racing dogs and finding an overgrown fifty-year-old trail, but the business end of a race was definitely not his forte. Johnson and Huyck knew they needed more help.

Within this group of motivated and active volunteers was a young lawyer, Terry Aglietti, who caught the spirit of Joe's race. "At the time I was traveling around the state writing education grants," said Aglietti. "This was a transition time in the villages from the dog teams to snowmachines. Joe saw the sled dogs fading from the cultural life-style of the people in the villages and I saw that, too." Aglietti agreed to work for them as a lawyer, making sure their fund raisers were legal and helped promote the idea that would help preserve the sled dog culture in Alaska.

They really needed some good publicity. The press was not very supportive of the idea and seemed to focus more on the problems rather than looking for the good. They needed to figure out a way to get mushers interested. So they hired a public relations man, Steve Smirnoff.

One of the first stumbling blocks they discussed was Iditarod. Where in the world was Iditarod? Nobody had heard of the place. They needed to come up with some place that mushers could get excited about—a place that had a magical ring. Then somewhere in the conversation the town of Nome hit the thought-waves. Why not run to the old gold rush town of Nome? They had dog races in the early 1900s between Nome and Candle. Nome—everyone knew where Nome was.

Joe was fired up! When he got home late that night and got the dogs fed, he called his friend, Mackey. Midnight seemed to be the best time for these friends to visit.

"What do you think about runnin' to Nome?" Joe asked.

Before Joe finished, Mackey was already on board. With the enthusiasm one has for a new adventure, Mackey said, "Well, I'll be the second one to sign up."

"What do ya mean?" Joe asked.

Mackey replied, "Aren't you signed up yet?"

"I sure am," Joe laughed.

Now there were two mushers and a sled dog race to Nome.

At this point they had less than four months to pull off the impossible. This race would be a one-way race, not an out-and-back race, as all the other races had been in Alaska, and they had no idea how many miles it would be—at least 1,000 miles, if not more.

"Joe and Tom [Johnson] and others would meet at my office," said Aglietti. "The first year was very informal. We really didn't know what we were doing." But these few men were making a grand effort to make the race happen.

Getting word out to the mushers was crucial in their minds. Joe wanted very much to get dogs and dog mushing back into the villages.

Mackey asked what he could do to help. So Joe had him writing letters about this new race to mushers and the villages along the trail route.

Joe was making constant trips into Anchorage. After Johnson's and Huyck's teaching day ended, their Iditarod work started. "We would go into Anchorage three or four times a week," said Huyck. They tried to drum up support for the race and met with Aglietti, Smirnoff, and other interested volunteers. Vi was holding the homestead down, taking care of the dogs, running errands, writing letters, and doing whatever Joe asked her to do.

They needed money in the bank for the race purse and to pay expenses. "I went to the banks and they turned me down cold. They said, 'Joe, you're crazy.'"

Johnson remembered, "We went to big corporations and we got zip, nothing, zero. I imagine that as far as they were concerned, this was a hare-brained idea that would never happen."

"No one wanted to support a catastrophe about to happen," said Huyck. There were fund-raisers, but they weren't bringing in what was needed for the big purse.

They also had to have strong support on the other end of the trail in Nome. On December 9, 1972, Joe wrote a letter to his friend and fellow dog musher, Howard Farley. Howard ran a team of dogs for tourists during the summer and was the only man to have a dog team in Nome for some years. The letter started, "I thought you might be interested in this race. I need some help on that end. Let me know if you are interested …" And Farley was. Farley sent the letter on to Leo Rasmussen. Then the Nome Kennel Club got involved. Their tireless teamwork and generosity proved to be invaluable to the Iditarod Race. Now Joe had the support and help he needed from the other end of the Iditarod Trail.

Joe found that many who raced dogs were intrigued by this new idea. They may not have believed it could be done, but they were intrigued.

The entry fee was $100. Their committee did not want money to deter any racers from signing up. And Alaska's native community did show up for this race. Mushers came from Nome, Unalakleet, Teller, Noorvik, Tok, Shishmaref, Fairbanks, Seward, Huslia, Anchorage, Talkeetna, Palmer, Delta Junction, Wasilla, Ester Dome, Akiak, Montana Creek, Houston, Red Devil, and Point Hope. The more mushers that got involved, the more enthusiastic they became. The possibilities of this race began to dawn on the minds of the planners. They could see it becoming a nationwide, even worldwide, sled dog race.

Governor Bill Egan was very supportive. He helped Joe get a place for bigger meetings at the Gold Rush Hotel in Anchorage. Also, in 1972 the State Legislature made dog mushing the Alaska state sport.

They needed race rules. "I wrote the rules in about half an hour. I think some of the stuff is still in there today," Johnson recalled. Dan Seavey worked on the rules with him. "We took the old Alaska Sweepstakes Race rules and modified them to fit the first Iditarod." At the same time, Joe, Vi, and Mackey were eating at the Kashim in Wasilla. They wrote their rules on a napkin. Combined, these veteran mushers had come up with rules for Joe's new race.

Still another big job was getting the trail ready. "Joe was the guy that could do it," Johnson said. "He knew where the real trail was and spent countless hours out there working or flying in his Piper Cub over the route. In December we didn't even have a trail and in March was the race. He got ahold of some army buddies."

Joe, Johnson, and Huyck took turns having more meetings at their homes. They would pour over the map of Alaska figuring out the route for the race and checkpoints. A partial trail was marked between Knik and Farewell Lake, part of the old mail trail to Iditarod. From there they could go through Athabascan

U.S. Army Chinook helicopters landed on Knik Lake unloading ten alpine, double-tracked snowmachines. Their purpose was to test them for extreme arctic military maneuvers and brake trail for the first Iditarod Race to Nome. General Gettys thought this race would be an excellent test for his soldiers and these machines.

The army's winter camouflaged snowmachines are lined up by Knik Bar on Knik Lake ready to brake trail.

villages from Farewell Lake up to Ruby on the Yukon River using the village trails. Then they could follow the Yukon River Trail down to Kaltag and take the Kaltag Portage Trail over to Unalakleet. Between there and Nome were a number of Eskimo villages and they could follow the Coastal Trail between those villages with the finish line in downtown Nome.

Time was getting short. Finally, at the eleventh hour Joe again called for help from the army. Less than a week before the race Joe and Vi were in their home at Knik when they heard a low thrump-thrump-thrump sound getting louder and louder. With a nod to Vi, Joe headed out the door and down to Knik Lake. U.S. Army Chinook helicopters had landed and the military were unloading ten alpine, double-tracked snowmachines. To the army these white, camouflaged machines were being tested for extreme arctic military maneuvers. General Gettys thought this project of Joe's would be an excellent test. That was the way they wrote up the order for this venture and that's how they got away with making the trip. To the planners of this race, they would be helping to blaze the old trail to Nome and set a trail for the mushers to follow.

Joe said, "Everythin' kind of worked together. Things fell into place as it went along." Joe was proving one step at a time, that when there is a right idea and the motives are good, nothing can stop that idea from happening. The arrival of the military snowmachines showed this to be true.

There was one huge issue that still needed to be addressed. Johnson and Huyck took Joe aside not long before the race was to begin and said, "You can't go, Joe. We need you here. We still have $50,000 to raise."

"No one knew that we didn't have the prize money yet," said Huyck. Most of the money they had raised had already been spent on unexpected expenses. A drawing, guessing the number of days, hours, and minutes it would take to get to Nome, was one idea for raising money, but it required legal papers to be filed with the State. Aglietti said, "This was a drain of unexpected expenses." And there were many more.

Sadly, Joe admitted, "You're right. There is still too much to do." Once the prize money was guaranteed, he said he would use his Piper PA-11 and help keep the race running from the air.

The Gold Rush Hotel in Anchorage was buzzing with activity the Thursday night before the 1,049-mile race was to start. Joe said, "We came up with the number of miles because we knew the trail was at least a thousand miles and Alaska was the forty-ninth State—1049 miles."

The small Iditarod Committee threw a banquet for those helping with the race and the thirty-four daring mushers. A spirited "can do" atmosphere filled

Muktuk Marston with General Gettys right behind him at Knik Lake. These men were taking in the moment and this incredible long-distance sled dog race that was about to take place.

the room. How? No one knew for sure, but Joe's confidence that the dogs would get the mushers to Nome was starting to rub off on those around him.

At the same time, "There was a lot of doubt at the banquet," said Huyck. "Some were afraid the money support for the race wouldn't be there."

Johnson and Huyck took Joe aside at the Banquet. "We call you the silver-tongued fox," said Huyck. "You need to convince them that it will happen."

And that is just what Joe did. He met their challenge. He said the money would be there when they got to Nome and the mushers believed him.

Rules for the race were read and then each musher came up one at a time to draw a number for their starting position. Then Mayor Dan Renshaw of Nome spoke and promised a great party at the end of the trail.

Most people didn't realize Joe would not be running the race as he had dreamed, at least not this year. Joe asked Raymie if he would run his dogs. He really wanted his team on the trail. He told Raymie, "I didn't send my dogs' food out to the checkpoints, but I will air-drop you what you'll need."

Not prepared, but having the Redington spirit, Raymie said, "Well, the dogs are trained. I might as well take 'em and go."

Racing the 1,049 miles to many was a far-fetched idea. It had never been done before. Was it even possible?

CHAPTER 23

1973 Iditarod Trail Race to Nome

If you can trust yourself when all men doubt you,
But make allowance for their doubting too;
If you can force your heart and nerve and sinew
To serve your turn long after they are gone,
And so hold on when there is nothing in you
Except the will which says to them: "Hold on!"
Yours is the Earth and everything that's in it,
And—which is more—you'll be a Man, my son!

RUDYARD KIPLING

Joe slept very little the night before the big day. His mind was spinning with all the details of this incredible race. Before dawn, he loaded up the truck with his dogs and gear and headed into Anchorage. As he drove across the Matanuska and Knik River bridges, he saw open water. Not good he thought. All this warm weather and little snow cover was going to be another obstacle to cross. But the race would go on. The mushers will have to use the bridges. Volunteer race officials will have to redirect traffic. There was no way they could cross these rivers today.

Other volunteers had been sent out to the checkpoints along the trail. Ham radio operators were ready to communicate the news of the race. Dog food had been sent out to the checkpoints. Hundreds of details were put in place. Hopefully, they would be enough to help get all the mushers and dogs to Nome safely. But Joe still needed a vet. He had asked a friend in the air force, but that didn't seem possible. Then orders came down through the channels, thanks to General Gettys. Terry Adkins recalled being told, "Doctor Terry Adkins was going to be the vet for the Iditarod for as long as it took."

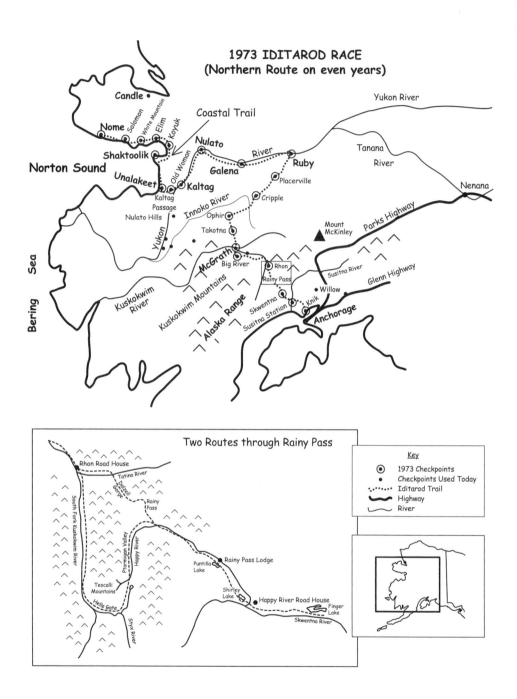

1973 IDITAROD RACE
(Northern Route on even years)

Yukon River

Candle

Nome
Solomon
White Mountain
Elim
Koyuk

Coastal Trail

Shaktoolik
Nulato
River
Ruby

Norton Sound
Galena
Tanana
River

Unalakeet
Kaltag
Nenana

Kaltag
Passage
Old Woman

Placerville

Nulato Hills
Innoko River
Cripple

Yukon
Ophir
Mount
McKinley
Parks Highway

Bering Sea
Takotna

McGrath
Big River
Rhon
Susitna River

Kuskokwim
River
Rainy Pass
Glenn Highway
Willow

Kuskokwim Mountains
Skwentna
Knik

Alaska Range
Susitna Station
Anchorage

Two Routes through Rainy Pass

Rhon Road House

Tatina River

Dalzell Gorge

Rainy Pass

South Fork Kuskokwim River

Ptarmigan Valley

Happy River

Rainy Pass Lodge
Puntilla Lake

Teocalli Mountains

Hells Gate

Styx River

Shirley Lake

Happy River Road House
Finger Lake

Skwentna River

Key

1973 Checkpoints
Checkpoints Used Today
Iditarod Trail
Highway
River

"I had two hours to check thirty-four teams," said Adkins. "Today there are thirty vets and they start looking at dogs three weeks before the race. I pulled one dog out before the start of the race."

This overcast, history-making day was Saturday, March 3, 1973. The Tudor Race Track, now called the Tozier Track, in Anchorage was buzzing with excitement, wonder, and utter disbelief. Families bundled up their children and headed to the dog race.

"Look at the size of those sleds!" folks gasped.

And what an array of sleds there were. Some freight sleds weighed over 400 pounds. The smaller, shorter, but common sprint sleds, were modified to hopefully meet the unknown and, no doubt, very rugged trail conditions to come.

"I wonder how the dogs will fare? Do you think they will make it?" many asked.

Sprint dogs were used to racing short distances over packed trails. This race was well over a thousand miles long. And much of the first half of the trail would take the mushers across two mountain ranges and unfamiliar terrain, not to mention an unpacked, soft trail.

"At least," said other, "there will be some used trails once they get to the Interior villages."

One disbeliever announced, "They'll never get that far. They'll turn around before they even get to the mountains."

A dog enthusiast said, "Joe Redington says the dogs can do it. And he has pulled freight all around Alaska with his dogs. I trust Joe's judgment."

"I hope the rivers are frozen over," another supporter stated.

"Would you look at all that gear," many people muttered.

Mushers were packing and repacking their gear trying to decide what to take and what not to take. Actually, no one knew exactly what they needed. So just to be on the safe side, everything the mushers thought they would need to survive in the wilds of Alaska, they stuffed into the canvas bags on their sleds. The result was sleds piled high with sleeping bags, dog food, stoves, pots and pans, five-gallon Blazo cans, extra clothing, a wide assortment of people food, tents, tarps, axes—you name it, someone surely had it.

Interested spectators continued to comment:

"Some of those sleds look like they weigh a ton."

"How will those dogs be able to pull those heavy freight sleds over the mountain ranges?"

The mushers must first conquer the steep passes and treacherous gorges of the Alaska Range, of which Mount McKinley was a part, and then cross the Kuskokwim Mountain Range.

Dog mushers, sled dogs, sled dog mushing fans, and curious Alaskans filled the Tudor Track for the first start of the first Iditarod Race to Nome in 1973.

"Who in their right mind would want to run this race? What's the point?"

"Look at those beautiful dogs. Golly, there sure are a variety of dogs here. Some of them don't even look like race dogs, do they?" one dog lover commented.

"Look at them pull at their harness. They really want to go!"

Hundreds of supporters and skeptics alike were milling around the Tudor Race Track just to see how all this was going to unfold. Could Joe and a handful of people actually pull off this race? Could the mushers make it safely?

And what about the mushers who came from around the state? What were they thinking and feeling? The questions and doubts racing through their minds were too numerous to record, but one thing was certain—they all were in this first-ever Iditarod Trail Race to Nome for two reasons: the pure and grand adventure of it all, and their great love for dogs and dog mushing.

Joe didn't race this first race of his dreams, but he sent mushers to Nome with a promise and a piece of his adventurous dream in their hearts. He staked his reputation on the belief that these tough Alaskan sled dogs could do it.

"Ten-nine-eight-seven-six-five-four-three-two-one. And they are off to Nome!"

Dick Tozier, the race marshal, along with a longtime musher, Orville Lake, and Joel Kottke, the judge, sent the mushers up the trail to Nome at two minute intervals.

The number one sled was an honorary position set aside in remembrance of Leonhard Seppala's achievements as a dog musher. The first Iditarod musher out the chute, wearing the number two bib, was Bud Smyth. Raymie Redington with Joe's dogs left in twenty-first place. Also running were Isaac Okleasik, Dick Mackey, Dan Seavey, Herbie Nayokpuk, Howard Farley, Dave Olson, and many others—thirty-four in all.

At the same time mushers were leaving the Tudor Race Track, five volunteers left Knik on snowmachines, following the trail of the army's double-tracked snowmachines. They needed to be just ahead of the teams to pack any newly fallen snow and keep open the trail the army had made earlier that week. These snowmachiners were equipped with saws, axes, ropes, nails, and brawn. If they found toppled trees on the trail, they moved them out of the way. If there was an open creek, they built a make-shift bridge. Any other obstacles that would interfere with the mushers, they tried to fix them, too.

By the time the mushers got to Knik, it was starting to snow lightly, and before long six inches of snow and freezing rain covered the ground. Still the mushers raced on. The weather cooled the farther north they traveled, making dogs and mushers much happier despite the poor weather conditions.

Dave Olson got as far as the Little Susitna River. As he was resting, Dr. Hal Bartko and Howard Farley stopped.

"How are things going?"

"I don't seem to be feeling too well," was Olson's reply.

"Here, let me check you out," Dr. Bartko said. After a few moments he said, "You have pneumonia. You don't belong out here on the trail. You'd better head back to Knik and go home." He knew Olson really didn't want to quit. "There will be another race next year and you can run that one."

That's when Farley added, "And say, would you ask Joe to round up a pair of boots for the Doc. His aren't warm enough and are falling apart. He'll never make it to Nome with these."

Olson took the good advice, turned his team around and headed back to Knik. Once in Knik he gave Joe the message. Joe wasted no time in rounding up a pair of warm bunny boots, those big, rubberized, cold-weather boots that look like huge white marshmallows. He landed his little Piper-11 in a space about the size of a basketball court on a little lake about 200 miles up the trail. Walking through a thin curtain of fog, Joe handed the boots to a very surprised and grateful musher.

Dr. Terry Adkins is standing by Joe's PA-11 along the Iditarod Trail. Adkins was the only vet in the first Iditarod Race. He was flying and checking dogs every waking hour for the entire length of the race.

Airplanes were integral since there were no roads through most of Alaska. Pilots volunteered their planes and time to help out. One pilot was Art Petersen from Palmer. He knew Joe and Dick Mackey way before the 1973 race. "Dick called me to haul some gas to Skwentna at the first of the race. Then they needed help with a radio. I hauled that. They needed dog food at McGrath. They twisted my arm and I went all the way to Nome."

Joe flew Adkins, that is, until Joe flipped his plane in some deep snow. Adkins flew the rest of the race with Petersen. "Him and I spent a lot of time in the air. I was the only pilot from McGrath to Nome. We made every stop between McGrath and Nome. If Terry hadn't seen a team for a while, we would meet them on the trail and check out everyone. I think some days I had thirteen takeoffs and landings."

Between flights up and down the Iditarod Trail, Joe was in Anchorage talking to people and working to get the race purse filled by the time the mushers got to Nome. Joe's first break came when he talked to Colonel "Muktuk" Marston. Muktuk was a good friend of Joe's. He was a longtime dog musher and also organized the Alaska Eskimo Scouts during World War II. He listened to Joe's story, became very enthused about the idea, and was the first to put up land valued at $10,000 in support of the Iditarod Race. The newspapers were very critical of this deal and questioned the value of his offer. So in public Muktuk presented Joe with a check for $10,000.

Now, perhaps the ball would get rolling. This very generous gift gave validity to the race that was badly needed.

Bruce Kendall, a gentleman in the hotel business, got caught up in Joe's vision and could see that Joe wasn't in this for the money. "Bruce Kendall and I cosigned on a $30,000 note," said Joe. "He believed in Alaska and believed in dog mushing." Frank Murkowski, president of Alaska National Bank of the North, who later became governor of Alaska, authorized the note in support of this race. "Bruce paid that off himself," stated Joe.

"That was the best loan I've ever made," said Murkowski years later. "We used to do things based on the character of the individual."

Thanks to these three generous men, who saw Joe's vision, the Iditarod Race was finding its rightful support. Without their financial backing, the race would surely have died.

Now Joe could devote the rest of his time to the race. The small group of planners and volunteers continued their dedicated work in support of the race. And the people in Nome were preparing their town for a big welcome.

There were no phone lines in rural Alaska, so communication was done through the use of ham radio operators around the state. Roy Davies worked hard to keep communications going. Ham radio stations were set up in Anchorage at the Gold Rush Hotel, along the trail at village checkpoints, and in Nome. Tom Busch was the manager of KNOM Radio in Nome and a ham radio operator. "I gave the Iditarod Committee unlimited long-distance calls and use of my office during the race." He sent the first race standings of the first Iditarod Race into the Associated Press teletype wire and continued his support of the race until his death in 2010.

Then Joe heard that the army snowmachines could not get through Rainy Pass because of deep snow and too much brush. He flew out to survey the situation. He called in to say an alternate route could be used, farther south through Ptarmigan Valley. It was a better and more passable route, but it was rough and about twenty miles longer. The teams would have to travel over bare rock and dirt or glare ice.

"The mushers were going to be in for a real roller-coaster ride, that's for sure," Joe reported. "But once they got to the South Fork of the Kuskokwim River they would have smooth sailing into the Rohn River Roadhouse."

By now, mushers were bunched together in groups of two or more. They helped each other along and took turns breaking trail during the day. At night they camped together repairing broken sleds, and sharing what they were learning about this new trail, or telling how they barely managed to get through two or three feet of overflow. The warm campfire, friendly conversation, and cups of hot tea did wonders to the mushers' morale. This was more of a winter camping trip than a race.

Two mushers said they were sitting around their campfire resting and chatting away when the dogs began to get nervous. They discovered pairs of yellow eyes moving on the outskirts of the firelight. Wolves! They were probably trying to figure out who these strangers were and what they were doing out there. The mushers didn't take long to decide they'd had enough campfire chat.

Time to move on.

The difficulties the small committee encountered to man a race of this size were unimaginable. There were many snafus along the way—some big ones to mushers who had the mindset of the short sprint races in larger towns that were able to supply whatever the mushers needed. But this was no twenty-five mile circuit they were mushing with their dogs. This was over 1,000 miles through untamed wilderness with only a few communities along the way. This race was really testing their woodsman skills. And at the checkpoints the volunteers did their best to help the mushers.

And what kept Joe going through all this?

Trust—a deep sense of trust that getting a dog team up the Iditarod Trail was possible. Joe had trust in the sled dogs based on all his years of experience with his own dogs. Joe had trust in the mushers based on the grit these men had already shown in previous mushing experiences. Joe had trust in the volunteers because he sensed they had picked up the spirit of this sled dog race and would work to make it happen. Really, it all boiled down to a deep-seated basic trust in dog and man alike. Trust is what got Joe through this.

Raymie Redington was having his own set of problems. Just out of Knik he broke his dentures. That cut what he could eat to almost nothing. He ended up eating the warm, soft, nutritious meal that he fed his dogs. When Joe found out, he stuffed a new pair of teeth in a 10-pound bag of dog food and air-dropped them to Raymie. Then thirty-some miles before McGrath, Raymie and several other mushers got hit by a horrendous blizzard. The trail got blown over by snow and they wandered around for hours looking for it. Some snowmachiners from McGrath found them and made a trail back into town for them to follow.

Finally Raymie decided to scratch from the race. "I'm going to take them home and rest them up," he said. At the end of the race Raymie was unofficially awarded the "Guts Trophy".

By the time the rest of the mushers and their teams had gotten to Nome, they had met and conquered snow and ice blizzards that made the trail absolutely invisible and either grounded the dog teams or sometimes allowed only the leader's good sense of smell to move them forward; minus thirty-degree weather with bone-chilling winds; deceptive overflows along lakes and rivers where near-freezing water had seeped upward from the depths to the surface, camouflaged in a snowy blanket, just lying in wait to suck in any unsuspecting dog team and musher; icy trails wind-blown so smooth the dogs feet slid out in all four directions. But despite all the fierce challenges, friendship between musher and dog and musher and musher grew and would last forever.

Through it all, the mushers learned what Joe knew all along—these dogs could go the distance and so could the mushers.

The vet, Dr. Terry Adkins, said, "I am amazed at the durability and recuperative powers of the dogs," and "the very humane care and treatment the mushers give to their dogs."

March 23 marked the beginning of the end of the first Iditarod Race to Nome.

"Musher in sight! It's Dick Wilmarth! He's looking good. No other teams in sight," radioed a spotter who was posted three miles out of town.

Wilmarth, a miner from Red Devil with Hot Foot, his five year old leader, headed into Nome with eight of his eleven dogs still in harness. Soon he heard the Nome fire siren blaring across the tundra marking his arrival.

As he was mushing down Front Street, an Eskimo woman ran out of the crowd, surprising everyone, and hung a bell necklace around Hot Foot's neck. Wilmarth had no idea what was going on, but just continued down the street to the cheers and hollers of the crowd. The Nome school band was playing its heart out for the musher. At the last minute someone realized there was no finish line, only the yellow banner they had hung across the street in Anchorage, which read: STARTING LINE on one side and WELCOME TO NOME! on the other side. They ran into one of the buildings and came out with some red Kool-Aide and sprinkled it across the snow to make an official finish line. Wilmarth and his team had been on the trail 20 days, 40 minutes, and 41 seconds.

Wilmarth said of his dogs, "They saved my life!"

Between White Mountain and Solomon he'd run into a blizzard. He could see nothing, but Hot Foot knew where he was going and inched his way through the blinding snow to bring Wilmarth and the rest of the team to safety as the first musher and dog team to win the world's longest sled dog race. And Hot Foot became the first Iditarod dog hero.

At the 1973 Iditarod Race finish line in Nome was a banner that had STARTING LINE on one side and WELCOME TO NOME on the other side and Kool-Aide poured across the snow for the official finish line.

General Gettys on the left and Muktuk Marston on the right are having a good laugh with Orville Lake at the finish line in Nome. Gettys and Muktuk are two outstanding men who believed in Joe's dream and helped to make it happen!

Wilmarth later was told just how important Hot Foot's bell necklace was. A law had been made in 1905 that all leaders of dog teams must have a bell on them, so that the team wouldn't come unexpectedly upon townsfolk. That law still existed. This Eskimo woman had overheard some men talking about this law and quickly made a bell necklace for the leader of the first team into town. She had the spirit of the Iditarod in her heart when she did this simple, selfless act. As it turned out, this was all a practical joke being played by those men on Wilmarth, but from that moment on Joe's vision of the Iditarod Race belonged to all the people who loved dogs, dog mushing, and that wonderful sense of pioneering adventure.

Mayor Renshaw of Nome was very supportive of this race. He was at the banquet before the race began and greeted all the mushers as they crossed the finish line. It didn't matter if it was windy, cold, or in the middle of the night, he was out there with open arms to welcome to the great city of Nome these daring, hardy men and their teams of tough sled dogs.

The weather was still bad and the ceiling was very low when Art Petersen flew into town with the vet. "I called Nome radio and they said we couldn't land because they had a medivac coming in," said Petersen. "Then I saw two snowmachines coming out of town. I told Terry their headlights aren't bouncing. That must be a pretty good stretch of trail. So I followed them down and landed. Then I taxied several miles into Nome." Just then the airport radioed Petersen that he could land. Petersen responded, "I'm parked."

"Where?"

"Between two big barges beached back there."

Adkins laughed and said, "That's the longest taxi I ever had!"

When Joe got to Nome at the end of the race to present the prize money to the first twenty mushers, he was still short a few thousand dollars. Wilmarth's winning purse was $12,000. Second place was Bobby Vent with a prize of $8,000. Seavey placed third winning $6,000. But before the checks were awarded, Joe took Seavey aside and said, "Seavey, I'm going to end up a little short for the purse. Could we use some of your winnings? You're the only one with a job when you get home."

Seavey was quick to respond, "Sure." He said later, "I felt like I was part of the instigators and we had a responsibility to all the mushers." So Seavey lent him $2,229.63 to top off the purse. Just another of the long list of selfless acts people made in support of Joe's dream. It took several years to get paid back, but Joe made good on his promise.

The twenty-second and last musher to cross the finish line was John Schultz of Delta Junction. He received the Red Lantern. The Red Lantern is an important

Raymie in Ruby just before
he scratched out of the race.
Freckles is his leader.

Dan Seavey at the finish in Nome. He
generously and without a second thought
lent $2,229.63 in order to meet the $50,000
purse. *From the Dan Seavey Collection.*

part of dog racing, the history of Alaska, and now the Iditarod. During the dog-freighting days it was first called the "Widow's Lamp" and was hung outside roadhouses when a musher was on the trail between villages. The lamp was not taken down until the musher had reached his destination safely.

It was always Joe's belief and hope that the media would pick up on it, too, and recognize and report on all the mushers in the back of the pack. Joe felt that each musher who entered the race was just as important as the fastest. Each musher and his dogs were undertaking a feat that required courage, strength, endurance, ingenuity, brotherly kindness, and a great sense of adventure. Each musher had a story to tell, and each musher in his or her own way was promoting the vision Joe had of keeping the Alaskan husky and dog mushing alive, preserving a vital part of Alaska's history for Alaska and the world.

George Attla, a well-noted sprint dog musher and winner of many races in Alaska, said, "One thing the race has done for the outlying villages where the race passed through is that the people have started thinking dogs again instead of snowmachines."

Hearing a comment like that coming from a man who did not believe this race was possible made Joe Redington Sr. smile his bashful smile and breathe an unheard sigh of satisfaction. His dream did come true.

The governor of Alaska, Governor Bill Egan, had planned to attend the end-of-the-race banquet but had to cancel at the last minute. He did have someone read his tribute to Joe, though, which in part recognized Joe who "envisioned the historic race and labored through it all." Bob Scott speaking for the governor, said, "He made an Alaskan dream come true."

It was also noted that the Iditarod was the "longest and most grueling and demanding sled dog race in history!" And all the mushers smiled in total agreement.

At the end of the banquet, Joe asked, "Is there anyone present here tonight who would like to see the race run next year?"

From the packed banquet room at the Nugget Inn came a loud and resounding cheer from everyone, "Yes!"

"We'll have one then, and I promise you, it will be bigger than ever."

Joe Redington's "impossible" race was a success and a miracle!

"It was fun and exciting, something really cool. And it actually happened," said Aglietti.

"The villagers," said Johnson, "were just fantastic."

After the race Joe knew he needed to start advertising for the next race. He wanted a little magazine about the Iditarod Race, like the Fur Rendezvous had every year. The magazine would be informative and be a money-making project. Joe and Vi talked. There was one person they knew who had a passion for preserving history just as they did—Dorothy Page. So putting aside past differences and only wishing to go forward with a good idea, Joe contacted Dorothy Page to see if she would be the editor of this new magazine idea. The result was the Iditarod Annual.

"Dorothy got all the photos together from all the different photographers and did lots of historical research," said Brit Lively. For ten years Brit, who owned Mapmakers Printing, took all the materials Dorothy gathered for the Iditarod Annuals and prepared them for the print shop. Vi also worked on the annuals for a number of years. "Dorothy put the race in the historical perspective and Joe could make people believe in the race."

"As things got to lookin' better, after they saw we made it to Nome, there were more people willin' to jump in and help," said Joe, with a hint of satisfaction in his voice.

"They called Joe the silver-tongued fox," said Seavey. "He was so believable. The reason he was so believable was he believed in himself."

Joe smiled his lopsided smile and said, "I don't know why they believed me, but they did."

"Joe is a rugged, never-stop kind of guy," said Olson. "He liked to follow through on whatever he gets started. He is a good promoter and gets people to follow."

The Iditarod Race was founded on this man of his word.

CHAPTER 24

1974 Joe's First Running

Energy and persistence conquer all things.

BENJAMIN FRANKLIN

True to Joe's word and despite the unending challenges, the second running of the Iditarod Race took place on the first Saturday in March 1974.

Muktuk Marston greeted all the mushers at the Mushers' Banquet held at the Captain Cook Hotel in Anchorage and said, "The race is the most grueling contest in the world. It's the age-old desire to pit yourself against the elements and win." Then he went on to say that they would be crossing two mountain ranges, break through twenty-foot snowdrifts, cross overflows, and endure bitter winds. "Like Rudolph the red-nosed reindeer, you will go down in history."

Later, each musher came up to draw his or her starting number for the race. This year two women would be running the race, Mary Shields and Lolly Medley, both from College, Alaska. And they had their first dog musher from out of state, Tim White from Taylor Falls, Minnesota. This pleased Joe very much.

Prior to the banquet, Joe and Vi had a very busy year. Vi had started working at the Goose Bay Nike Missile Site at the end of Knik Road, serving food in the dining hall and cleaning. This she did for the next six years. On July 24, 1973, Knik Hall, the Bjorn cabin, and the acre of land Joe had been given was listed on the National Historical Registry.

By now the Iditarod Trail Committee had more volunteers who got caught up in the spirit of this new race and were working hard to make a second race happen. They were trying to find sponsors. During the first race many expenses were charged to the Iditarod Trail Committee, which had to be paid somehow. Hundreds of other details that arose during the race needed attention to make this second race run more smoothly. One big detail was to find a new race chairman. Joe realized that if he wanted to race his dogs in '74, he had to delegate some of his workload.

After the '73 race Jay Bashor, enthralled by this incredible race, walked up to Joe and asked him, "Is there anything I can to do help with next year's race?"

Joe's eyes twinkled and he grinned his quiet, wide grin. "There sure is. I'm lookin' for a new race chairman."

Bashor in turn called his friend, John Norman. Norman said, "Things were in disarray. They needed a lawyer and an accountant. He asked me for some help." This is how the Iditarod was perpetuated—through word of mouth. The spirit of this idea spread by word of mouth from one friend or acquaintance to another. The idea grew. People felt compelled, for any number of reasons, and wanted to help. Not for money—there was none—but because of the idea. "I plunged into it going through the piles of paper. There were some lawsuits that had to be resolved. I did my best to bring order to the confusion. One man who had recruited many volunteers also ran up a long trail of unauthorized bills. An accountant, Ron Veltcamp, worked with me, too. We set up a plan to get everything paid. Then I met with Joe. Once the bills were paid and paperwork was cleared up, we made plans for the next race."

"For me," Norman continued, "this began as just another civic activity. But I was gradually drawn into it. Joe was such a wonderful person. You couldn't say no to him. At least I couldn't."

At the next meeting of the Iditarod Trail Committee, Bashor was elected the new chairman. And did he have his work cut out for him. Joe, of course, was still on the committee and still totally committed to the unending details of a race of this size, but now he felt he could devote a little time to training his dogs.

Joe had learned much from that first race. One thing he discovered was that dogs burned more calories than anyone expected in a race of this length. Getting a proper diet was a big challenge for all the mushers. Commercial dog food just wasn't enough. So Joe came up with his special "gourmet" canine treat. He ground Purina dog food, water, tallow, salt, sugar, beaver, and halibut together and made 2 1/2-pound meat patties. Each dog got two patties a day.

Another challenge was finding better ways to protect the dog's feet against the often rough and icy trail. Ointments of different kinds were used and booties or socks were taped over their feet. He knew that Scotty Allen, a musher in Nome in the early 1900s used flannel for his dogs' feet. Some Eskimo mushers had used sealskin booties in the '73 race.

Joe spent lots of time promoting the race, talking to people to get financial support and had many, many, many organizational meetings to attend. Being creative, thinking outside the box, chewing on one idea after another was a constant activity for Joe. And right beside him through it all was Vi. Sometimes Vi drove into Anchorage with Joe to these meetings. On one occasion Joe's ingenuity was put to the test. Joe related their adventure to the folks at the meeting.

"We headed to the meetin'. We got down to Eklutna Flats and had a flat tire, but I had no spare. So I took my axe and went out into the woods and cut me a real long pole. I always carry an axe. Then I tied it to the front bumper and ran it back to the rear and about six feet behind. The tree was about as big as I could carry—eight to ten inches at the base. Then I took the wheel off and we came on into Anchorage."

Vi giggled as she looked at Joe, "We ran into Anchorage on three tires and a pole."

"Yep," confirmed Joe. "I put the jeep in four-wheel drive and we got here. It wore the pole down to about four inches, but the drum never did touch the ground."

Joe and Vi were simply an unstoppable team.

Always striving to find ways to get the trail recognized, another idea was hatched at one of the many meetings. The Iditarod Trail was a mail trail, so why not have each musher carry mail? An arrangement was made with the U.S. Postal Service to carry cachets, packets of letters, over the Iditarod to Nome. Joe asked his artist friend, Bill Divine, if he would design an Iditarod Trail logo for the envelopes. These would be postmarked in Anchorage and Nome and used as a fund-raising project.

At a prerace meeting this idea was presented to the mushers. Surprisingly, it was met with some resistance. There was already enough to do. Carrying mail was too much to ask. Joe did not react, he responded in a good way, and came up with a solution—"I'll carry yours," was all he said.

"He was one of a kind," said Norman. "Joe had such a unique, easy way of looking at things."

His positive attitude turned the whole negative thought around. To have the U.S. Postal Service support the Iditarod Race added credibility, recognition, and needed funds. And Devine's logo became the official Iditarod logo.

The first Saturday in March finally arrived. The race would again start in

Anchorage, but the teams would be leaving from Mulcahy Park. The weather was not very good and a big winter storm was gathering up steam. Joe had twelve dogs hitched to his sled, with Tennessee and Ready as double leaders in his team. Joee and Raymie and their teams joined their dad in this second Iditarod race.

As the mushers raced north out of Anchorage, the wind and falling snow increased. By the time they reached Knik they were in a full-blown winter blizzard. The Redingtons spent the night in Knik, heading out the next morning at eight o'clock. Their sleds were so heavily laden with gear that they were hard to control and tipped over all the time. Enough of that. When they got to Susitna Station, they stopped, pitched a lot of stuff to lighten their load, and headed up the trail again. This gear would be flown back to Anchorage by the volunteer pilots helping with the race. About ten that night they stopped and built a fire, fed the dogs, and then sat down for a nice hot cup of tea. Refreshed, they crawled into their sleeping bags and slept in their sleds.

Their next stop was at Skwentna about twenty miles down the trail. Joe was looking forward to visiting with Joe Delia. They had known each other for years and Delia sure helped blaze the Iditarod Trail around Skwentna. When

This is an old picture of Joe Delia. Joee said he didn't like to use anything mechanical in his younger days.

the Redingtons arrived, they checked their dogs, gave them snacks, then went inside the Delia home to have some tea and a friendly chat.

Joe had first met Delia when he was pulling a crashed army Beaver up on the airstrip years before. Then he couldn't help but add, "Gee Joe, what is it about your house that all these planes keep crashin' around you?"

"Well, I'm at the end of the airstrip!" laughed Delia.

Soon it was time to move on. The mushers readied their teams and headed up the trail.

They crossed many frozen lakes surrounded by stunted black spruce as they headed north toward the Alaska Range. Many miles up the trail Joe stopped on the edge of an unnamed lake to snack his dogs and give them a short rest. While he waited, he pulled out his ever ready camera and took pictures of the beautiful mountains, the snow-covered beaver house on the lake, and his team. A snack in their bellies, most of his team started looking around wondering why they weren't moving up the trail.

Stowing his camera securely away near the top of his gear, Joe gave each dog a loving and encouraging pat, then walked back to his sled. He lifted his snow hook and yelled out to Tennessee and Ready, "Okay boys, mush." The team loped eagerly up the trail.

The closer to the mountains they got, the rougher the trail became. All the mushers struggled to keep their sleds upright. Tipovers were frequent. Pots, pans, food, thermos bottles littered the trail! Joe found himself stopping to pick up the "lost" gear, hoping to find the owners later. But all his efforts were for naught, because he was also tipping over and being jostled like popcorn in a hot pan. By the time he got to Shirley Lake he had lost everything he had picked up and even some of his own stuff including his coat, which a musher grabbed off the trail and returned to him later. That stretch of the trail got its first name by the mushers—Suicide Gulch.

All the mushers stopped at the lake for rest. They tethered their teams, fed them, and checked the condition of each of their dogs before they took care of their own needs. Then Joe found out that Happy River was not frozen, like last year, and a new trail needed to be blazed.

Frank Harvey was one of a number of volunteers that were trailbreakers. They were responsible for making sure the trail was open and right now he was flummoxed. Finding the old Iditarod was not easy.

Harvey asked Joe, "Would you mind taking a ride with me in our helicopter and help me find the old trail?"

"Very good. Let's do it," was Joe's instant reply.

Once in the air, Joe was able to spot a number of different land features that

"Tennessee is an Alaskan husky," said Joe, "and he had real good feet."

Ready is leading Joe's team along the Iditarod Trail. Behind him is Tennessee Stud. He was also a good leader. Note Joe's stuffed sled bag! A beaver house and the Alaska Range are in the background.

The mushers decided it was time for a chat along the trail. Joe and Ron Aldridge are in the forefront and Ken Chase is up by the huskies.

marked the original trail. Now Harvey and his crew of trailblazers knew what to look for when they continued opening the trail for the mushers to follow.

When Joe got back to Shirley Lake, his team was one of the few remaining teams to head out. Joee and Raymie had already left, so when Joe set his team in motion, he was determined to catch them. But the trail had other plans.

Joe came to a fork in the trail. A spruce tree blocked the route he thought he should be taking.

Hummmm, don't know why that is there, he thought. Guess I'll head off to the left. "Haw," he hollered to Tennessee and Ready.

The trail was rough and slow going. Two mushers passed him and then all three of them came to a dead end. This must have been where Harvey had stopped because he couldn't make out where the trail should go. So the teams turned about and headed back to the fork in the trail, meeting some other mushers on the way. They turned around, too. When they got to the fallen spruce, they moved it across the left trail, preventing all the other teams from traveling it, and took the right one.

Tim White and Joe were mushing along the trail together. "We were heading out in the afternoon in Ptarmigan Pass and the wind started to pick up," White said. "Joe took off his glove and was eating a candy bar and dropped his glove on the trail. He didn't notice he had dropped it. Joe would get so focused on some things. He wanted to catch the front runners and didn't notice his missing glove." Tim found it and gave it to him later.

The towering mountains surrounding the Alaska Range became dark shadows holding the frigid air down on the trail. Joe looked at the thermometer he had hanging on his sled. It read minus thirty degrees Fahrenheit. The winds started to roar, stirring up a fierce storm. Joe's only desire was to get through the pass so he could catch up with his sons.

White said, "I'm going to stop and get out of the wind." He wished Joe luck, then went to the side of the hill near a creek, took care of his dogs, dug himself a cave in the snow, and got a good night's sleep out of the wind.

Joe continued on. The temperature was now about minus fifty degrees and the wind was howling about forty-eight miles per hour. Before long he was mushing in almost whiteout conditions. Joe could see nothing. He knew where he wanted to go, but the dogs did not want to head into the wind and kept veering to the right and then to the left to avoid the icy fingers of the north wind. He constantly had to walk to the front of his team to get his leaders to lead the team in the right direction, only to have them veer off the trail again.

"That's it. Time for us to take a break." After six hours of tough, sweating labor, Joe finally gave up.

Hooking his tether line, a long chain with short pieces of chain, to his sled, he threw it downwind, tied up his dogs, and gave them a snack for all their hard work. Then with food in their tummies, the dogs scratched holes in the snow, turning in a tight circle, and snuggling down with their noses tucked tightly into their tails. The cold wind spread a snowy blanket of warmth over them and their body heat stayed inside their furry ball. They didn't move until morning.

Joe dug out his Denali sleeping bag, which was good to minus sixty degree temperatures, and jumped in, coat, parka, boots, and all, to hunker down for a very much needed rest—rest, but not sleep, not in minus sixty- degree temperatures. He spent the rest of the night wondering how far they had actually come. How were Joee and Raymie? Had he made the right decision to travel through the storm at night?

Later he recalled, "I had so much clothes on I even got sweaty. I got a little bit cold, but not bad. But anyway, I stayed awake and when it got daylight, I got up and harnessed 'n all. I looked down and I was about a hundred yards off the trail and here comes Tim White. So I mushed right down there and I caught up with Tim and I said, 'How long ago have ya left camp?' He said fifteen minutes. I mushed all night and only gained fifteen minutes."

Joe just shook his head. What could he say?

Daylight made traveling easier—easier to see, but not easier to travel. The wind in Ptarmigan Valley was still playing a game of "How much havoc can we wreak on a dog team?" Snow whirled all around their legs, pushing back on them, making it a challenge to move forward. Then rounding a bend the wind pounded on their backs. Hoping for some reprieve once they got to the South Fork of the Kuskokwim, they persevered.

By evening Joe and White had reached the end of this miserable section of the trail. The front-runners had stopped for the night at Hell's Gate, and everyone knew why the early mapmakers had given this break in the Teocalli Mountains its name. The mushers had a rip-snortin' fire going and nothing looked more inviting. Joe took care of his dogs, then joined the other mushers for a lively conversation about everyone's trials that day. The camaraderie was great and everyone had stories to tell.

Joe added his own. "The worst wind I ever seen was up at Granite Mountain. That was probably 1956. An old-timer named Otto Wurm, who ran the first cats and stuff in Nome—he was a miner—him and I went out on Granite Mountain to take a Beech 21 helicopter off the mountain. It blew for three days and it was fifty below and a fifty-mile wind. You just had to stay in the sleeping bag. That's the worst one." He thought a minute. "Until now. I used to think there was some places a dog team couldn't go, but now I know better."

Herbie Nayokpuk of Shismaref and Isaac Okleasik from Teller stopped at Rhon Roadhouse on the north side of the Alaska Range. Time to repair sleds, get some nourishment, rest, and, of course, tell stories.

Art Mortvedt was a volunteer ham operator in the 1974 Iditarod Race at the Rhon Roadhouse.

191

The next morning Joee and Dick Mackey led the teams out of the camp. "It was quite a sight watching all those teams plowing through deep snow down to the riverbank," Joe commented.

On the South Fork of the Kuskokwim there was no trail. Everyone bunched up. It was drifted and there were holes in the ice. So the mushers had to snowshoe in front of the dogs. "We all took turns," said White. "The teams could go no faster than a person snowshoeing."

But the wind still had another trick up its sleeve. Farther down the valley the wind had turned the river into glare, slippery ice, making it the perfect place for tossing the teams back and forth between the riverbanks of trees and willows. Two teams got pitched sideways tangling in the thick, frozen willow brush. Then the river presented some open water just to add a little more excitement to the day. Reaching the Rohn Roadhouse the exhausted, bone-weary mushers found a warm meal and hot drink to bring comfort to a long, hard day. They were all very grateful for the thoughtfulness of the volunteer checkers.

The winds finally ceased, but in the wee hours of the morning the temperature had dropped. That didn't stop these hardy, adventurous mushers. They harnessed their teams and headed up the trail.

By the time Joe got to Ruby on the Yukon River, he had made a decision. He was going to change the material on the runners of his sled to accommodate the cold weather. But even as he was doing this, the weather was starting to warm up and before morning it had started to snow.

Each village they came to, the mushers were greeted by laughing, running, cheering children and adults. The schools shut their doors to welcome the mushers. Coming into Nulato, the high school students cleared areas for the teams to bed down. "The school kids used to cut spruce [boughs] for us, but Ready didn't want anything to do with 'em. He went right over and laid on the snow."

And they made signs that they put along the trail. One sign read, "Only ten miles to NULATO—you can make it!" If the mushers chose to stay in the village to feed and rest their teams, the villagers opened their homes to them, feeding them until they could eat no more. The hospitality all along the trail was simply outstanding. It was like time had been turned back to older days. Everyone was having fun with the arrival of mushers in their villages. Seeing their joy confirmed Joe's vision of the importance of preserving the use of sled dogs in Alaska's villages.

By the time Joe got to Unalakleet, it started raining. He was running his dogs along the sea coast of Norton Sound. His sled was really dragging. Joe realized he probably shouldn't have changed the material on his runners.

"The school kids in Nulato used to cut spruce boughs for the dogs," said Joe. "We didn't have no straw in those days. But Ready didn't want anything. He went right over and laid in the snow."

Out of Shaktoolik "the ice was terrible on their feet," said Joe. "We cut up blankets and different things. I found some blankets in a big building, the Loman Brothers building used to butcher reindeer." By the time he left Elim, the dogs were having a very difficult time pulling the sled over the sea ice. Joe had been talking to an old Eskimo the night before, who said that ivory was the best material for sled runners along the coast. But Joe didn't have any ivory. Mulling this over in his head he thought of how he used to put wax on his kid's sleds to make them go faster, so he decided when he got into Golovin, he would get some wax and try that out. And by golly, his sled pulled much better.

With less than eighty miles to Nome, the rising temperatures melted the ice so some of the rivers were running open, making crossing a challenge.

"At Fish River, the water was running swift and about knee-deep. I tried to go upstream but it was open all the way—about twenty feet of water between the shore and ice. Finally, I stepped out into the water, but the dogs wouldn't follow.

I pulled the two lead dogs. All of a sudden, they decided to go, and jumped right against me. I sat down in the water—but not for long—it was cold."

Joe decided to let the wind dry his clothes since it was a balmy thirty degrees out, but that really wasn't warm enough to dry ice-cold, soaking wet clothes. After several hours, he stopped, built a fire and started drying out his clothes and drinking tea. "I must have had twelve cups of tea before I felt normal," smiled Joe.

"By the time I got close to Nome," Joe remembered, "I began to look like the Pied Piper. At least seventy-five kids were trailing me, begging for a ride. I gave about twenty-five of them a ride. They sure loved that."

Joe finished his first Iditarod Race with eight dogs and in eleventh place. They had been traveling 23 days, 10 hours, 15 minutes, 57 seconds.

Vi so wanted to be in Nome to see Joe. "We had no dog handlers then," Vi remembered. "Too expensive. So I stayed here and took care of the dogs."

CHAPTER 25

1975 Galena Crash

*You have to be a survivor. For everything you
do, there is a consequence. You have to consider
all possibilities of whatever you choose to do.*

BOB KALLENBERG, ALASKAN TEACHER

AND COMMERCIAL FISHERMAN

In January, 1975, the Nome Kennel Club sponsored a rerun of the 1925 Serum Run to Nome in celebration of its fiftieth anniversary. They invited Joe to take the first leg of this run. "I took Ready in the Serum Run. I had him from Nenana to Tolvana, fifty-three miles, same section that Wild Bill Shannon ran." It was a fun time for him, especially because he got to be a part of a reenactment of Alaska's history.

Then the first Saturday in March was the Iditarod. Joe raced it with Joee and their friend Herbie Nayokpuk. Joee came in third, Nayokpuk fourth, and Joe fifth. They had a great race, although these first races were more like great winter camping trips until they got close to Nome.

Off the trail the existence of the Iditarod Race faced challenges. The race was in trouble. The *New York Times* had been bombarded by a barrage of hundreds of letters from animal rights groups on the East Coast about the alleged "cruelty" being inflicted on sled dogs in the race, demanding that the race be stopped. This led to a major oil company dropping its generous sponsorship of the race and this in turn posed a huge threat to the survival of the Iditarod Race.

At a meeting of six men held in Anchorage, Joe was told there was no way they could hold the '76 race. "Joe, this can't be done."

"What do you mean?"he asked.

"It isn't doable this year," he was told. They needed to wait a couple of years to build up their coffer.

This was just not acceptable to Joe. He went around the room one by one asking what each man thought. These men had put their all into volunteering their time and energy and money to make the race happen for the past two years. There was no staff—just devoted individual's willing to work. But this setback was just too much. No one had a large amount of wealth to fill the huge void. The last man he asked was John Norman. "You, too, John?"

"No, if you think we can do it, I'll stick with you." Then Norman wrote a check. "It was a small amount, but probably helped get things started."

With a pleased smile Joe said, "He never quit me."

"It was just through Joe's sheer will-power," said Norman, "that we had a race that year."

The issue with the animal rights group needed to be addressed because they were determined to shut the race down completely. The group's intention to look out for the well-being of the sled dog was good, but they didn't understand that the husky is a working dog. And they didn't realize that one of the reasons Joe was promoting this race was one of the very same reasons they were trying to shut it down. This breed of dog was dying out and being replaced by snowmachines. The sled dogs were unique dogs. They were intelligent, strong, devoted to loving masters, and had saved many, many lives in the Arctic. They must be preserved.

Alaskans were in utter disbelief at such uninformed statements flying across the country. Many were very, very angry. But Joe, being Joe, hunkered down and worked to set the record straight. The rest of the country needed to get accurate information about the sled dog. And they could work on the race rules and procedures for the race to make them better. The trick was whether people would listen. The Iditarod Race would just have to prove itself.

Even without a major sponsor, the race was run in '76, but with a much smaller purse. The mushers didn't care. They loved the long-distance race to Nome. And so did Alaskans. The volunteers in Anchorage, the villages, and Nome continued their dedicated work. Everyone was exhausted. But again, the Iditarod Trail Committee and all the volunteers pulled it off.

Another issue that Joe was indebted to Norman for establishing was a trust fund that was separate from the race. The two men talked at length.

"Joe was concerned about the growth of the race and ensuring it could go on in perpetuity. At one point there was threat of a lawsuit that could have taken the entire purse," Norman stated. "I recommended they create a fund held by a separate entity distinct from the Iditarod Trail Committee—as backup."

"Let's do this," said Joe.

"If he hadn't said that," said Norman, "nothing would have happened."

So a trust fund was established for two reasons: (1) to establish a separate legal entity with money that could support the race in an emergency, in other words—"Not to have all the money in one basket," and (2) to allow investments to continue to grow and provide income to help support the race.

With determination and optimism Joe moved forward. This mind-set was to help him with what came next.

Dr. Jim Scott, his veterinarian friend, said of Joe, "He was not the kind of man to get caught out on a sled and freeze to death. He was always prepared. If he were to lose his sled with his gear, he would have whatever he needed in his pockets. He didn't like to be rescued. He would use his head, think about what had to be done, and try and get out on his own. Or if he knew he couldn't get out, he would sit right there until someone came and found him. In this day and age we need more thinkers like Joe."

The second week in November, 1975, fifty-eight-year old Joe was flying from Anchorage to Galena in his PA-11 Super Cub for a meeting of Iditarod mushers. The meeting was to discuss raising money, improving the course, instructing prospective mushers who would compete in the race, care of dogs, what to expect on the route, and historical trail status, which would qualify them for federal funds.

But Joe never showed up for the meeting.

"We were going to fly up together Friday for the meeting on Saturday," remembered Dick Mackey, "but Joe called and said he would fly up later. I went to the meeting and got back Sunday night. Joee called me Monday and asked, 'How'd the meeting go?' 'Fine. How come your dad didn't show up?' 'What?' Joee said. 'He left Friday.'"

Joe had always told Vi and his boys, "Give me a week so I can get myself out. If I'm not back in a week, call our friends, because I've had a little trouble."

Joee said of his dad, "He knows how to handle himself." But he was concerned.

"We need to call someone," said Joee.

But Vi was quick to respond, "Don't do that. Joe wants us to give him time to get himself home."

Joe landed his PA-11 in the spruce trees on his second emergency landing. He had to cut the trees, lower the plane, and then begin the repair work. The bent prop was the biggest mend that needed to be made. His skills from work in Reclamation came in very handy using a Spanish windlass to help straighten the prop.

Joee said, "She wasn't worried a bit. She was pretty mellow and used to that." But Joee went looking for him but without success. On Tuesday they called the Search and Rescue.

An HC 130 Hercules search plane, part of the 71st Aerospace Rescue and Recovery Squadron, left Anchorage to fly over Interior Alaska searching for Joe's white, black-trimmed plane. On board the Hercules was an instrument used to pick up emergency locator beacons. Joe had one on his plane. These emergency locators had been originally designed to spot space capsules as they reentered the earth's atmosphere. Now they were used to help find downed planes.

Also the Civil Air Patrol and volunteers were searching. The weather was very poor in Rainy Pass, so they flew two other routes Joe might have taken.

At the scene of the crash, Joe checked to see why the engine quit. He discovered the carburetor had iced-up, causing the plane to lose power. Fortunately, he was able to land the plane with no damage. Now he had to get the plane

Joe used the cut trees to build a hot fire to repair his prop.
Then he repaired the landing gear and wings for another
successful take off after four days of work.

up in the air again. Joe dug out his axe and began cutting trees and brush to
make a runway for his plane. Once that was done, he started the plane, and
took off.

Then his engine iced up again. Joe glided his plane into a black spruce tree forest.

"It was even a steeper angle than that," Joe said using his arm to show the
steep angle of the plane. "Straight up and down. You don't usually fly them
into the ground that way," Joe said. But he was gliding very slowly. "The trees
bent right over and lowered it down." So there he stood, looking at his plane,
nose down and tail straight up.

He said, "I sat myself down on a log and I gave myself a little talk." Not
unlike the many *sit-down talks* he and Vi had had over the years. "You got
yerself into this, you can get yerself out. I don't want to hear a word about
being hungry or uncomfortable."

He took stock of the situation and began working out a plan. In one of his
numerous pockets, Joe found a chocolate candy bar. He proceeded to break

it into small pieces and decided he'd eat one piece a day. Then he focused his attention on the job of getting his plane out of the trees, fix the prop, and just get the plane into the air. He gave no heed to a growling stomach. He also had a pocketknife, pliers, baling wire, and, of course, matches and a few other things in his pockets. These would come in handy.

Joe looked at his plane hanging from the tree. All the weight was put right on the prop and that weight bent the prop badly. "I had to cut enough branches out of the way and lowered the tail of the plane out of the trees and down to the ground," said Joe. He had an axe and a nylon rope in the plane.

With the airplane out of the trees and the fire nice and hot, he started the tricky work. He had to heat and carefully bend the prop of his plane back into place using the rope and a technique called a "Spanish windlass." Then he repaired the landing gear with a snare and duct taped the wings. Once that was competed to his satisfaction, he got busy cutting through trees and brush to make a runway. After four days of hard work, Joe became airborne again. His destination was no longer north to Galena, but east to Nenana, near the only road system through Central Alaska.

Joe was grateful for the progress, but then for the third time the engine sputtered once, then twice, and Joe's white plane headed for the earth again! Joe had just about had it, but he did not let frustration or fear enter his thinking. "That sure won't help a thing," Joe muttered.

The temperatures were still way below zero and the engine just wouldn't do its job. Joe was headed for another emergency landing. He searched the open expanse of tundra for a safe put-down spot. There were no soft trees to set the plane into this time, but there was a frozen lake straight ahead. Unfortunately, his glide pattern was a hundred yards short. He hit the hummocky tundra with a couple of hard bounces. The leading edge of his wing ripped right off the plane.

With one bite of chocolate for the new day, a deep breath, and his unswerving determination, he set about winching the plane a hundred yards to the lake and lowering it down the twelve foot bank. Then he began fixing the broken ski and wiring it back to the plane and then patched the wing.

Now, plane, just do what you were made to do and get me to Nenana, Joe thought as he climbed in for the takeoff.

The little plane headed down the lake and slowly lifted into the cold winter air. Six days had passed since he'd begun his flight to the dog mushers meeting. He still had a couple of pieces of chocolate in his pocket. And he had one more day until he knew Vi would be calling for help to find him.

For the third time he got the plane repaired and managed to get it in the air. This time when he landed, it was because he wanted to. The roadway at Nenana was straight ahead.

When he set the PA-11 down and got out of his plane, someone said, "Hey, you must be the guy they're looking for." That's when he discovered that the search and rescue was out looking for him.

"I don't know why they didn't see me. I was burning eight-foot logs."

He made a beeline to the nearest phone and called home to say he was safe and sound, and to come and get him. "I've had enough of this plane for awhile," he said. Joee and Vi jumped in their truck and drove to Nenana, picked Joe up, and headed home.

Feets at the front of the team of 200 sled dogs jumping with excitement trying to get the show on the road.

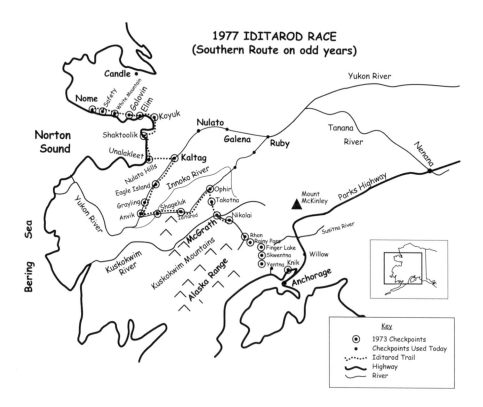

1977 IDITAROD RACE
(Southern Route on odd years)

Candle

Nome
Safety
White Mountain
Golovin
Elim
Koyuk

Norton Sound

Shaktoolik

Unalakleet

Nulato
Galena
Ruby

Yukon River

Tanana River

Nenana

Kaltag

Nulato Hills

Eagle Island
Innoko River

Grayling
Shageluk
Ophir
Takotna

Anvik
Iditarod
Nikolai

Mount McKinley

Parks Highway

Yukon River

Bering Sea

Kuskokwim River

McGrath

Kuskokwim Mountains

Rhon
Rainy Pass
Finger Lake
Skwentna
Yentna
Knik

Susitna River

Willow

Alaska Range

Anchorage

Key

⊙ 1973 Checkpoints
• Checkpoints Used Today
⋯ Iditarod Trail
〜 Highway
— River

CHAPTER 26

"The Last Great Race on Earth"

Let me tell you the secret that has led me to my goal. My strength lies solely in my tenacity.

LOUIS PASTEUR

Timmy read in the paper where somebody in Michigan said they were going to hook up seventy-six dogs to celebrate the 200th anniversary of the United States. Tim looked at his dad and said, "Why don't we hook up two hundred dogs?"

"That's a great idea. We'll do it."

Joe was proud of being an American. He said, "I have a lot of pride in the United States. A lot of people cuss the president. I don't. I may not like him, but he's still president of the United States."

When this country needed him, Joe enlisted. He didn't wait to be drafted. He felt it was important to support his country in this way. Times were rough, but he did the very best he could. Celebrating the United States 200th birthday was important, too.

The team was billed by the local newspaper as "The World's Biggest Dog Team." A total of two hundred sled dogs made a 900-foot-long dog team, pulling a thirty-eight-passenger bus, stretched out in front of Joe's homestead. Mushers from all over hooked their teams up with Joe's to break the record of seventy-six dogs. Handsome Feets was the lead dog. Joe had a walkie-talkie

The 1976 Bicentennial of the United States of America was celebrated in Knik with a 200 sled dog team of Alaskan huskies pulling a bus down Knik Road. Mushers from all over brought their dogs to build this unique team. Feets was the leader. Joe had a walkie-talkie tied to his neck to give him commands from the back of the team.

Nikki was the star in the Walt Disney film *Nikki, Wild Dog of the North*. Nikki was a Siberian husky from Joe's kennel.

connected to Feets so that his leader could hear his commands. "Mush," said Joe. The 200-dog team headed down Knik Road. The gimmick also made people think about the next Iditarod Race in 1977, which was the first time the southern route was to be used going through Iditarod.

Nikki, one of Joe and Vi's malamutes, was a star in a movie *Wild Dog of the North*. In celebration of the United States bicentennial in 1976, Larry Janis' seventh- and eighth-grade students at Iditarod School in Wasilla carved a totem pole and Nikki was on that pole because he was "the most famous movie star" from Wasilla and Knik. The totem pole was put up in front of the Eskimotel and Kashim in Wasilla for the Fourth of July celebrations.

Joe was a champion promoter of the race, always talking to people and getting them excited about the Iditarod. In between times he tried to find time to train his dogs and that was usually at night. "When I'm training, I feed late at the end of a trainin' day. When the moon comes up—time to go out trainin'," he grinned.

Across the state Alaskans gathered around the ham radios to hear news about the Iditarod Race. Then they heard a fellow with a British accent come on, "All day the huskies have been toiling up the terrible gradient that gashes through the Alaska Range like a white-walled Khyber Pass.

"Men and dogs rested overnight at Ann Budzynski's Sprucewood Lodge, eating moose steaks, twelve to a table, and sleeping twenty-nine to a single fetid room. By dawn they were gone, crawling thirty miles upwards and westwards at four miles an hour."

Ian Wooldridge, the *London Daily Mail's* columnist of the year, and renowned sports reporter, was on assignment to cover the Iditarod Sled Dog Race. He followed the mushers by airplane, stopping at checkpoints along the route and sending out his reports by ham radio. People across the state were tuning in to hear his coverage—the best that had yet been done for the race.

In a small Eskimo village schoolhouse along the Kobuk River, teachers, villagers, and kids were listening to hear news of their favorite mushers. One teacher was especially interested in two mushers—Joe Redington Sr., who was now being called the Father of the Iditarod, and Pete MacManus, a fellow teacher from Ambler. He was a friend, and she helped sew many, many dog booties for his team. How she wished she was in one of the villages along the trail route, but being able to hear on the ham radio of the happenings was good, too.

The 1977 race was the first race where the route took a southern bend and went through the old town of Iditarod. Joe and others felt it was important to include more villages in the race and so this southern route was set. From

Joe has Joee on his sled and a volunteer riding a tire behind his sled to add needed weight as they head out of Anchorage. Joee's wife, Pam, is in the crowd in the front row wearing a bandana.

now on, odd years took mushers through the southern route and in even years mushers followed the northern route meeting at Kaltag on the Yukon River and continuing to Nome.

On the first day of the race, not ten miles beyond his Flat Horn Lake, part of the trail just before the Susitna River had been blocked, so a new section of the trail had to be put in at the last minute. The trail took a steep drop coming off a cut bank down to the river. When Joe and his team came around a corner, he and his team flew off the lip and tumbled end over teakettle down the hill, breaking his sled and impaling a splinter of wood into his leg just below his knee. Out of breath for a moment, he lay crumpled in a tangle of dogs, sled, and harnesses. He shook his head, surveyed the mess, and immediately began to untangle his dogs and make sure they were okay. Finding that everyone was shipshape, he bent over to tend to the damage in his leg.

Darn, ruined a good pair of new long johns, he thought.

The deep wound was a bit of a mess. He tried walking. Though he never complained, pained tears said everything. There was only one thing he could do. He sat on the basket of his full sled, tied himself down, and yelled in his soft, low, but commanding voice, "Hike! We're movin' on to Finger Lake."

Finding Gene and June Leonard's checkpoint cabin took a sharp eye, however, as it was buried in deep snow. Gene had to keep adding a new step out the front door with each new snowfall. Joe felt like he was walking, or rather limping, down into a snow cave. Once inside, with happy smiling faces and luscious warm smells wrapping around him, he sat and relaxed for a nice friendly chat and tended to his gashed leg.

"Say, thanks again for the use of your clothes pin last year," Joe said gratefully.

"Clothespin?" someone asked.

"Yeh, I camped a little too close to the trail last year and durin' the night a team passed me and a dog bit Ready on the lip. I didn't realize it at first and when I did, it was still drippin' blood. Just wouldn't stop. So June let me use one of her clothespins. That stopped the blood from drippin' and caused it to finally clot."

"Who'd ever think a musher would need a clothespin on the Iditarod Trail," mused Joe.

Everyone got a chuckle out of that story. Joe just shook his head.

Then Gene said, "Sorry you had to scratch last year." He was referring to the 1976 race when Joe withdrew from the race 131 miles from Nome.

"That was quite the race. Missed a corner at night. My headlamp was dead and I didn't see Mackey's trail in front of me. Ended up goin' over the bank into waist-deep water and was pulled downstream with the dogs into an ice jam. Tough getting' out with the dog lines all tangled. Built a blazin' fire and for eight hours worked on getting' everyone dried out, but didn't do such a good job on me. Then headed to Rohn. By the time I got there, my boots were frozen. Dick Tozier knocked the ice off so I could get out of 'em. For the first time in all the years I've lived in Alaska, my feet were frostbitten. I felt terrible. But a little rest and a warm cabin sure helped. Mackey and I broke a lot of trail and ran into six- to eight-foot snow drifts out of Poorman."

"How were your dogs doing?"

"Oh, they were strong. Feets is a strong leader and Candy is a sweetheart and exceptional leader, too. Good dogs. Bonnie went into heat, so that slowed me a bit. Ready and Buster and Sunny and Two Bits—they were all working hard. It was me that was having a hard time. By the time I got to Elim, I knew I'd just about had it. When I went out to hook up the dogs, Bonnie only opened one eye. She looked up at me as if to say, 'Do we really have to go already?'

"Right then and there I decided it was time to quit. In dog mushin' it's important to know when to go and when to stop. I knew I had enough dog power to get to Nome, but I also knew I wasn't going to be able to help them much. I couldn't see myself ridin' the runners all the way. I just quit."

Then he smiled. "I got to Nome before Mackey though. Never thought I'd be flyin' into Nome."

They all laughed.

Rested, and feeling a little better, Joe headed up the trail. This year the trail took the teams through Rainy Pass. It was a tree-crashing, body-wrenching ride through the valley to a small cabin out in the middle of nowhere—Rohn Checkpoint.

Several mushers were already there resting their teams, including Terry Adkins, the only vet in 1973. He was now mushing his own team of dogs. Adkins sewed up the gash in Joe's leg.

He said to Joe, "I'll treat you just like I would my lead dog."

Joe leaned back and smiled, "I can't ask for more than that."

Later, the mushers were sitting around repairing their sleds and sharing trail tales through Rainy Pass.

"It was the fastest five miles I ever traveled. I just fell," Joe related to Mackey.

"There were some mighty big holes," Mackey remarked.

Joe grinned and said "I made most of them with my head."

Even with his mishaps, Joe blazed the fastest time in the race's history to McGrath. That's when fierce east winds from Siberia swept in and hammered the teams. Thirty miles out of Ophir was a sign that read, DO NOT PROCEED PAST THIS POINT UNLESS YOU HAVE 5 HOURS OF DAYLIGHT. Good visibility was needed to see the trail flagging, and over several wind blown passes there was absolutely no protection from the wind storms. Coming into Anvik, a village along the Yukon River, was another sign, WELCOME MUSHERS.

Each village had lookouts straining their eyes down the trail looking for the next dog team. The town church bell would ring the musher's entrance into town and all the folks would come out and cheer them in. Kids scurried around to help teams if needed. Village community halls and families were ready to feed mushers hot, home-cooked meals of moose stew or ptarmigan stew or blueberry cake or sourdough pancakes. What a happy time for everyone. Leaving Anvik, the trail headed up the Yukon to Kaltag, then climbed the Nulato Hills and down to Unalakleet. This was Joe's favorite part of the trail—"just plain old beauty" he'd say.

Joe met up with Wooldridge, the British reporter, in Unalakleet. He reported on Joe, "He arrived after fifteen hours on the trail from Kaltag, fed his dogs, and gave every indication that he was going to join his rivals in an eight-hour sleep before the final assault.

"While they bedded down, Redington harnessed his dogs discreetly and slipped out of town.

"He is a tiny, soft spoken man of great courtesy and gargantuan modesty … and when he sledded out of here he had not slept for more than twenty-two hours, and had spent all but four of the preceding sixteen nights out of doors in temperatures ranging from twenty to fifty-five degrees Fahrenheit below freezing."

Joe was haggard-looking and fatigued, but very determined. He was not going to scratch this year. He still had all thirteen dogs he'd started with and they were doing fine.

Coming around Norton Sound across the ice, Joe said, "It was simply terrible." The temperature dropped to minus seventy-two degrees Fahrenheit.

Joe finished fifth—a black eye, gouged leg, crusted lips, scratches, bruises, and all. And beside him were all the thirteen devoted sled dogs that were with him when he left Anchorage 17 days, 1 hour, 26 minutes, and 30 seconds ago.

After the race Ian Wooldridge spoke to Joe about the tough conditions of the race. In typical Joe fashion he said, "You only get one shot at this life and you might as well make the most of it! I don't think we're here to take things for granted. A race like this reminds you that the world doesn't necessarily owe you a living." Everyone who ran the race this year, whether they finished or not, was a winner. They had braved the very best and the very worst of conditions and they survived. And standing right next to them were their hardy, stout, courageous canine companions.

In October 1977 Joe and Vi were awarded the Humanitarian of the Year Award by the Alaska Society for the Prevention of Cruelty to Animals for all their efforts to insure the best care be given to all the dogs who took part in the Iditarod Sled Dog Race. This year there were five vets moving along the Iditarod Trail caring for the dogs. And for every musher, the care of their dogs always came first before anything else. Joe exemplified the best of the best.

And what about Ian Wooldridge, the reporter, the schoolteacher, and Pete MacManus? Ian Wooldridge coined the phrase that will be forever attached to the Iditarod Dog Sled Race—The Last Great Race on Earth. The school teacher continued teaching in Alaska and following every race hoping, like many other Alaskans, that Joe would win his race one day. Pete MacManus finished the race in very good standing in thirteenth place. Joe said, "Pete was a fine man and a very good musher. We sure miss him." Pete went down in a plane crash a couple of years later on his way to race the Iditarod again.

CHAPTER 27

A Dream Takes Form

*To accomplish great things, we
must not only act, but also dream;
not only plan, but also believe.*

ANATOLE FRANCE

Now we need to go back in time for just a bit. Joe had come up with some pretty wild ideas in the past, which caused some folks to call him Crazy Joe, and this seemed like another one of those wild ideas. But one thing was for certain——Joe Redington Sr. never tested the fates. What he did was based on what he had already experienced and learned and proven. This is what set him apart from others. He had the courage to match his convictions. He was an adventurous scientific explorer. He read, studied, observed, planned, and then went forward with his ideas.

He said once, "I don't do anything just to do it or because it is there. I always have a reason."

Because Joe loved dogs and he knew what they could do, he also knew that someday an opportunity would arise where he could prove just what the Alaskan sled dog was fully capable of doing.

In the spring of 1969 when the salmon started their swim up Cook Inlet to fill the rivers and streams with their flashing silvery dance, the Redingtons headed out once again to their fish camp along the Susitna River. And it was there that a new idea took form in Joe's mind.

Joe and Vi were working at their fish camp when a fellow not much taller than Joe strode into their camp and said in a big, booming voice, "Hi, I'm Ray Genet!"

Joe grinned and shook his hand. As they stood there talking, Joe was racking his brain thinking, "Where in the heck have I heard that name?" Suddenly it came to him. This was the man who had, just two and a half years earlier, become the first of a three-man party to climb Mount McKinley in the winter and stand on its summit. Dave Johnston, Art Davidson, and Ray Genet had summited on February 28, 1967.

Mount McKinley is the tallest mountain in North America. The Indians named the mountain Denali, which means "home of the sun" or "the great one." In 1896 it became known as Mount McKinley when a prospector decided to honor the twenty-fifth president of the United States. McKinley has two peaks and it was the southern peak, the tallest, that Ray Genet climbed.

On this day, Genet needed a ride across Cook Inlet to Anchorage and Joe, being the man he was, naturally took him. For two hours these two adventurers palavered. They seemed to hit it off, probably because both men lived for a challenge and could only think in one way—big. Vi watched as a sparkle glinted into Joe's eyes.

What was he thinking now? she thought.

In the end, Joe's enthusiastic and convincing manner burst forth with a new and intriguing question for Genet, "Would you guide my dogs and me up to the top of Mount McKinley next year?"

Ray Genet thought a minute and then slowly said, "Yes, I think so."

Joe had a reason for wanting to take his dogs to the top of McKinley. People had been telling him since the '50s, when he worked for the army, that dogs could not go to higher elevations. Yet Joe's dogs did.

Veterinarians told him, "Joe, their blood cells won't change. They can't possibly go that high."

Still, Joe disputed that idea. He said, "I don't believe that. I think these dogs can go higher than a man can go. They're tough. Maybe their blood cells don't change. They don't need to."

Here was an opportunity Joe couldn't pass up. He loved these Alaskan huskies. He knew their abilities. So he said, "I want to take my team to the top more or less to prove what these dogs can do."

But when the next year rolled around, Genet found himself with too many paying clients wanting to climb the mountain and not enough time to guide Joe and his huskies to the top of McKinley.

For ten years Joe kept asking Ray if this was the year they could go to the top and each year Ray was too busy leading other climbing groups. Finally, January 20, 1978, Joe took the bull by the horns and announced publicly in the *Anchorage Daily News* that he, Joe Redington Sr., was taking his team of dogs up Mt. McKinley in the spring of 1979.

"I know them dogs can make it. They are tougher than us and some of them are smarter than us. They got better lungs," Joe told the *Anchorage Daily News*. "I never climbed McKinley, but I've had dogs up pretty high in airplanes before and I worked Rescue, and I used to put those dogs up some pretty steep places."

Joe was not going to wait for Ray Genet to say he was too busy again.

Veterinarians said, "It can't be done."

Dog mushers said, "It can't be done."

Folks in the army said, "It can't be done."

But again Joe said, "It can be done."

Now Joe had never climbed a mountain just to climb a mountain. He always had a reason for doing whatever he did. He had taken dogs up and down Mount Susitna and other mountains many times on specific jobs that needed to be done. This McKinley adventure was no different. Joe had a specific goal. For ten years Joe had dreamed of proving once and for all that a dog team could climb to the top of the 20,320-foot summit of Mount McKinley. And now he was going to do it.

Joe had been asking Vi over the years to go with him up McKinley, but Vi's only reply was, "No way!" Mushing dogs was fine, but mushing them up that dangerous mountain—no way.

The previous summer Joe had met a young, adventurous veterinarian technician working with musk oxen in Unalakleet in 1977. Her name was Susan Butcher. She had gone to see one of Joe's slide shows on the Iditarod race. She was fascinated. Afterwards she started talking to Joe about the race. Her enthusiasm grew and she said, "Some day I would like to run in that race."

"Well, come down and train with me and see our dogs."

Not much time had passed and Joe and Vi got a phone call asking if she could come down for a couple of weeks.

"Sure," was their automatic reply.

So Butcher packed up her belongings and dogs in her little Volkswagen Beetle and drove down to Knik. She became a dog handler for Joe and was learning all she could from him. Joe gave her a leader and some dogs to add to her young team and she entered her first Iditarod race in 1978 coming in nineteenth place. That was great for a rookie.

The 1978 race was also the closest dog race in Iditarod history. Tom Busch announced the wild sprint down Front Street of two mushers who had just raced over 1,049 miles to finish neck and neck. Dick Mackey beat out Rick Swenson by a dog whisker second! Busch's coverage earned him the unofficial title of "Voice of the Iditarod." Joe wished he could have been there to see that take place, but he was a couple mushers behind them, coming in fifth.

Butcher ended up staying in their little cabin across the road from their house off and on for the next four years. Joe took her under his wing providing a wonderful opportunity for her to experience dog mushing from the master. She helped take care of the dogs, watched Joe, and had her questions answered. She was learning what Lee Ellexson had taught Joe and gleaned all the years of Joe's experiences.

She soon developed a good eye for spotting good race dogs and leaders. Joe talked about the importance of puppies having a strong appetite. "That's number one." Also, good leaders love to run and are a free-style runner, not stiff, they are ready to go and are energetic, and they have a good attitude."

One little puppy in a litter Joe saw had great potential and he was really keeping an eye on him. Apparently Butcher was, too. "She wanted him so bad," said Vi. Finally, Joe gave in and gave her the dog. "Granite was about a year old and a very healthy dog," said Vi. Butcher and Granite became fast friends. Joe always had a great desire to share his love of dogs with others and to promote dog mushing. He generously gave her dogs for her growing kennel in return for her work in caring for Joe's dogs. Butcher left with about sixty dogs and Joe's encouraging tutelage. In later years he would give an entire trained dog team to a Japanese musher. Everything was about promoting these Alaskan huskies to Joe.

One day Joe and Butcher were talking. He asked, "Say, do you think you'd like to take your dog team to the top of McKinley with me?" The Iditarod Race was in its seventh year and they would leave right after the race.

"Yes," was her enthusiastic reply.

"One thing though, Susan, when we start, we're going to the summit no matter how long it's going to take us."

That was fine with her.

Later Joe was to say, "I never dreamed it would take us forty-four days."

When Joe told Vi that Butcher was going with him, Vi had mixed feelings. She knew Butcher was tough and could do it. To be exact, Vi said, "Susan was ready for anything."

The Burled Arch finish line in Nome was made by Red "Fox" Olson of Fairbanks. He received the Red Lantern in the 1974 Iditarod Race when he finished in last place. He thought the race needed a distinguished, permanent, finish line.

But even though Vi had known about this mountain adventure of Joe's for many years, she was never happy with the idea. She did not want to go up McKinley and she didn't want Joe to go up either.

This was the only time she was ever really concerned about Joe. "I know what can happen on that mountain. That bothers me. Those storms come up so suddenly. No matter how you looked at it, no matter how prepared you are, that mountain is a dangerous mountain to climb," she said with an uncommon hint of worry in her voice. The storms on McKinley bring fierce winds and frigid temperatures and could come with very little warning. And it was steep. She just did not like the idea of Joe climbing it one bit.

Vi was not happy at all.

Joee, on the other hand, referred to his dad as his "intrepid father." He said, "If anyone could do it, Dad could."

The 1979 Iditarod Race took the 1,161-mile southern route to Nome. This was Joe's sixth race and Butcher's second. Their attention was focused only on the race at hand. Racing from Kaltag to Unalakleet, they faced fierce winds and snow, making travel a challenge. They drove their dogs into Unalakleet at the same time, tying for ninth place. Then heading out of town on their way to Nome, they encountered more snow and fierce winds and continued to battle whiteout conditions.

In typical Joe humility he said after the race, "Susan was my leader. If it weren't for her, I'd still be out on the ice." They finished the race eighteen minutes apart, Butcher coming in ninth place and Joe coming in tenth after just under seventeen days of mushing. Teamwork, hard work, determination, camaraderie, and their love and trust in their teams set the stage for an even greater challenge to come.

And it was during this race Joe talked to a photographer, Rob Stapleton, about their expedition up McKinley. Stapleton met Joe in 1976. "I was working at the *Anchorage Daily News*," said Stapleton. "Then I went back to Knik with Joe. He showed me his kennel and explained about the race." That's when Stapleton said, "I bummed my way out on the trail." He flew a Cessna 185 to Fairwell and started taking pictures of the Iditarod Race. Joe was impressed with his photography. And that is what led Joe to ask if he would be interested in taking photographs of the huskies on the mountain. Stapleton definitely was interested but everything was spoken of in general terms. No definitive plans were made and they both went their individual ways. But that was not to last.

Joe and Butcher didn't hang around in Nome long. They needed to get back to Knik, to restock their provisions, and gather mountain-climbing gear for their next marathon. This trek would take them close to four miles up into the earth's thinning atmosphere.

Joe's route up Mount McKinley. *Photo by Brian Okonek.*

Mount McKinley
West Buttress Route
April 17 - May 27, 1979
Memorial Day Summit

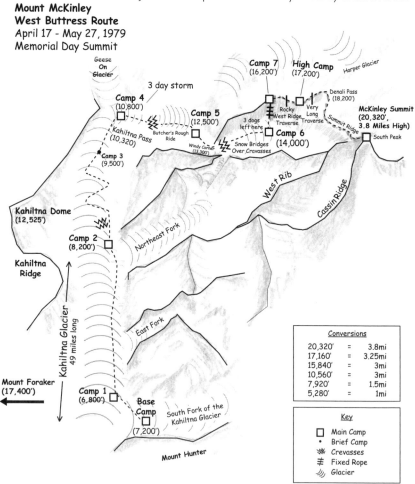

Geese On Glacier

Camp 7 (16,200') High Camp (17,200') Harper Glacier

3 day storm

Denali Pass (18,200')

Camp 4 (10,800')

Camp 5 (12,500')

Rocky West Ridge Traverse Very Long Traverse

McKinley Summit (20,320', 3.8 Miles High)

Kahiltna Pass (10,320)

Butcher's Rough Ride

3 dogs left here

Summit Ridge

South Peak

Windy Corner (13,300')

Snow Bridges Over Crevasses

Camp 6 (14,000')

Camp 3 (9,500')

West Rib

Cassin Ridge

Kahiltna Dome (12,525')

Northeast Fork

Camp 2 (8,200')

Kahiltna Ridge

Kahiltna Glacier 49 miles long

East Fork

Mount Foraker (17,400')

Camp 1 (6,800')

Base Camp (7,200')

South Fork of the Kahiltna Glacier

Mount Hunter

Conversions		
20,320'	=	3.8mi
17,160'	=	3.25mi
15,840'	=	3mi
10,560'	=	3mi
7,920'	=	1.5mi
5,280'	=	1mi

Key	
□	Main Camp
•	Brief Camp
⚡	Crevasses
‡	Fixed Rope
◞	Glacier

CHAPTER 28

Huskies Summit McKinley

*The devotion of thought to an honest achievement
makes that achievement possible.*

MARY BAKER EDDY

In the sixty-second year of Joe's life, he set out to finally prove the last obstacle the Alaskan husky had to proved—that they could ascend to very high elevations without being affected. Joe and his team of huskies would begin their ascent of the tallest mountain on the North American continent, Mount McKinley. With the spring sun casting long shadows across the diamond-studded snow, Joe and Butcher loaded their ton of gear and drove from Knik to Talkeetna. They chose their seven best huskies. Joe brought Lucas, Candy, Buster, Shadow, and Sunny. Butcher brought Tekla and Merryberry.

Meanwhile, back in Anchorage a conversation was taking place.

Stapleton was in his dark room processing film when his phone rang.

"Stapleton. Stapleton. Are you ready?" Ray Genet was calling.

"Ready for what?"

"To climb McKinley," Genet replied.

"When?"

"Tomorrow."

This was a conversation Stapleton was not expecting and he most certainly wasn't prepared. He and Genet met at a downtown restaurant and Genet handed him a list of all things he needed for the climb with Joe Redington.

"I went downtown to the Sixth Avenue Outfitters," Stapleton said, "and bought just about everything I needed."

The next day he was headed up to Talkeetna to meet up with Joe and Butcher. Genet had all three of them unpack all their gear and then sorted through it all discarding what wasn't necessary and the rest was repacked into their bags. They left Talkeetna with three sleds loaded to the hilt carrying all their gear including 800 pounds of dog food and 800 pounds of people food. The seven huskies were eager to start pulling up the trail. With the late start, they were only able to travel a couple of miles before it got dark.

The next morning snow was falling. Joe and Butcher took off with the sled dogs. Stapleton followed on snowshoes.

"It was snowing so hard, I couldn't see," said Stapleton, "but I kept going because I didn't want to lose the trail." Later that afternoon Genet met up with him. Stapleton was glad to find out he was still going in the right direction.

"We had to mush in twelve miles. Stapleton had never had snowshoes on. He'd never had a pack on his back, and he had twelve miles to go." Joe was impressed with Stapleton's determination. "He stuck with it. When he got there he had blisters on both heels."

Genet had built several small log cabins on Pirate Lake, which is right at the base of Ruth Glacier. This was where his climbing parties bided their time until he could guide them up the mighty Mount McKinley. Outside their small log cabin, Joe and Butcher piled their gear, bedded the dogs, and went inside to wait. Almost all their gear was well-tested winter gear used on the Iditarod Trail. They were prepared to meet the wind, cold, ice, and steep hills. What they didn't have on the Iditarod Trail, though, was crevasses. Crevasses could pose a major problem for a dog team on the mountain, so they rigged up a unique harness with a belly band for their lead dogs in case they should fall in one. The belly strap would prevent the dog from slipping out of the harness.

The climbers waiting for Genet were continually engaged in doing all kinds of exercises. That is, with the exception of Joe and Butcher. The Iditarod mushers relaxed, playing cards. Everyone knew they weren't mountain climbers and they'd say, "Boy, you'd better exercise or you'll never make it!"

Joe simply responded with a twinkle in his eye, "Oh, we want to rest. We don't want to exercise. We just came off the Iditarod." Joe figured *all* his miles of dog mushing across the wintry Arctic was plenty enough exercise for him.

Within a few days Joe got a note from Genet saying he couldn't take them

Joe standing outside one of Ray Genet's cabins at Pirate Lake with all of their gear waiting for the go ahead from Genet. *Photo by Rob Stapleton*

up McKinley. He had too many paid groups he had to get up the mountain. But Joe had other plans. He hadn't waited ten years and gotten all geared up just to be told he couldn't go again. So when Genet flew into camp, Joe confidently walked out to meet him.

"We're going to go on our own. I'll be in charge."

Genet looked him square in the eye. He knew Joe was tough and resourceful, and not fool-hearty. The wisdom gained from all his past experiences was definitely to Joe's advantage. "Well," said Genet, "that's good. That's okay. I'm sure you can do it. I'll be with you as much as I can. I'll try to help you in the bad parts."

Before Joe's small group left, Genet instructed them in how to use their climbing gear and some important mountain survival techniques. Joe was all ears. He didn't take his eyes off Genet as he told them how to use the jumars, a mechanical device with "teeth" that would enable them to ascend a rope, and how to use their ice axe to self-arrest, or stop themselves, if they should fall.

Later Joe said, "I paid particular attention to that. You'll never find a picture

Buster with saucers-sized eyes looks as if he is saying, "Is this what we really want to do?"

Don Lee, the pilot, and Joe with Merryberry are scooting over to get Buster into the back seat. Buster was the youngest of the huskies. *Photo by Rob Stapleton*

of me, I don't think, when I'm movin' without that ice axe in my hand. I had to use it several times, too."

The temperature was minus ten degrees the day they left for McKinley. Don Lee, an Alaskan bush pilot from Talkeetna, had just purchased a Super Cub PA-18 in Canada and flew Joe's expedition from Pirate Lake to the southeast fork tributary of the forty-four-mile long Kahiltna Glacier. Joe left first. Lee strapped two of Joe's sleds to the struts of the wings—one on each side of the plane, then stuffed in a bunch of gear and four dogs.

"Normally we put dogs in a gunny sack, but these dogs just jumped right in," said Lee. "They were well-behaved."

Joe managed to find enough space to squeeze in and shut the plane door. There wasn't much room to even wiggle his toes.

Lee said that with all the moisture from the dogs breathing and the low

"The acrobatics Joe talked about is more like a ballerina doing a pirouette," said Geeting. "The plane does a pirouette on the top of the glacier. If you go too fast the right ski gets buried or too slow the left ski gets buried. The balance has to be perfect, and then the skis go right into the ski tracks on the glacier and the plane comes to a stop facing downhill."

Doug Geeting landing on the East Fork of the Kahiltna Glacier.

temperatures, they had to scrape the windows to see out. So they ended up flying with a window open up to the landing strip at the 7,250-foot level of the Southeast Fork of the Kahiltna Glacier.

Lee dropped Joe off at the Base Camp and headed back to Pirate Lake for another load. Meanwhile, Doug Geeting, another pilot with a larger Cessna 185 loaded up more gear, Butcher, Stapleton, the rest of the dogs.

"Joe was kind of a character—quiet, not overly excited, at ease, just takes his time," remembered Geeting. "Susan was a little frustrated, but she was still learning."

After seven or eight trips all their gear was on the McKinley.

Below Joe's feet the slow, grinding dance of Kahiltna's ancient glacial ice as it slowly ate away at the mountain was a strange thought for him to contemplate. The Kahiltna, the longest glacier in the Alaska Range at forty-four miles, was a buzz of activity. Climbers were setting up camps, unpacking and arranging gear, and exercising.

Joe's biggest kick was watching the planes land. Every pilot seemed to have his own unique way of landing. Some came in to land, misjudged their air speed and the landing strip, and the plane plowed off the packed tracks into the snow. Joe and other climbers grabbed their shovels and helped dig them out. Then "Another pilot would come in with a 185, do an acrobatic roll, and then land. We didn't have to dig him out." That was Doug Geeting. The glacier was humming with activity.

Joe's climbing party of three and seven dogs grew to six climbers and seven dogs. Joe and Butcher hooked up their dogs to start hauling their first load of gear. The dogs just wanted to hit the trail. Joe securely anchored his sled into the snow and it was a good thing, too.

"Look at that Buster," Joe mused. "He just screamed to go." Buster was pulling so hard, his front feet were clear off the snow. "He was one heck of a dog, that Buster."

Then all the dogs were jumping up in the air with all four feet off the ground anxious to start pulling. And off they flew. The load they pulled didn't slow them down a bit. That's when Joe realized he'd probably goofed.

"These dogs had too much power," he said, shaking his head. They had brought their strongest dogs, but the work they were doing on the mountain didn't even compare to what the dogs had done on the Iditarod.

Their first carry was to take their gear from Base Camp down to Camp One at 6,800 feet in elevation on the Kahiltna Glacier. One of the three sleds they'd brought broke up right at the get-go on the rough glacial terrain. So they proceeded up the mountain with two sleds.

Then it started to snow. "We really got hammered with snow," Stapleton remembered. "It snowed and snowed." There were lots of snowstorms on the lower part of the mountain that kept them pinned down for prolonged periods of time. But that didn't bother Joe. He was patient. He was in good company and they were in this for the long haul.

After the first snow flurry, they hauled gear up to Camp Two at 8,200 feet at the base of Kahiltna Dome. Sometimes Joe had four dogs and Butcher three, sometimes Butcher had four and Joe three, or sometimes they hooked all seven of them together, depending on what they were hauling. Genet did have one rule—he didn't want them traveling at night. There were times when they took a load up to the next new campsite and it was getting on into the evening, too late to head back to the main camp. So they rolled out their sleeping bags, cooked the dog food, and spent the night there.

But then Joe clarified Alaska's spring, "The nights are shorter and not very dark in the spring. Each day was gettin' longer." In fact, there are about eighteen hours of daylight in May and twenty-one hours of daylight in June. So every day was getting longer and longer.

One trick to climbing tall mountains was the importance of getting acclimated to the mountain environment. Their bodies needed to adjust to less oxygen in the air at the higher elevations. The weather and the trips back and forth between camps with their gear and supplies provided time for this to happen.

Joe and Butcher used the dogs to haul heavy loads and Stapleton packed heavy loads on his back and pulled a red plastic sled up to the next camp. "I climbed most sections three times," he said.

Joe took a lot of extra food because he wasn't sure how long they would be on the mountain and he wanted to have enough to ensure they could stay long enough to summit. And he wasn't sure what the dogs' diet would require at those altitudes, so there was lots of frozen fish and other food for the canines. He came prepared for anything. Not unlike any trip he went on into Interior Alaska or any race he ever entered in the Iditarod. This meant many trips. All in all, their bodies became well-acclimated.

Over the years Joe had done a lot of experimenting with stoves trying to make them more efficient for heating large amounts of water for the dogs' food while he was out on the trail. Now he was very grateful for that experimentation. Joe discovered that even in the thinning air, his specially built Coleman stove could boil five gallons of water pretty fast from snow.

"The dogs needed lots of water. We had to water them pretty often. They would dehydrate pretty quickly on the mountain." Then Joe smiled a little and said, "The other mountain climbers were usin' their little stoves. They would fool around for hours tryin' to get a little bit of water boiled. By then, I'd have the whole team watered."

It wasn't long before he found himself helping them out, boiling water for eight or ten people in Genet's party of climbers.

"That was another thing that amazed Genet, how good a stove we had," said Joe. "It was special built for the Iditarod."

When they were hauling gear between Camp Three at 9,500 feet and Camp Four at 10,800 feet (that's almost two miles up in the air), they encountered an odd curiosity. They noticed their dogs started to sniff the snow. When they stopped their teams, the dogs started digging for all they were worth.

In no time at all, Buster's head popped up and hanging from his mouth was a frozen Canada goose!

Joe walked up and took it out of Buster's mouth. "Now would ya look at that. How'd he get clear up here?" Joe muttered.

The "Clapping Mountains", an old Eskimo legend, had an answer.

The legend tells of two young Canada geese that were getting ready to migrate south in the fall from the Yukon River Delta. They joined up with the honking V-formation of hundreds of geese that were also heading south. That's when the pair first heard tales of the terrible Clapping Mountains.

The Clapping Mountains were two very tall mountains that were quite close to each other. All the migrating birds from the nesting ground along the Bering Sea must fly through them. These two geese became quite fearful.

Then an old gander talked to them. They listened carefully to his instructions. He told them when they needed to fly and that they must fly very fast. Those that made it through would be the strongest and fittest geese for the migration south and their children would be strong. Those who flew too slowly and were too weak, would be caught between the mountains and crushed.

So heeding the advice of the gander, the two young geese ate a good meal and rested the night on a sandbar. The next morning they flew towards the Clapping Mountains to be tested.

The mountains clapped. The gander called, "Fly. Fly strong. Fly fast. Don't stop until you're through!"

So the young geese flew. They flew with all their might. One began to fall back, but her partner pushed her on. Then the mountains began to shake. Just before they clapped together the two geese flew out the other side into the clear blue sky. Sadly, there were some who did not make it and they remain on the mountain.

Brian Okonek, a guide working for Genet, who later helped Joe's party, said, "Migratory birds are following the Kahiltna Glacier." The glacier ascended to Kahiltna Pass, the lowest place in the range between Mount Foraker and Mount McKinley. "It's quite often cloudy and windy there. They'll be flying in zero zero conditions with no visibility at all. You'll hear geese honking continuously as they fly through the mountains. They must be echo-locating their way up through the peaks."

In any case, the dogs were having a heyday.

Joe said, "There were dozens and dozens of them that the dogs would dig out of the snow."

"Then at 10,800 it snowed again," said Joe, "and we got buried."

This fury lasted three days. They whiled the time away playing cards, with their gloves on, telling stories, and visiting. They kept warm using both their

Coleman stoves which brought the temperature inside up to a "balmy" minus 1 degree Fahrenheit.

There is a reason some call Mount McKinley the Weathermaker. She can whip up a storm and throw in frigid temperatures with 60- to 100-mile-per-hour winds in the blink of an eye. Then all you can do is hang on for dear life and wait it out. These violent gales may be a short 15- or 20-minute blow followed by a quiet calm, or other times the blast will last for hours, even days. There is no predicting this mountain. So the storms slowed Joe's expedition up McKinley, allowing them to get well-acclimated.

They built thick, heavy, snow-block walls around their tents and hunkered down to wait out the winter tempest.

Even though it was taking them a long time to ascend the mountain, Stapleton said in an article by Brian O'Donoghue in *Mushing Magazine,*

"… there was never any doubt in my mind whether we would make it. Not with Joe there—he's such a survivor."

The temperatures on the mountain varied a lot. But Joe was used to layering. When it was cold, he wore several layers of clothing, like he did on the Iditarod, and bundled himself in his warm navy blue parka and heavy-duty pants with only his white, zinc-oxide nose barely showing. His beaver skin hat was a tremendous help, since the head was where the most body heat was lost. For his feet he wore the military's warmest boot—the clownish, white bunny boot.

"My toes did get cold if I didn't move much. So I kept movin'. My fingers didn't get cold though. I had good mittens, a couple of different layers of mittens. They were commercial mittens, same as I wore on the Iditarod. I never did like beaver mittens. When they get wet, you can't dry 'em out," he stated.

And then sometimes he was just wearing a thin shirt—that was when they were running gear between camps and they really worked up a sweat.

The dogs wore no booties on this trip. Their feet were tough and not a dog complained. They were in tip-top condition.

After Camp Four they put away their snowshoes and used crampons, as the glacier became more precipitous and windblown, and there were more crevasses to be avoided.

When they came to a very steep grade, the dogs gripped the side of the mountain with their toenails, put their heads down, and slowly moved up the mountain. Joe jammed his sharp claw-like crampons and ice axe into the ice and snow to keep the sled from going back down the hill.

"Ice cleats made mushing very difficult," Joe recalled, "but we wanted to stay on the mountain, not slide down the mountain. My ice axe was never out of my hand."

Genet was not with Joe's party much of the way, but he was looking out for them. He was like a yo-yo between all the climbing parties. "Genet told us where to go," said Joe. "He didn't want us wanderin' around. In places he set up flags as a boundary for walkin'." These flags were on thin willow wands jammed in the snow.

"We didn't have to use gee and haw much, just mush." The trail was pretty much straight forward and up, no turning left or right.

Windy Corner and Beyond

The dogs were hauling heavy loads of gear up to Camp 5, just below Windy Corner, to stock pile. Beyond Windy Corner at about 13,300 feet, they hauled lighter loads for shorter distances because of the difficulty of the terrain. Here they were going to get some help from Brian Okonek, an experienced guide on McKinley. Joe met him at about the 12,700-foot level.

"Ray asked me to help Joe get his expedition around Windy Corner. It involved some belaying to get their loads of gear around the corner," Okonek said.

"I thought that was a good deal," remembered Joe. They chatted awhile and continued on their way.

A load of gear had just been deposited at Windy Corner and Joe said the sled needed to be rough-locked before they went back down to Camp 4. Rough-locking involved wrapping a chain around the sled runners, which helped brake the sled going down icy slopes, so it wouldn't run over the dog team. Joe had used this safety technique often in his reclamation work and now that the trail was hard and icy, he told Butcher the same technique needed to be used here. But that never happened. Butcher was getting ready for the return trip. Then the unthinkable happened.

Okonek recalled, "One of the dogs got a wild hair and everybody took off. Susan leapt for the sled and was able to get ahold of it, but not to stand up on the runners."

Joe grimaced as he recalled that moment. "Rob and I ran down the hill after her and our fears were confirmed when we saw her gear strewn all over the trail."

Joe and Butcher coming around Windy Corner with a crevasse to the left. *Photo by Ray Genet.*

"She was getting drug down the mountain and it is steep and icy and she wasn't going to let go for anything," continued Okonek. "Susan's got a good voice and she can holler loudly when she needs to. And she's yelling for the dogs to whoa and they were not stopping."

The dogs had let out all their stops and were headed pell-mell down the slope below Windy Corner. Butcher was hollering to stop, but the exhilaration of this race was all that was on the dogs' minds. Then the sled started to catch up with them. The happy yelps sung for the pure joy of running stopped. Tekla knew this was not good, but by now the seven dogs were out of control. Butcher was bouncing all over the place as the sled careened over the rough-ridged sastrugi, and hanging on for dear life. One most important rule for mushing dogs on the Iditarod—never let go—rang instinctively in her thoughts.

Joe felt completely helpless and mightily concerned for her safety. But fortunately, Tekla was one sharp leader. She saw Genet below them. The sled and team came very near a crevasse, but then Tekla swerved over towards Genet. He saw the team coming, jammed his ice axe in the side of the mountain, and planted his feet in the snow. As Tekla brought the team towards him, he grabbed the rope between Tekla and the swing dog. Using all the brute strength and determination he could muster, he swung the team around, bringing them all to a screeching halt!

Everyone was safe. Butcher had some bruises and one rough ride she would never, ever forget. And everyone was counting their lucky stars. However, the sled was broken and had to be repaired before they could continue. That's when the unused snowshoes came in handy. "We had to rebuild the sled several times," said Joe. "We got the snowshoes tied along the side of it to hold it together." Then he added with a little grin, "Ya use what ya have."

By the time they got to Windy Corner at 13,300, only Joe, Butcher, Stapleton, and the seven huskies remained to continue. The extreme conditions and long days on the mountain with minus forty-degree-Fahrenheit nights were taking their toll on the other climbers in their party. Joe was especially conditioned for this type of weather, Butcher was young and tough, and Stapleton was simply determined to record this unheard of venture of Joe's. These three strong-hearts stayed on the mountain.

Beyond Windy Corner was the most spectacular West Buttress. The glacier calves off a cliff of solid rock, bending the bed of ice, making it rougher with more crevasses adding to the difficulty of the ascent. Just as the dogs could feel on the Iditarod Trail the strength of river ice beneath their feet and not go out on it if it was bad, so they could feel unstable snow beneath their feet. Tekla, especially, could sense weak snow-cover.

But even so, as they took the dogs up and around each crevasse, the front dogs were clear of the deathly crack, but sometimes, because of the curve of the gang line in making the corner, the wheel dog's feet would punch through momentarily.

"They were having to jump the crevasse," Okonek said. "And then the sled goes across the crevasse right at the end. They were narrow enough that they could get across, but it was definitely risky business. You can't always tell where they are and how fragile the bridges can be even though they appear so strong."

Joe said, "The dogs could sense the danger in advance, and barked when they came too close."

Everyone's senses were alert to this.

Other times they used their ever present ice axes to test the snow and see if it was solid underneath the top crust. If the axe handle went through the snow, they knew a crevasse was buried below. They had to see the size and then determine whether to jump over or go around.

"They never had a foolproof system for protecting Susan and Joe from the crevasses," Okonek grimaced. "They were pretty much solo on the mountain,

Joe at 14,200 feet having a cup of hot Tang and enjoying the spectacular sights with Mount Foraker in the background. *Photo by Rob Stapleton*

because while they were handling the dog sled, they were not roped up with a partner."

Another time they went the wrong way. They headed up a gully only to find they could go no further. So they had to backtrack and see where they went wrong. That was nothing new to Joe. The Iditarod sent out false trails, too. That was all part of the adventure.

Between Camp Five at 12,500 and Camp Six at 14,300 was Windy Corner and just around the corner were crevasses. They had to traverse by them without sliding into them. "We had a line tied right to the front of the sled or it would have slid right down the hill," Joe said. "Susan was holding the line. I was on the sled. The dogs really have their feet planted in the snow." Their sled was tilting on one runner at times and it was like the dogs were walking on a tightrope trail. But that was one thing dog mushing taught you—good balance. And Joe and Butcher did have that.

Camp Six was at 14,200 feet. Six climbing parties were scattered across the snowfield waiting to summit. Everyone had dug out holes in the snow to set up their camps and on McKinley it is common practice to build snowblock walls around tents for protection from the unpredictable winds. Colorful tents dotted the side of the "The Great One."

The dog sleds came in very handy up to Camp Six. The dogs were able to pull heavy sleds up to this point transporting all the expedition's equipment and food.

Joe and Butcher would have mini races and see who could make a relay of gear up and back in the fastest safe time. The dogs loved it. "Joe and Susan were definitely living life for the moment," Okonek said.

"We went back and forth a lot," said Joe, "hauling tons of gear."

Genet told Joe, "I am convinced that the dogs were really useful at 10,000 feet and even at 14,000 feet. I am amazed at how much they can haul."

Joe laughed to himself because he was thinking the same thing about Genet. "He would carry two five-gallon cans in his pack and that would be at least eighty or ninety pounds. He could carry more than anyone I ever seen! But then we could haul four five-gallon cans with the dogs."

Genet's comments warmed Joe's heart and confirmed what he already knew. But now these Alaskan huskies were proving to all who saw them that they could climb to great heights.

But Joe had to really watch the dogs because they would try to spin around and head back down the mountain. "But we had good leaders. I had Candy and Susan had Tekla. They weren't much on whoain', though. They were eager to go. I don't think they realized it was dangerous. They just wanted to go wide open."

At Camp Six, the glacier leveled out into a big flat basin. Joe and Susan decided it was time to power down their dog team and take only their calmest dogs. They needed total control for the rest of their climb. They already had first-hand knowledge that too much power could pull them off the mountain. They needed to be able to stop on a dime. They did not want any dogs that might bolt. Candy was Joe's sweet and good leader. Tekla was Butcher's sharp leader. Lucas was the youngest. And Buster had a determined spirit. These were the four dogs that went with them to the summit. Leaving Camp Six the dogs pulled an empty sled as the terrain was too steep. Here the climbers carried the dog food, including frozen fish, and their gear to High Camp.

From 15,500 feet to 16,200 feet, Camp Seven, are seven hundred feet of fixed ropes. Three-foot pickets were anchored in the very steep, ice-covered granite wall about seventy-five feet apart and attached with a sturdy rope. "The fixed ropes were maybe at a seventy-degree angle," said Stapleton. "The process was like climbing a ladder." Jumars were used to ascend the precipitous incline. The jumars had metal teeth that opened to slide up the rope and then clamped down into the rope to allow the climber to pull up. This was an invaluable device to ascend a steep cliff.

"When we got to Camp Six, Joe got ill," Stapleton continued. "Genet and I set out together leaving Joe and Susan in camp. We set up a camp at the top of the fixed ropes." They put up a large expedition tent and anchored it really well with ropes to the rocks, because the winds could get really bad up there. "We chopped ice away making an eight-foot-by-eight-foot platform to put our tent. We spent hours putting up camp."

"It is an incredibly exposed area," explained Okonek. "You must dig into a steep slope to build a secure camp."

A four-man team came down the mountain and stopped for a short visit. Before they started their descent on the fixed ropes, Genet gave them a note and said it was very important that they give it to Joe. "His camp is the one with the dogs," Genet said. The note told Joe and Butcher to wait until he came down to help them up the fixed ropes.

Joe never got the note.

Genet left the next morning to go up to High Camp and check on some other climbers and then he would come back to help Joe and Susan. Since Joe didn't know this, he and Butcher hitched up their four dogs and headed to the fixed ropes.

"We had a jumar on Susan up front, one on the lead dog, one on the sled, and one on me," explained Joe, "and every arm length, we moved the jumar up." They kicked their ice-crampons into the ice, and set their ice axes securely into the ice with one hand while they moved the jumar up the rope with the other hand. The jumar was also attached to their seat harness with a sling and served as a backup safety if they slipped. Then using all their body strength they pushed and pulled themselves upward. They slowly moved a foot or two at a time.

But they had difficulty with the dogs getting tangled in the ropes, when they got to the pickets. About two-thirds of the way up, Joe had enough. He unharnessed the dogs and they scampered right up to the top of the headwall. Then he hooked the sled to the rope with a carabineer and he and Butcher worked their way to the top one step at a time. Hours had passed since they left Camp Six.

"It was dusk about two o'clock in the morning when they got up there," remembered Stapleton. "Susan was having a hard time. Joe was struggling also, because he still wasn't feeling well."

Stapleton and Buster at Camp 6, which is at 16,200 feet.

Climbing along the West Ridge up to High Camp. *Photo by Rob Stapleton*

"Susan froze her feet a little bit there because your ankles are bent so bad that you don't get no circulation [in your feet]. It's steep," Joe said.

"We anchored the dogs down good by some big rocks," said Joe. Then Stapleton put Joe and Butcher in sleeping bags and went down the fixed ropes to retrieve the sled and their sleeping bags. About two hours later he crawled into their tent for some much needed rest. Everyone was safe and sound.

The next day Butcher and Stapleton were out tending to the dogs and Joe was in the tent. "It was sunny and nice and you could see forever," said Stapleton. "Then we heard an odd sound, kind of like a jet going to come buzz us, but the sound was more like a freight train. Then WHAM! It [an incredibly intense blast of wind] hit us. Susan yelled at Joe to get out of the tent. When he poked his head out of the door, some of our gear was sucked right out. He went back inside and laid flat on the ground. The tent was really anchored well to the rocks, but it looked like a parachute trying to fly off the mountain.

"Susan and I were crouched with the dogs as low as we could get, behind rocks," continued Stapleton. "That 100-mile-per-hour wind lasted perhaps a half hour or a little more, then it just stopped."

The next day Genet and Okonek joined them. They continued their ascent of the West Buttress to High Camp at 17,200 feet. They had to cross a very long, icy and rocky traverse. "It was hard going with crampons because the teeth would break through the ice and hard-packed snow and hit rock," said Stapleton.

At that elevation the body is operating on half as much oxygen content in the air. They had to pace themselves. "You must concentrate to keep a pace of one step per one breath. But it has to be a concentrated effort. The body slows down, but," Okonek said, "Joe and Susan were doing fine and the dogs were as energetic as ever."

"He and Susan acclimated very, very well." Okonek was impressed. "They were doing fantastic."

Then another storm with high winds grounded the climb to a halt for a couple of days.

On Memorial Day, May 28, they made their final drive to the summit. Genet joined up with them again. Joe was going strong. His goal was at his fingertips, but in typical Joe Redington fashion, he didn't make a big fuss about it or get real excited. The dogs were in great condition and eager to go. He just knew they could get these dogs to the top—weather permitting.

The day was crystal clear. Genet was up at 3 a.m. getting ready. As many times as he had climbed the mountain, this day had to be the most beautiful in his mind. They all left High Camp for the Summit with soaring spirits.

Joe on the West Ridge with climbers heading down. *Photo by Ray Genet*

This is going across the long traverse to Denali Pass with Joe on the sled and Butcher holding the safety line above the dogs, Lucus and Buster. *Photo by Ray Genet*

Okonek wrote this in his mountain diary, *Myself, Stapleton, who has never climbed before this trip, ropes with me ... In an hour and 40 minutes we're to Denali Pass.* They left ahead of the others in order for Stapleton to take photographs.

"That's really good time. Generally it takes two hours with a guided group," remarked Okonek.

Joe said, "Going to Denali Pass between 17,200 and 18,200 feet, we just had a narrow walkway about a foot wide that would hold only one runner. The other runner would stick out over the edge into thin air. We'd hold the sled upright. It was the most dangerous spot. That's where Ray wouldn't tie into us. He said, 'You guys go ahead. I don't want to go with you. I'll hold all I can hold and then I'll turn you loose.' So it was just Susan and me and the dogs. We were all tied together through that area. We had a line tied right to the front of the sled or it would have slid right down the hill. Susan was holding the line. I was on the sled. You slip there and you'd go about 2,000 feet. The dogs had their feet really planted in the snow across there."

Joe is on the sled with Buster, Lucus, Candy, and Tekla following Butcher across a corniced ridge. McKinley's summit is the peak beyond the cornice.

Stapleton is taking pictures. They reached the summit.

And the look on their faces said, "We don't want to go down that way!"

At one point the sled started to slide sideways down the hill. Thinking quickly, Joe jammed his ice axe in between the runners to stop the team and sled from sliding down the mountain.

"You had to be alert all the time," Joe said.

All the way across the diagonal traverse Joe was leaning right into the snow. The leader had his ears laid back. Lucas was the most nervous. Joe was always talking softly to him and encouraging him along.

"He talked in a real even voice," said Okonek. "This helped greatly."

Then Butcher took over on the sled with the four dogs. She really had to hustle to keep up with them, but she never gave up.

The dogs' pace was way faster than one step one breath," said Okonek.

Butcher would run for a distance, then stop to get her breath. Then one of the dogs would bark, not wanting to wait, and off they'd go again. This twenty-four-year-old had the stamina and willpower to match these four-foot Alaska athletes. But it was not an easy way to summit McKinley.

Joe's energy level was also very high. The fortitude of this Alaskan, again, was unfaltering. He felt like a teenager with sixty-two years of experience behind him. He, too, had a concentrated pace of one step and then several breaths, then another step.

He said, "The last 1,000 feet of climbing along the corniced ridge near the top was pretty good walking." There were two types of cornice on Summit Ridge—one was an overhanging shelf of snow formed by blowing snow on the downwind side of a mountaintop or ridge, and the other was formed on the windward side of a ridge by supercooled water droplets that froze to the surface of anything they touched, making cauliflower-type formations called rime. This rime could build up on a pencil-thin willow wand, turning it into baseball-bat size or bigger. But to Joe it felt good to be walking where it wasn't as steep as where they had just been, even if he was on a cornice.

In Okonek's diary he wrote, *The traverse went super smooth. The steep icy spots above the pass go like a snap. Above that the dogs pull the sled with both Susan's and Stapleton's pack in it. We take a third break at Kahiltna Horn … Laying around in the warm sun and calm air munching and drinking … It was really neat to watch Susan and Joe mush along the summit ridge with Genet protecting them.* By "protecting them," Okonek meant that Genet had a rope tied to them to protect them from falling, if they should slip.

"In places, the Summit Ridge comes to a peak. You walk right on the crest—one foot in front of the other," he clarified. "And in other places you have to put one foot on each side."

We summited at 4 p.m., no wind, minus 8 degrees Fahrenheit, clear as a bell everywhere ... All in all, we ended up spending about four hours on top.

"We made it!" Joe exclaimed with great joy.

Looking down on the earth from four miles up in the sky, not a cloud could be seen on this dead calm, crystal clear day. A more spectacular day could not be had. "It was absolutely a bluebird-perfect day!" Okonek exclaimed.

Butcher sat in the snow by Tekla, and Joe stood there waving to the world.

Joe couldn't sit down. There was just too much to be seen. He spent the next four hours walking around that small 8-by-10-foot summit taking in all the wonders of the Alaska Range and for that matter, Alaska.

He had flown and mushed over so much of Alaska and to see it from the top of McKinley fascinated him. "I was real curious about where places were," he said. "Just look at all those mountains below. You can see all the way to Anchorage and the Kenai Peninsula hundreds of miles to the south!" He could see the Yentna River coming out of the range. He could see the route of the Iditarod Trail crossing the Susitna Valley floor and where it entered the mountains starting across the Happy River Gorge. Then turning and looking northwest, "And there's McGrath!" he declared, with excitement seeing the bends in the Kuskokwim River.

Okonek said, "He knew the state so well. It must have been great for him to survey it. It was a stellar day. I've never seen such a day."

Joe's thoughts were interrupted by the dogs barking. "Would you look at that Buster. He's really putting out," laughed Joe.

He snapped a picture of Buster barking for all he was worth—his mouth wide open. It was as though he was saying, "Hey, where do we go from here?" These huskies really wanted to go, but there was no place to go except down.

Speaking of Joe, Okonek said, "He was just like a little kid. He had that great grin."

Joe made the summit on Memorial Day 1979. Standing right beside him were four Alaskan sled dogs. He proved what he set out to prove! What a memory he had.

Genet got out his radio phone to try and get ahold of someone in Anchorage and let them know the first ever dog team had arrived at the top of Mount McKinley. However, everything was closed in Anchorage for the holiday. He finally managed via a ham radio link to get hold of a reporter for the *Anchorage Daily News*. One of the first statements Genet made to the reporter was, "I underestimated Joe Redington!"

The *Anchorage Daily News* wrote that Joe said it was "the most beautiful day of my whole life. I'm feeling great."

Four Alaskan huskies, Buster, Lucus, Candy, and Tekla, the only dog team to ever summit Mount McKinley, and, of course, Joe and Butcher. Joe had Rob Stapleton's photo made into a postcard so that he could sign it and give it to people as proof of what these huskies could do. This is the signature Joe always took special time to scribe for people. *Photo by Rob Stapleton*

Meanwhile just below the summit another undertaking was being attempted.

"Bill Divine and I hired a plane to take us up, so Bill could take pictures of Joe on top," said Vi. "The pilot had a brand-new Bonanza."

They asked if he could get them to the top. He replied, "Oh yeah, we can get you up there."

But he only got them up to about 19,000 feet. Joe could see the airplane circling around and around the mountain peak. So he stood there and waited and waited and waited. The pilot had flown bit by bit to higher elevations to acclimate the three of them to the thinning atmosphere, unfortunately, he had forgotten his oxygen mask. Vi and Bill had theirs. When they realized this, Bill and Vi gave their masks to the pilot, so that he could fly the plane. They didn't fully realize what occurs to the body in thinning air and they were becoming extremely uncomfortable. Bill did manage to take some pictures

Butcher is resting by Tekla and Candy, Joe could not possibly sit down, there was just too much to see from the top of the North American Continent, AND at long last, these Alaskan huskies proved altitude does not affect them. *Photo by Rob Stapleton*

Candy, Lucus, and Buster on top of Mount McKinley. Stapleton is by the sled.

of the top of the mountain, but he couldn't see anything. Both of them were having a hard time staying conscious. The pilot finally pointed the nose of the plane down the mountain. He had run out of oxygen. They just couldn't get up to 20,320 feet.

In Joe's words, "They pretty near killed themselves. They were feeling wheezy and had extreme headaches."

It wasn't until much later, when Bill was examining his photos that he discovered he actually had gotten pictures of them just before they got to the top. There they were, no bigger than the smallest of ants, all lined on the top of McKinley: Joe Redington Sr., Susan Butcher, Rob Stapleton, Ray Genet, Brian Okonek, and the four Alaskan huskies, Candy, Lucus, Buster, and Tekla, the only huskies to ever summit McKinley at 20, 320 feet!

The Descent

As Joe stood in awe of all their magnificent surroundings, Genet asked how they planned on going down. That is when Joe realized he had no plan as to how to get the sled and dogs down the mountain. All his thought and energy had been spent on how to get up McKinley, not down. To say that Genet was not very happy about that is an understatement. These dogs were full of energy. They had traveled only one short distance that day and were raring to go.

But now it was time to seriously think about heading down. There were poles at the summit. Joe wanted to leave the sled securely anchored at the top and bring the dogs down loose, but Genet said no. "You brought it up here and you can take it back." Joe didn't argue. It made perfect sense to him. He definitely did not want to be a part of making a junkyard on top of this great mountain.

The descent is probably the most dangerous part of any expedition up tall mountains. Climbers are tired. They have reached their goal and are anxious to get off the mountain. But they must remember one thing—the same concentrated effort that got them to the top of the mountain must be maintained in order to get them safely down the mountain.

Joe knew this and was cautious. He knew firsthand the importance of taking your time in dangerous situations. He would continue doing what experience had taught him.

He rough-locked the sled runners and tied ropes to the sled. "We also put a piece of angle iron across where you stand on the sled runners that would dig in," said Joe. They needed as much braking ability as possible. Then they slowly guided the dogs down the way they had just come.

Some of the time they had to calmly talk to the dogs, ride the brake and use the cleats on their boots to slow the team down. Sometimes Joe walked calmly by the lead dog with Genet holding a rope to the sled to belay the team and Butcher walked in the middle of the team.

Okonek explained, "Going down from Denali Pass was very tedious, very, very tedious. You had to go down and across at the same time. And that was really hard. Side-hilling with a dogsled is tricky, very, very tricky. And side-hilling on the type of slopes they were on with the killer exposure below you is terrifying."

Step by supremely careful step their determination held them to the mountain.

Genet was belaying. "He would be up above them and then they would do short spurts, you know, they would go down and across the slope for a while and then stop. Genet would reposition," said Okonek. "It was pretty serious terrain. It's definitely not a place to get out of control. There's been a lot of fatalities on this section of the route over the years. It's steep."

Later, when Joe was asked if that part of the climb scared him he said, "I don't scare very easy. I pretty well know my limitations. I know what I can do and what I can't do, so I don't let it bother me."

Okonek concurred. "He never got panicked or afraid or anything. You could see it in his eyes—he was really having fun."

They made camp around midnight on Harper Glacier just below Denali Pass. Okonek got busy making soup for everyone, but by then everyone was sleeping.

The next morning they packed up and headed down to High Camp. They camped there for the night, then packed up all their gear to head for the fixed ropes. Their packs were very heavy, but they didn't want to make two trips.

Twenty-one people were bottle-necked at the fixed ropes waiting to go down. Genet took a short power nap, not unlike Joe's famous fifteen minute power naps. The dogs got lots of attention as they waited. And the rest of the folks were waiting for their turn.

Back at the camp, the three dogs left behind saw their owners clear up the mountain. With determination Merryberry had chewed through the team line and the three dogs escaped to join the rest of their team. In ten minutes those happy pups had reached the base of the fixed ropes. But they got tangled in their harnesses and a picket and were stopped.

"They dug themselves in a hole and were pretty content," read Okonek from his journal. *"It was a long descent with them critters leaping ahead pulling me in full belay."* Stapleton, Butcher, and Okonek took a dog and headed down to Camp Six.

Just as Joe got to the bottom of the fixed rope, he let out a whoop. He slipped on some blue ice. "I had too heavy a pack. Too high," he later said. Better to slip there than where they had just been! This also pointed out how important it is to be totally alert at all times, even on your last step.

They got back to camp sometime after six o'clock. Now it was time to have

Joe coming down the fixed ropes followed by Butcher, the four huskies, and Okonek. Joe's nose is white because he covered it with zinc oxide to protect it from sun burn off the glaring snow. *Photo by Rob Stapleton*

a cup of hot Tang, some food, and relax. They sat around talking and visiting. "Joe had the darndest stories about some things," laughed Okonek.

Then a young lady from one of the other parties saw something fall and told Genet that she saw a sleeping bag or something tumble on down the mountain. Joe saw this, too.

Genet said it wouldn't be a sleeping bag.

Joe Redington Sr. with the summit of McKinley reflected in his sunglasses. *Photo by Rob Stapleton*

Joe ate lots of oatmeal and drank lots of Tang on his McKinley expedition. *Photo by Rob Stapleton*

In a flash Genet and Okonek were headed up the mountain to see what it was. They found three Korean climbers lying in the snow. These climbers were one part of an experienced Korean team that had summited just after Joe's team. One of them was the only Korean to have climbed Mount Everest.

These three men had fallen down a 2,500-foot couloir, or gully, off the West Ridge of McKinley on their descent. One man was dead, one was barely alive, and one was obviously alive but badly frostbitten. Genet and Okonek put one man in a sleeping bag in a tiny snow cave to bring down on their next trip and lowered the frostbitten survivor down on a sled. Joe met them at the bottom of the slope with his dog team and took him into camp, where there was a doctor waiting. The surviving Korean was put in Stapleton's tent. Other climbers helped recover the two bodies, as the second survivor of the accident had died. Joe and Butcher and the dogs helped on the flat terrain of the basin with the other two men. Genet radioed down the mountain for help and the next morning an Army Chinook helicopter came and flew out the Koreans.

But all that night they were awake trying to help the one surviving climber. They had an awful time trying to keep the climber from putting his hands into his sleeping bag, because when he became conscious he wanted to get them warm. However, the doctor told them not to let him put his hands in his sleeping bag. That might sound odd, but in order to save the man's hands, they had to stay frozen until they were at the hospital, where they could be thawed out in the proper way.

The remaining Korean climbing party made it safely to the camp.

Later, Joe was given a plaque of gratitude from the country of Korea thanking him for the help he gave the Korean climbing party on McKinley.

After the Koreans were flown off the mountain, Joe, Butcher, and Stapleton loaded up their gear, harnessed the dogs, and headed down the mountain. Doug Geeting flew his 185 to Base camp to fly them back to Talkeetna. "He came in, turned like a corkscrew, and rolled his plane in to land," Joe grinned with admiration. "Doug crammed us all in there—dogs and everything." Geeting pointed the nose of the plane down the mountain.

"Flight plan is closed," said Geeting, as the plane rolled to a stop at the tiny Talkeetna airstrip.

When the climbers wiggled out of the plane, there was Bill Devine holding some peaches for them. Joe's weathered face was bearded after over a month on the mountain. His lips were cracked and dry. The tips of his fingers were numbed by the nip of frost, but overriding all this was a huge grin of great joy, accomplishment, and satisfaction. Everyone was smiling and laughing.

Looking back at the mountain he had just climbed, all he could see were clouds and the bottom of Mount Hunter. No matter. He knew it was there and he knew what he had just accomplished. And he knew what he had just proved. These Alaskan huskies could physically go to the top of the world's highest mountains.

Devine handed the fearless climbers tasty peaches with the words, "Congratulations. You did it!"

That peach tasted mighty good to Joe after having eaten mostly oatmeal, Tang, and lots of water on his climb.

Looking at the dogs, Joe said, "You just can't keep up with them there. They are too strong. Look at them. They look better now than when we left!"

Joe would always remember with a sense of humble pride what Genet said, "I sure misjudged Joe Redington. That's the toughest man I ever saw."

A much relieved Vi said, "I was glad he was back down. Joe wanted to go back and climb with Ray [Genet] again. I told, Joe 'If you go, I won't be here when you get back.'" And Joe told Genet, "If I go, I have to get a divorce." This continued to be a big joke with them. Butcher and Stapleton did return to climb the mountain again. Stapleton went several times taking many, many pictures of that magnificent mountain.

Genet called Joe later and said that he was off to climb Mount Everest. He would see him when he got back, but he never made it back. Tragedy struck as he was descending the 29,032-foot Mount Everest and claimed the life of that great mountaineer. But his legend lives on and Genet will always be a part of Denali, the mountain he so loved.

Rob Stapleton petting Tekla, Susan Butcher, Ray Genet, and Joe Redington at Talkeetna after having taken the first and only Alaskan huskies to the top of Mount McKinley. *Photo by Bill Devine*

When Joe had left to climb Mount McKinley there was two feet of snow-cover on the ground. The fifteen-day trip stretched into forty-four days. Spring had arrived. Fishing time was upon them. The king salmon run was due to arrive any day. Time for Joe and Butcher to head for Emmonak to manage the fish processing plant.

CHAPTER 29

Blueberry Patch

*Live your life so that whenever
you lose, you are ahead.*

WILL ROGERS

The king salmon were running. They had no time to lose. Joe and Butcher traded in their warm mountaineering gear for rubber pants and rubber boots, left Sunny Knik, and headed into Anchorage to catch the next plane north to Emmonak, a small Eskimo village at the mouth of the Yukon River.

He was managing a fish plant and had to get it set up and ready to take in the season's salmon. Butcher had worked with Joe the previous summer and decided to join him again this year.

"We got there just in time when they brought in the first kings."

The previous summer, in 1978, Joe had been hired by Whitney-Fidalgo to manage this plant. He certainly had proven himself in Unalakleet. And he got Butcher a job as a header. Headers cut off the heads of the salmon. "I ran the plant and she was one of my headers."

"You know, that was something," reminisced Joe about the previous year. "There's only a few people that know that when I went to Emmonak, they dumped king salmon by the thousands, [because they could not process all the salmon.] So when I went there, I told Whitney-Fidalgo the only way I'll do it—we're not throwin' no king salmon away. I'll buy every king salmon they bring to me."

He was not going to be a part of gross wastefulness due to a lack of processing capabilities. Waste was not a word in Joe's vocabulary. In fact, Joe and Vi never threw out anything that could possibly be used for something.

Joe continued, "They said, 'Well, you can't handle them.' I said, 'Let me try.' And we made history down there.

"So when I went there, they sent a man down there. Just as soon as I started buyin' salmon, he said, 'Okay, it's time to shut it down.' I said, 'There's no way I'm going to shut it down. We're going to buy every salmon in that line out there and I'll figure out how to get it to market.'

"He said, 'I don't want no part of it!' He took an airplane and went back to Anchorage."

Then Joe explained what was happening back at the processing plant.

"A little Eskimo was back there in one of the boats that was all lined up, ya know. Here, I've got king salmon layin' everywhere, fish everywhere, but I'm also on the phone callin' airplanes. And this little Eskimo come up and he said, 'Are you still buyin'?' I said, 'That's right.' He said, 'My boat's back there. Will you still buy when I get up here?' I said, 'That's right.' He looked at me and said, 'You got more money than brains!' That's what he told me," Joe laughed. "And I never lost a fish."

"They figured we'd mess up," he added.

Obviously they didn't know Joe Redington.

"But ya know what I did? I hired all the dog mushers I could hire. That's why we was successful. I had good workers. I knew they would work twenty-four hours a day, if we had to. Wherever I could get a good Iditarod musher, I'd hire him. This was good summer money. I even hired one fellow who was said to be real lazy. I asked him, 'Can you get up by noon?' He says, 'Oh, yeah.' Okay, ya go to work at noon then."

"And ya know what? He was one of the best workers I had. He turned out to be real good and he'd work 'til midnight or later."

Each day Joe continued buying salmon. "Sometimes there'd be twenty boats lined up to sell their fish," he said.

Joe's determined spirit took hold. He said he could handle all those king salmon and by golly, he would do everything in his power to keep his word.

When Joe had a spare moment, he called a man in Nome who owned an airline business. This man had a World War II bomber he had made into a freighter.

"We've got lots of fish and we've gotta get them outta here. Can ya do it?"

"Sure," came the reply.

That helped, but he needed more planes—anything that could fly 200 pounds of fish from Emmonak to Unalakleet or Nome. He called every pilot he knew to fly for him. "I had planes comin' outta Nome and Anchorage, wherever I could get an airplane, no matter how small or how big. I had 'em haulin' fish into Unalakleet or Nome."

The airfield wasn't the greatest. It had a huge mud hole right in the middle. But that didn't stop anyone. Planes would fly in empty and fly out loaded to the gills with fish.

Meanwhile, Butcher was heading fish fast and furiously. The fish heads flew.

"No one could beat Susan headin' fish. She would work so hard all day long," Joe stated with admiration. "She was a real worker. She would butcher the kings faster'n anyone. She could head two fish to everyone else's one. Sometimes at night I would have to peel her fingers off of the knife. She couldn't turn loose of the knife."

He got more workers from Unalakleet to help. Then the unthinkable happened—his two freezers quit running. He had to work fast to get them fixed. Joe had cutting tables set up on the beach. Stacks of fish were scattered up and down the shore of the Yukon River. To keep them moist and cool Joe had workers lay a thick cover of freshly cut green grass over all the salmon.

"I never lost a fish. We proved that we could handle all the salmon. We was the first ones that would say we'll buy whatever ya have," stated Joe. Emmonak's fish plant would take in 300,000 fish for Whitney-Fidelgo that year.

So now Joe was in his second year at Emmonak. He hoped to do as well this year; after all he had just had a great Iditarod race, took his dogs to the top of North America's highest peak, so why shouldn't he have a good fishing season?

And they did have another very successful fishing season. "Susan, she was a worker, so the second year I put her in charge of the plant and I went buyin' fish all up and down the Yukon and bringing them to Susan."

After the salmon stopped running, the co-managers started closing up the plant. Joe had a very responsible foreman, who said, "I'll close up everything and it will be good. There isn't any reason for you to be here."

"Well, okay," replied Joe. He thought that would work out fine. He had 150 dogs to attend to back in Knik and they were anxious to get back home.

So in the middle of August Joe and Butcher chartered a Cessna 185 floatplane out of Nome to fly them back to Anchorage. They loaded the plane up with a thousand pounds of "stuff"—gear and dried fish for the dogs. Joe took the seat next to the pilot and Butcher with a young fox she had been given and cared for all summer, piled in the back.

Everything was fine. Then about eighty miles from McGrath the engine quit. The pilot was very nervous and excited and said, "What do I do now? You've put planes down before. We're on floats and there isn't a drop of water around for miles!"

"Well, see that little bit of trees over there?" said Joe. "I've had real good luck puttin' them real slow right into the trees."

"No! I know better than to put my plane in the trees." Then the pilot declared, "I'm not going to put it in those trees."

"Well, you're the boss, but you're goin' to have to do somethin' pretty quick. See what you can do."

Joe didn't panic or get excited. What good would that do? What they had to do now was get themselves through this crash alive. He could get nervous later, if he wanted.

"So he made a circle and he come in across, instead of goin' with the slough that was there," said Joe. "He comes in crossways and I look ahead and there's a bank, a straight-up-and-down bank. I said, 'You sure picked some place to put it.'

"And that scared Susan. So she's diggin underneath everything. I had $30,000 in cash that I was very careful with, in a satchel. I put it up over my face and we hit that berm and the airplane flipped over on it's back."

The Cessna hit the top of the bank, bounced a few times, and flipped the plane up and over landing on its back in the boggy arctic tundra. All three of them found themselves hanging upside down by their seat belts.

"He's hollerin' to get out, it may catch on fire or somethin'. I undone [my seatbelt] and I dropped out and I reached back to help Susan. She had a fox and it bit the heck out of me, and that's the only injury I had."

They scrambled and somehow got disentangled from all their gear. Standing in the middle of the tundra, they surveyed each other. They had a few cuts and scratches and bruises, but other than that they were just fine. Joe's only injury was a bloody hand where the fox bit him.

However, they did have one big problem. They had parked their fish-loaded plane smack dab in the middle of a grizzly bear fruit stand. Big, ripe, juicy blueberries and grizzly bears were everywhere.

An old sow with her three cubs did not like the idea of anyone taking over her berry patch. The four bears came charging straight towards these invaders to keep them away from their eating ground. (Bears sense of smell is far superior to their eyesight and they were investigating these newcomers.) They

Flying from Emmonak to Anchorage the engine in their airplane quit. The plane crashed and flipped into the tundra, right-smack-dab in the middle of bears and blueberries.

stopped less than a hundred yards from the downed plane swinging their heads from side to side and sniffing the air.

Joe saw the sow lumbering heavily across the muskeg and in his understated manner said, "I think we'd better move to higher ground."

The highest point around was the bottom of the floats, which at that time were trying to touch the sky. Joe and Susan and the pilot scrambled as quickly as they could up the struts and onto the floats and hung on watching the bears from their high aluminum tower.

As Joe looked around he commented, "We couldn't have picked a better spot, if we have to stay here awhile. We have everythin' we need. There is a stream right over there, hundreds of pounds of dried fish, and loads of ripe berries."

Susan made a deck of cards from envelopes. They played cards and ate salmon and blueberries until someone came to rescue them, scrambling every now and again up to the top of the floats when bears got too near.

When they didn't refuel in McGrath as their flight plan indicated, search planes were sent to search for them. The next day they were spotted and it wasn't long before a helicopter arrived and picked them up.

The unfortunate part was the local paper wrote a rather thoughtless article that sensationalized the incident. When Joe read it he jumped in his truck and drove all the way into Anchorage to the newspaper office.

"Who wrote that article about me?" he asked.

When he found the man, he lambasted him in his strong, quiet voice, "Now look, I'd rather crawl on my stomach for a mile than to ask to be rescued. And I wasn't teaching anyone my old trick about being rescued. I didn't ask to be rescued. I want that corrected."

So the next day there was a little apology in the paper for not correctly stating the facts.

Chapter 30

1981 Inaugural Parade of Ronald Reagan

*Choose a job you love, and you will never
have to work a day in your life.*

Confucius

"The Case of the Hot Dogs" hit the January 1981 newspapers, televisions, and radio stations in Washington, D.C.

"Valued at more than $5,000 each Feets, Candy, and Joey ... disappeared a few minutes after midnight from a Damascus farm where they had been staying since being flown here," wrote Martin Weil of the *Washington Post*.

Someone had taken three very valuable Iditarod sled dogs, just a couple of days before the 40th United States president, Ronald Reagan, was to be sworn into office.

Before all this happened, Vi remembered, "Jay Hammond's office called the Iditarod Headquarters and asked for suggestions for someone to represent Alaska in the Presidential Parade. Joe and Herbie Nayokpuk were contacted." Colonel Norman Vaughn also joined the group.

Joe, the Father of the Iditarod Race and constant promoter of the Last Great Race, was ecstatic over this invitation. Nayokpuk was a loved Alaskan musher and Inupiaq ivory carver from Shishmaref, north of Nome. This gentle and very competitive man was always and forever smiling. He placed second in the 1980 Iditarod. Colonel Norman Vaughan had also run in the

Iditarod. As a young man, he had accompanied Admiral Richard Byrd on his first expedition to Antarctica, and he was in the U.S. Army Air Force Search and Rescue with dogs during World War II. This would be his third Inaugural Parade, having been in President Gerald Ford's in 1973, and President Jimmy Carter's in 1977. So he knew how special this event was. These three tough gentlemen mushers had so much in common and were good friends. What an adventure this would be.

Joe asked Dick Mackey and Bill Devine to help with his team.

Mackey said his wife, Cathy, "was the office manager and made all the arrangements for the flights for everyone. Everyone went commercial except for me. I flew with the dogs. And lo and behold, we flew in a 747 with the Flying Tigers! " Mackey exclaimed. "The pilot had been flying before World War II."

He asked Mackey, "Do you fly?"

"Yah, I do," he responded with interest. And they talked about their flying experiences. Then the second officer excused himself. Recalling what happened next brought the biggest grin to Mackey's face.

"The captain asked if I wanted to sit in the right seat? You know, it's no more difficult than your Cessna 180, just heavier. I flew it for a few minutes. It was the height of my flying career. It was quite a deal." Mackey was flying high in every sense of the word.

Mackey, the dogs, and their gear flew into Philadelphia, then got on a truck and drove to a horse farm owned by Walter and Nancy Hughes in Frederick, Maryland. "We had nine dogs apiece," said Joe proudly. "They was good Iditarod dogs."

"While we were there, we were running around seeing Washington, D.C., when someone came in and stole my two lead dogs and Colonel Vaughan's lead dog. It was the biggest hunt you ever seen. It was on all the televisions. They was stopping vehicles as far as up in Pennsylvania looking for our dogs."

The Montgomery County police used bloodhounds and traced each telephone call it got in order to find the missing dogs. This search for the missing Iditarod sled dogs filled everyone's thoughts for the next twenty-four hours.

"I can't believe someone would do that," Vi said, shaking her head.

"Someone must have known what they was doin' because only our leaders are missin'," said Joe.

Meanwhile, Joe, Nayokpuk, and Vaughn were on the Hill in front of the Capitol Building giving demonstration sled dog rides to Alaska's only representative, Don Young, other U.S. senators and representatives, and other people that were present.

Joe was decked out in the beaver fur hat he had made, plaid flannel shirt, and knee-high fur mukluks. In fact, all these Alaskans were wearing their furs,

Joe and Vi in the sled at the National Mall.

Herbie and Elizabeth Hayokpuk by the Capitol Building in Washington, D.C.

256

where the majority of folks were wearing suits and fancy business shoes. They had one thing in common though—everyone who was near the Iditarod mushers and dogs was wearing a big happy smile.

Joe had to do it without his leaders Candy and Feets. "Usually a swing dog will make a temporary leader." The swing dog is the second dog behind the leader. And that is what Joe did. "They weren't good, but they did alright."

The next day, not too long before the parade was to begin, a lady called the police and said, "I think we've got the missing dogs." Apparently she was ironing when she heard the news on the television of the three missing dogs.

The police went to her home outside Washington in Gaithersburg and sure enough, there were Candy, Feets, and Joey just as happy and contented as could be. They never barked. They just wagged their tails completely innocent of what was going on.

The lady's kids had stolen the dogs along with some dog food and put them down in their basement. It was purely an accident that they just happened to get the three most important lead dogs. The kids were taken into custody and the dogs were brought back to Joe and Colonel Vaughn just in time for them to be put in the harness and head down Pennsylvania Avenue for the presidential parade. Everyone was much relieved and very, very happy to have all the teams together again.

However, the parade did not start on time. "They were late getting started because of the hostage situation coming to an end," stated Vi. The Iranian Hostage Crisis had started November 4, 1979, when sixty-six hostages were taken captive at the U.S. Embassy in Tehran, Iran, by some radical Iranian students. They were finally released after 444 days in captivity, just moments after President Ronald Reagan was sworn into office. This was such good news for our whole country.

The ride through this nation's capital was a grand experience for all of the Alaska troupe. Joe headed down the street with Vi in the sled basket.

"We had to keep so many feet apart from the horses up front. And we had to have a rope leading and following each team," stated Vi. "Dick Mackey was in the front with a rope tied to the leader and Bill Devine was in the back. The parade officials didn't want any wandering." The dogs were great.

Vi was known for her hats. She loved to wear hats. And the one she wore in this parade was a hat that represented part of Alaska's history which only a few were aware of. Vi smiled so proudly when she said, "I wore Charlie Evans' hat." Then her eyes twinkled, "But it was way too big. Every time I turned my head, the hat would turn the other way."

All of Joe's dogs finally together again, lined up, and ready to go. They are Feets, the leader, Lucus, who went to the top of McKinley, is the swing dog on the left, Bee, the swing dog on the right, Candy, who also went up McKinley, is behind Lucus, and Knik is beside her, Seward is behind Candy. The remaining three we don't know, but Joe sure would.

Joe in his fancy tuxedo and Vi in her lovely pink gown are all set to attend the Presidential Inaugural Ball.

But that didn't matter to Vi. Charlie was a true hero in her eyes. In 1925 Charlie Evans was the twelfth of twenty mushers to carry the life-saving diphtheria serum to Nome in order to help stop the epidemic. Wrapping the serum in an extra blanket of rabbit fur, he left Bishop Mountain to mush thirty miles to Nulato. Heavy waist-high, ice fog blanketed the Yukon River. He couldn't see his dogs, but trusted them to sniff out the trail route. There was no turning back! The temperature dropped to minus 64 degrees below zero. Less than ten miles from Nulato, one leader collapsed and then the other, due to the extreme cold. He put the dogs in his sled, tied himself to the team, and continued down the river making a Goliath push to move the serum safely along his leg of the journey. He succeeded valiantly.

Dick Mackey, Joe Redington Sr., Congressman Don Young, Norman Vaughan, Senator Ted Stevens, Vi Redington, Elizabeth Nayokpuk, and Herbie Nayokpuk posing in Alaska gear in a very warm Washington, D.C.

And now, here was Vi wearing Charlie's hat, but in temperatures 120 degrees higher, in a parade for the President of the United States. What an honor.

In fact, all the Alaskans were melting in the 56-degree weather. Mackey said, "We were hot, too, decked out in parkas, mukluks, and fur hats. We were wringing wet."

"We were right behind the horses," Joe said with a hidden chuckle in his grin. "Some of the dogs were a little bit excited. We had wheels on the sleds and the regular drag brake and brakes on the wheels. And we stayed just to the right of the horses."

The three dogs that were kidnapped wore pink ribbons which matched their pink tongues that hung happily out their mouths as they ambled down

Pennsylvania Avenue. From the crowds all along the route they heard friendly, cheering comments. Everyone was waving.

"Glad you got them back!"

"Hello Alaska!"

"Sorry about your dogs. I hope they are alright!"

"Are you really from Alaska?"

When the three Iditarod dog teams went by the bullet-proof glass viewing stand in front of the White House, President and Mrs. Reagan jumped up so they could see all the dogs and mushers. They all waved.

The parade ended in the dark, but that was okay. Everyone was so happy and the night was just beginning.

All of them got dazzled up and went to a fancy dinner and a fancy ball. "We had tuxedos on," stated Joe with his impish grin. "That is the funniest outfit there is, you know. The shirt isn't even one piece. I couldn't believe it. It's a front. The one I had didn't even have a back. It's a phony deal." The men were even given top hats like Abraham Lincoln wore. You could hear the whole crew of Alaskan sourdoughs laughing all up and down the National Mall.

Vi had on a lovely pinkish floral gown and light matching blouse jacket. They were a pair of decked-out Alaska sourdoughs wearing smiles that just never quit.

"That was quite a deal!" Joe said.

And Vi said, "We had lots of fun!"

CHAPTER 31

Kamikaze Race To Nome

*It's not whether you get knocked
down, it's whether you get up.*

VINCE LOMBARDI

"Whoa! Whoa! Whoa!" Joe shouted fruitlessly to his leader, as he stomped his brake into the soft snow.

Joe's 18-dog team disappeared two-by-two over a rise leading down a bendy, blind hill dropping to Happy River.

"Whoa! Whoa! Whoa!" he kept yelling, as the steep hill catapulted his team rapidly forward.

He discovered too late that two other teams had careened headlong sliding down the steep drop-off colliding into trees, the snow bank, and each other, while trying desperately to stay on the trail and not plow into the team in front or go over the side.

First, Ron Robbins hit a tree and was lying unconscious for awhile, only to come to and see Betsy McGuire's team flying down the hill out of control right towards him. Not much later Joe's team followed.

Seeing his brake was useless, Joe flipped his sled to cause more drag, and collided with Robbins and McGuire going end-over-teakettle. Over fifty dogs and three sleds littered the trail.

"It was awful. We had three sleds right on top of each other," Joe recalled.

The twisting half mile descent is practically a vertical drop set with tight corners, okay for snowmachines that blazed the trail, but not so good for dog teams. They worked frantically untangling their teams, making sure they were okay, talking to the dogs to calm them, and getting each team back on the trail before another musher hurled down on them. Nursing their personal injuries came later.

These three mushers were not the only ones to find themselves dangerously out of control getting down to the Happy River Valley. So, it is not surprising that the 1985 Iditarod Race added a new name to the trail—Kamikaze Hill.

Meanwhile, fierce snow, sleet, and rain pelted the Alaska Range causing a delay in food and supply drops because the planes could not fly. By the time Joe got to Puntilla Lake and the Rainy Pass checkpoint, teams were bedded down throughout the spruce forest and on the lake. Mushers were recouping and taking it easy. He tied up his team, got dog food cooking, and checked to the welfare of each dog. Only then was he ready for a rest and tend to his bunged arm. (It's not easy to manhandle a sled with only one good arm.)

The next day Donna Gentry, the race marshal, called for a mandatory freeze on the race. They couldn't support the race due to the horrible weather conditions. Puntilla Lake was now home to 810 dogs and fifty-eight mushers with all their gear. They were stuck there until the storm abated and the race marshal gave the okay to continue.

Around the campfires mushers gathered and visited. Everyone was sad to hear of the destruction a moose had caused to Susan Butcher's team. Deep snows drove the moose onto the trail, a much easier place to walk. This moose was determined to protect his right to the trail. The moose fiercely stomped Butcher's team killing two dogs and injuring all but a few. She could not continue the race. But Butcher wasn't the only one with moose problems. Other mushers had stand-offs with moose, too, some lasting several hours.

Joe had his own moose story to tell. It happened a couple of years earlier, though, in 1983, the only year, except for the first year of the Iditarod when he was raising the prize money, in which he didn't race. And it happened on the infamous Nine Mile Hill.

Joe and his fellow dog mushing friend, Dave Olson, had to take a tent out to the Little Susitna and set it up for the Iditaski. The Iditaski was the new cross-country ski race over a part of the Iditarod Trail.

Joe said, "I hit the top of the hill and started down when a moose ran right out of the bushes and went right across the sled. It was comin' right towards us and kind of hit us at an angle and jumped right over the sled. I don't think it was a mean moose, because he went right on. But in goin' over the sled, I ducked down. It kicked me right in the back and broke three ribs. It just sent me a whirlin'. And when it did, I twisted my knee up. I was layin' there on the trail when Dave came by. The dogs had gone. I'm layin' there on the side of the trail with a terrible pain in my right knee. Dave loaded me up and we found the dogs about two miles down the trail. One dog had broken ribs. He recovered okay. But I was a year gettin' right again."

Joe's proof, that it was a moose that tripped him up and not a tree, was the perfect impression of a moose hoof mark on his back.

"But my team ran that year," he quickly stated.

At his Wilderness Camp in Petersville, he had a Norwegian musher, Roger Legaard, and his family, learning more about dog mushing from Joe that year. Joe wanted the race to become an international race and this was his way to help promote the idea. When Joe couldn't run, he let Legaard take his team and run in his place. Legaard did very well and went back to Norway with tenth place winnings in his pocket.

Joe loved to palaver with everyone and since they were stuck here, Joe made the most of his visiting time.

Three days later the freeze was lifted. There was a mass exit of rested dogs and mushers heading out of Rainy Pass, like a very long freight train heading through Dalzell Gorge and on to Rohn. Raymie was also running this year and left Rainy Pass in eleventh position. He said, "My dogs looked pretty good, so I just let 'em go."

Joe's team was looking good, too. He said, "I went outta there and I passed team after team after team. I never saw dogs perform any better. They just couldn't wait to get to the next team, to get by it. Even Herbie Nayokpuk, who has a real fast team, I went by Nayokpuk and he said it was just like he was standin' still. I got to the Rohn checkpoint first that year. It's quite a pleasure to have a team perform like that."

But even after a good run down the north side of the Alaska Range, rough trail lay ahead. Just before the Rohn checkpoint, his team fell through the ice crossing Tatina River. Joe stayed at Rohn tending to his team until they were ready to move on.

Teams checked in and out. When Joe left he was no longer in front, but he made up for lost time sailing through hilly terrain and then onto the notorious Fairwell Burn. Since the destructive 1976 fire that burned across 360,000 acres of spruce and tundra, all that remained were fallen trees, scorched spruce stumps, and two- to-three-foot high mounds of mossy tussocks. With the heavy snowfall this year, snow filled the deep holes between tussocks and fallen trees. The normally very dangerous section was passable with a fairly well-packed trail.

The trailbreakers were barely in front of the racers and having a dickens of a time keeping the trail open because of the heavy snowfall. Joe was gaining on the front runners by the time he got to McGrath on the bank of the Kuskokwim River. He fed and rested his dogs, then repacked his gear, and was just harnessing his team when the second freeze was declared, stopping all mushers in Ophir and McGrath from continuing on down the trail.

"Just fifteen minutes more and I'd have been outta there."

He shrugged his shoulders, turned around, and unharnessed his dogs. Raymie was ahead on the trail and that was good. One musher said Raymie's dogs looked like a Fur Rondezvous team because of their speed.

But Joe, not to be disgruntled, sighed, "Oh well, I'll just have to make up for lost time when we get started again." He knew he had started this race with the strongest team of eighteen dogs he had ever had, so he was optimistic.

With the freeze lifted he headed out only to be caught in another fierce blizzard out of Ophir.

"It was snowin' and blowin' so hard, you couldn't see anythin'," Joe said. "I had trouble findin' the trail. It took me fifteen hours to go forty miles."

This had been some race so far. "I've been banged up, had the flu, fell in a hole in the river, and spent fifteen hours in a blizzard." That never stopped Joe before and it wasn't going to stop him now. There were still hundreds of miles to go. The game changes all the time, and Joe figured he'd probably left the worst behind him.

"My team reminds me of a powerful Cadillac with no steerin' wheel and no brakes. I can go great, but I can't control where I'm goin' and I can't stop."

The Iditarod spirit beckoned Joe to the coast. Then just outside Shaktoolik another storm blew into the region. Raymie was traveling with his dad then and they decided to camp out in the Blueberry Hills until the wind died down a bit. "We built a fire and had some tea," said Raymie. When the winds calmed, Raymie took off followed by Joe.

Once down on the flats the winds were blowing as hard as ever. Joe could hardly stand up. After dragging over giant snowdrifts into Shaktoolik, feeding and caring for his dogs, he started to take care of himself and reflect.

Joe told folks, "I couldn't see in front of me. I went over a drop off about six or eight feet, and in the blowin' snow I couldn't even see it. When the sled came in after me, I fell on top of the sled. It broke one of my ribs, a little different than I'd ever broken 'em before. The health aide and veterinarian checked me out. They told me I should leave the race. I told 'em I would think about it. After I thought about it awhile, I decided they were right." Enough is enough Joe was the fifteenth musher to scratch in that year.

Joe's dogs were flown back to Anchorage. He sold his sled to someone in the village, and flew into Nome to meet Vi.

"It's been quite a race," Joe flatly stated.

"That's when Libby took off," remembered Raymie, "and made it through the storm."

And history was about to be made. News reached Nome that Libby Riddles, who courageously raced across Norton Sound in a blizzard, was in the lead. And, as Joe made a point every year since the race began to meet as many of the mushers as he could when they finished the race, this year was no exception.

"She's one of the finest mushers I ever knew. I'm goin' to be down there in the mornin' to see Libby, if I have to crawl there." And he was.

Fans poured onto Front Street and lined both sides for two blocks waiting to see her bring her team down the chute and under the famous burl arch— the first woman to win the Iditarod!

For Joe, her winning was the highlight of the race, far out-shadowing his personal disappointment.

Joe was also very pleased to watch Raymie finish the race in the money in nineteenth place, despite the fact that a seventy-mile-per-hour ground storm demolished the trail. Raymie said, "The wind was so strong. There was no control of the sled. The wind catches the sled's bag and blows you sideways. Can't stand on the break or you'll never move. Let up on the break and you can't steer."

Raymie and three other mushers lost their way between Shaktoolik and Koyuk, stopping to hunker down in their sleeping bags, their dogs turning round and round, trampling a saucer-shaped depression in the snow, and then burrowing their noses into their tails until the worst blew over.

Raymie asked his dad how he was doing and Joe replied with a hopeful lilt, "I'm very disappointed but I'm plannin' on next year already."

CHAPTER 32

Smokin' Joe

*'Tis not the dog racing itself that is important.
'Tis what the racing stands for.*

SCOTTY ALLEN (ALL ALASKA SWEEPSTAKES
RACE IN 1908)

"Wheeeee!" little three-year-old Bruce yelled, as he slid down the steep, snowy hill beside the frozen Eagle River.

"Watch me, Mom," hollered his older brother, Aron, his brown eyes snapping with excitement. They were trying to see who could slide the farthest while their parents and grandparents looked on. Watching all the Iditarod mushers start their long race to Nome was a family must every single year since the race began. Watching sled dog races had been the highlight of every winter for this family since 1952, when their grandparents, Grandma Billie and Bugga, moved to Alaska. Grandma Billie followed the Fur Rendezvous and the North American races every year. She wrote down every musher's name and their time into every checkpoint. The Iditarod Race was no different. Alaskans loved the spirit of sled dog racing.

Suddenly Grandma Billie shouted with excitement, "Boys, come here quickly! Joe Redington is coming down the hill. See, there he is. Doesn't he have beautiful dogs. How many does he have, Aron?"

"One, two, three," counted the five-year-old, "... fourteen, fifteen. Fifteen, Grandma Billie!"

Some children at Eagle River Elementary School
made this banner and had it hanging at the Eagle River
checkpoint, the VFW Hall. Schools in every community
in Alaska got involved with the race in some way.

Just then Joe's sled hit a big rock, sending him flying sideways, jarring him
so abruptly that his hat flew through the air.

The hat landed not far from Aron, who picked it up and ran to give it back
to Joe.

"Thanks," Joe smiled looking down at the little fellow. "I'm sure going to
need this."

By now the name Redington and Iditarod dog mushing were becoming
synonymous. Everyone in Alaska was watching Joe. This was the year Joe
would win. And the whole state was cheering for him.

Joe made good time out of Anchorage on the lightly snow-dusted, twen-
ty-mile trail, despite the temperatures being in the high 30s, much too
warm for a dog race. He called the first part of the trail the Banana Belt of
the Iditarod.

Vi was waiting with the dog truck at the VFW Hall in Eagle River, the
first check point of the race. Joe drove the team to their truck and lifted
each dog into their own compartment, each having their own little window.
Then they drove the thirty-four miles to Settler's Bay, where the restart would
take place.

The 1988 race would take the longer route north to the Yukon River
through Cripple and Ruby, down the Yukon River to Kaltag, and then out to
Unalakleet on the coast, and up to Nome.

Joe was in high spirits. "I'm looking forward to a good race," he told a reporter. "There's snow in Nome this year and that will help. Last year we went in on gravel."

This year Joe intended to save face. The last three years had been tough. This year he had a great team. Also, it pleased him that he had leased two Knik Kennels teams to student mushers that had trained with him at his Trapper Creek training school.

Joe left Settler's Bay, his dogs running well over a good trail through spruce and birch forests. At Skwentna Joe took his mandatory 24-hour layover.

"I stayed in Skwentna partly to see the mountain bike racers compete in the Iditabike," Joe said. He knew he would see someone come in within the next twenty-four hours because the bikers had left right after the last dog musher took off out of Wasilla.

Nayokpuk, the "Shismaref Cannonball," also took his 24-hour layover. He said, "The heat is bothering my dogs." So he gave them a rest.

Joe and Nayokpuk, twelve years younger than Joe, were the very best of friends, kindred spirits, and like brothers. This would be like old times when these two mushers would just sit around the fire, visit, and drink tea. Nayokpuk had run in eleven races, including the very first race in '73, and nine of them were with Joe, starting with the '74 race.

"Now that was a great campin' trip," Joe remembered.

They talked about the great shape their teams were in this year. Joe got another cup of tea and plopped in a few jelly beans, his favorite sweetener, besides honey.

"Ten of my dogs I ran on the Alpirod this year," he said. "I didn't have no trouble with their feet. I never used dog booties."

The Alpirod was a new 700-kilometer race in Europe, held in January. Mushers started in Italy, mushed through Austria, Switzerland, and France, and back to Italy. Each day they raced a short distance, loaded up the dogs and gear, drove to the next town, got some rest, and mushed another short race the next day. There were eleven stages to this race. Vi was Joe's chauffeur. There was lots of driving on very narrow roads through the Alps. That alone was pretty scary at times, especially when they met a bus coming towards them.

"There were a bunch of us that run the Iditarod and the rest from different countries in Europe. I came in seventh. The dogs was great. We had a lotta fun."

"I had Luna with me there," smiled Joe. Joe loved his leader. Luna was a wonderful leader. "I never heard him growl in his life." He was good with children and adults. He was honest, dependable, good-natured, a perfect gee-and-haw leader, and fast.

Vi, Joe's handler, and Joe talking to Martin Buser, an Iditarod musher from Big Lake, Alaska.

"Now over in the Alps, there's a lot of switchbacks and Luna and I could make a run right on the outside of the corners to give me more room. He wouldn't shortcut or anythin'. I'd say, "Gee over. Gee over." And that is what he'd do. Terrific dog."

With Luna leading Joe's team, anything was possible.

"That race and my new trainin' wheel and these dogs are ready for a fast race this year."

"What is your training wheel?" asked Nayokpuk.

"Well, you see, I wanted to find a way to keep the dogs fit when the weather was warm. So I built this contraption somethin' like the feedin' wheels I built way back when we first moved up here. I'd feed my dogs on it. Every time about feedin' time they'd get excited and start usin' it on their own power. The wheel would go around. They'd get exercise, and then I'd feed 'em."

"Good idea," responded Nayokpuk.

"Only this one is bigger and had a motor on it. It looks somethin' like a ferris wheel layin' down on its side with fifteen spokes. Each one looks like a long rafter. I took the rear differential from an old bus I had and a five-horse power electrical motor to make the wheel turn. I had a guy build it for me. It turns from three- to-30 miles-per-hour and will go in either direction. Pretty slick.

"The dogs didn't like it at first, but they got used to it fast. The best part is,

"I had one in 1949 down here on the bluff, but it didn't have any motor on it," said Joe. "I wanted a big one. This was 155 feet around it. It was real good fer trainin'."

Joe designed this dog training wheel. Some visitors were watching how it worked.

Both signs were designed by Bill Devine.

I can stand back and watch how the dogs move. Pretty soon the dogs would get to where they all kinda got in step. It was beautiful.

"When I first hook them up, they are jumpin' and barkin' their let's-get-goin' bark. Then I'd release the chain and they'd jump into pullin'. They'd outpull that five-horse powered motor and then they'd settle into a nice trot. It really ain't a workout 'cause they ain't pullin' anythin', but they're gettin' exercise and I can feel their bodies gettin' tougher.

"I run the dogs in two-hour stretches—one hour in each direction. When I took them up to my wilderness camp, I had twenty- to-thirty mile trainin' runs right at the git-go, instead of five-mile runs."

"Sounds like it really works."

"Yah, it's a good deal. I also had 'em out in the lake swimmin'—coolin' them down this summer and keepin' 'em in shape. So, I think we'll do pretty good this year."

These trail mates had the best time visiting. One can just imagine the tales they had to tell.

On Monday, fully rested, Joe and Nayokpuk got back on the trail that wound slowly up into the foothills of the towering Alaska Range towards Rainy Pass. There had been a heavy, wet snowfall and the front runners were bunched together slugging through deep snows. Then the wind started blowing and the wet snow turned to ice.

A trailbreaker on his snowmachine broke through a snow bridge tumbling down into a ten-foot pool of icy water. As he was struggling to get out of the overflow, mushers came by and saw his dilemma. Together with four dog teams they managed to turn over the snowmachine and get it to the top of the hill. Then they had to pack down snow to make a new snow bridge for all the mushers following to pass over.

By the time Joe and Nayokpuk arrived at Rainy Pass, the trail had been set, which was really to their advantage.

Tuesday, the seventy-one-year-old Joe grabbed the lead and took off. His dogs stretched out along the trail with happy dog grins on their faces. They ran with the spirit of the Alaska wind in their feet.

Luna was leading Joe's team at a very fast clip across the Farewell Burn through Nikolai and arriving first into McGrath. As Joe was caring for his dogs and talking to an ABC news reporter, he said, "I feel like an old fox bein' chased by young hounds."

Joe's team, running strong, arrived first at the halfway checkpoint at Cripple Creek. Joe with his lopsided, happy grin claimed $3,000 in silver ingots as his prize.

After checking in, Joe tended his dogs with loving care. He checked each dog's feet to see that no snow was balling up between their toes or cracks in their paws, applying salve if necessary.

Luna reached up and gave Joe a great, big, dog kiss as he was checking his feet. "He's a lover," grinned Joe. "He's always kissin' my face." Reporters and villagers watched Joe interact with his beloved leader. He told them, "He's easy to handle. I could unhook him, turn him loose, and he'd go right over and wait for me to tie him up. He would pay no attention to other dogs or anythin'. Perfect gentleman—just like Colonel Vaughan."

As he worked, people were asking many questions. He never stopped, but spoke quietly to each individual as if he or she was a good friend. Even when he was tired, he had a warm and friendly smile that said just as much, if not more, than the soft words he may have spoken.

Joe's race to Cripple was incredible. He and Luna set a new race record knocking off over twelve hours for the fastest time into Cripple, the halfway point of the race. He had gone about 524 miles in 4 days, 19 minutes, 14 seconds. This record held for the next seven years. His name was engraved on a perpetual trophy that is kept at the Iditarod Headquarters in Wasilla with all the winners of the halfway prize.

And then the brakes were put on his team.

When he pulled into the Cripple checkpoint, he discovered the trail setters had not left there for Nome yet. Joe couldn't remember a time when that had ever happened. But that didn't stop Joe. He wasn't going to let that slip-up dampen his spirits. He had broken hundreds and hundreds of miles of trail in the past. He could do it again. It just "made fer slow goin'," he said.

Joe signed his name at the checkpoint, had his gear checked, gave each of his dogs a love pat and word of encouragement and headed out despite the deep snow. He didn't get out too far before he had to turn back. The snow was so deep the dogs were swimming in the stuff. He could keep going, but he wanted to save his team's energy. So he decided to turn around, and see what could be done.

Joe was "kinda discouraged."

"I get discouraged real easy and then I say to myself, aw, to heck with it." He took a deep breath, and continued on doing the very best he could.

The Race Marshall flew in and said, "Joe, they sure messed you up. I'll get them back and get you a trail."

But that wasn't until nine hours later. By then the other mushers were pulling into Cripple Creek and a winter storm was brewing.

Joe and Nayokpuk left Cripple. "I tried to travel with Joe Redington from

Cripple, but he disappeared in a hurry. I never saw him again," Nayokpuk told a reporter. Joe's determination and his fast dog team still kept him ahead of the pack all the way to Ruby on the Yukon River. There he got the fancy Clarion Hotel seven-course gourmet dinner and $2,000 for being the first to arrive at Yukon River village of Ruby.

"Nobody came in while I was eatin' dinner either," he grinned.

His dogs rested a bit with good food in their bellies. Then they left the village and headed down the Yukon for Galena. And again he beat the other mushers. However, Martin Buser from Big Lake was right on his tail, followed by Butcher. Buser left Galena before Joe, but again Joe's team sped on past Buser along the river trail to Kaltag.

Joe got into Kaltag four hours ahead of the next musher who by then was Butcher. He left Kaltag to cross the Kaltag Portage, usually his favorite part of the trail, but another storm blew in fast and furious. Joe was caught right smack dab in the middle of that winter blow. Snow was whipping all around him and the visibility was very poor. He lost the trail. Then he passed some snowmachiners, who had set up a tent and were hunkered inside out of the blow. But Joe kept on.

He looked for the trail for a couple of hours but to no avail. So he decided it would be best to rest the dogs and himself and wait out the storm. The snowmachine folks invited Joe into their tent.

He gave each dog a honey ball. Joe's honey balls were famous. He had developed a high energy, 1600-calorie dog snack that "never freezes solid." He had shared his special recipe with many a musher over the years.

"I feed it in between checkpoints," Joe said, "The dogs eat it right up."

As Joe was going down the trail, his thoughts went back ten years to the famous 1978 Iditarod Race when Dick Mackey beat out Rick Swenson by one second. What a race that was. He wished he could have been there to see it, but he was having his own challenges and it was his honey balls that saved the day.

There are times when despite the drive to get the best race time, helping fellow mushers takes priority. Joe and Ken Chase had gotten caught in a snowstorm out of Topkok. Chase's light was broken and he wasn't sure where he was. Joe with his headlamp walked ahead of the teams straining to find the trail. This got them into Solomon. The next morning Chase left before Joe, but Joe soon caught up with him.

"His dogs were down," Joe remembered. "They wouldn't go. So I stopped and said, 'Ken, I got some honey balls. Let's feed 'em some and maybe you can get 'em goin'.' Ken said, 'You got a big advantage on me. You go on in

Honey Balls

250 lb. beef with less than 4% fat	1 gal. wheat germ oil
	10 lbs. Brewers yeast
60 lb. honey that hasn't been heated	10 lbs. bone meal with calcium
5 gal. Safflower oil	

Mix together and make into one-pound honey ball energy snacks for huskies.

There are at least 400 one-pound honey balls getting cool in the snow. Raymie remembers rolling out hundreds of these for each Iditarod.

and I'll muscle drive 'em in.' I said, 'It ain't that important to me, Ken. I'll stay here and help get yer dogs goin'.'

And that is what Joe did. Once the dogs were energized with the honey balls, Chase took off and Joe followed—all the way into Nome. Ken Chase came in fourth and Joe came in fifth.

Now here he was leading the 1988 race and thinking to himself with a smile, these honey balls are a powerful energy treat for dogs.

Now that his dogs had their honey ball snacks and were taken care of, he took the snowmachiners up on their offer, crawled into their tent, and promptly went to sleep. When he woke up, who should be in the tent with them? Buser and Butcher both sound asleep.

Meanwhile, everyone in the state was keeping their ears pinned to the radio to see who would arrive first. Would Joe be able to keep the lead? Everyone hoped so.

All three of them—Buser, Butcher, and Joe—headed out for Unalakleet together. Eager listeners were waiting. Night wrapped around the mushers, the wind was howling, and it was cold. Finally, the radio announced that Butcher and Buser were the first two into the Unalakleet checkpoint. What happened to Joe?

He was hot on their tail. His dogs were pulling a heavier sled than the others. Joe always had a heavier sled filled with more than ample gear, but necessary in his mind. He told the radio station in Nome, "I like a little bit of stuff with me just in case. I've been travelin' up here in the Arctic for forty years, and I've still got all my fingers and toes. I'd like to keep 'em!"

The northeast wind was still blowing strong, measuring thirty-five mile-per-hour and bringing the wind chill factor down even lower. Two more mushers arrived at Unalakleet—Swenson and Joe Garnie. The mushers and their dogs could smell Nome, about 250 miles away. Now the race was really on. Buser left first, followed by Butcher and Joe and later Swenson and Garnie.

By the time Joe pulled into White Mountain, his old friend Herbie Nayokpuk had caught up with him. Both were frosted, cold, and much relieved to get to this checkpoint.

"Out of Elim was the worst storm I ever seen," Joe said, as he was caring for his dogs. And if he said that, you know it must have been pretty horrendous. "It was Blackie, Nayokpuk's leader, that got us through that storm."

Nayokpuk agreed. "I think he saved us because that storm was pretty tough that time."

"It stormed so bad that we didn't know if we were goin' to make it or not.

Nayokpuk said he never seen anythin' like it, and he's seen a lot of storms. It was terrifyin', dark, dogs runnin' full bore, jumpin' over big clumps of ice and stuff and the wind about seventy miles-per-hour. It was somethin'."

They stayed at the White Mountain checkpoint four hours and then they were off to Safety, the last checkpoint before Nome. In the morning Buser, Butcher, Swenson, and Garnie were all back on the trail to Nome ahead of Joe and Nayokpuk.

After arriving at Safety, and conceding that the other four mushers would beat them to Nome, Joe and Nayokpuk talked things over and decided to have a race of their own from Safety to Nome. They had twenty-two miles to test themselves and their dogs until they reached the burled arch. Both mushers would give it their all.

Man and team went full bore, each jockeying to be in front. They were both kicking hard, one foot on the runner and one foot kicking the packed trail to give the team more boost. The siren in Nome sounded—music to all the mushers who were coming into town to complete their race over the famous Iditarod Trail! Joe was in the lead but just barely. Coming off Norton Sound onto Main Street, the crowd was jumping up and down for these two perennial favorites. They might as well have been racing for first place.

Joe crossed under the Burled Arch seventy-six seconds ahead of Nayokpuk for fifth place. To have raced 1,137 miles and be only seventy-six seconds apart—wow!

"What a great finish!" yelled Butcher as she watched the two friends race down the street. "This is fantastic. The best race within the Race!"

Susan Butcher placed first for the third time, Martin Buser was second, Rick Swenson was third, Joe Garnie was fourth, Joe Redington Sr. was fifth for the fourth time, and Herbie Nayokpuk was sixth.

"We showed a lot of young mushers how to drive the dogs," said Nayokpuk.

"I don't think anything was better for the race than to have Joe Redington and Nayokpuk out there in the front. I was really rooting for them. I wasn't standing on the break, but I was rooting for them," said Rick Swenson, a four-time winner.

Joe was the fox for most of the race, challenging everyone on the trail, and never daunted by the obstacles nature threw his way. For this he was awarded the Most Inspirational Musher Award and earned the name "Smokin' Joe." What made it the most fun for Joe was that Herbie Nayokpuk was also awarded the Most Inspirational Musher Award, chosen by the mushers in the race.

Perfect. A perfect ending to an almost perfect race.

School children in Nome walking by the Burled Arch with their special sign welcoming all the Iditarod mushers.

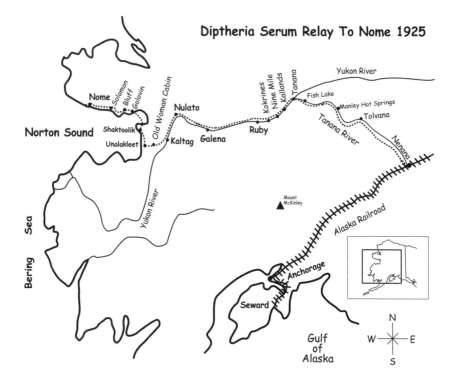

Diptheria Serum Relay To Nome 1925

CHAPTER 33

Always a Promoter

*I am only one; but I am still one. I cannot do
everything, but I can still do something; I will
not refuse to do the something I can do.*

HELEN KELLER

"Joe lives, breathes, and sleeps sled dogs," said Joe's friend, Dave Olson. "He is a rugged, never-stops kind of guy and a good promoter. He gets people to follow."

Joe was always encouraging dog mushers to try their hand at running the Iditarod and he was always willing to help anyone who was interested. In 1974 Tim White read about the Iditarod in a mushing magazine and drove the Alcan Highway from Minnesota to race. He placed twentieth and was the first musher outside Alaska to be a part of the Iditarod Race. The next year the Iditarod became an international race, when Chris Camping from Canada raced, coming in eighteenth. By the 1980s the Iditarod was gaining in popularity. This was also the year Joe received the Governor's Award for his tireless enthusiasm and effort to make the Iditarod race an important part of the culture of Alaska.

"We did a lot to make the race international," said Joe. One way was to support European mushers who wanted to come to Alaska to race.

In 1983 Roger Legaard from Norway brought his family to Alaska to learn more about dog mushing from Joe. An Italian, Armen Khatchikian, ran in three races in the mid-1980s then went back to Italy and started to put together a European long-distance race that was called the Alpirod. Jacque and Claire Philip from France came back for many years. The Iditarod and Joe Redington Sr. were now becoming legendary in the dog-mushing world in Europe. He began thinking about getting sled dog races in the Olympics. Norman Vaughan had talked to him about the 1932 Winter Olympic Games. The Games included dog mushing as a demonstration sport and he came in tenth place. Joe's thoughts would not let go of this idea.

Joe was always available to answer any questions prospective mushers might have. Wherever Joe went, the Iditarod somehow come up in the conversations. He epitomized the "Iditarod Spirit." You could find him at the Alaska State Fair, other dog races, and speaking to interested groups about dog mushing. His dog trucks had signs on them saying Knik Kennels, and carried the different sponsors he had for each of his races. He wore Iditarod patches on all his clothing and gear.

"Joe was the greatest promoter of the Iditarod Race," said Frank Smith. "He was a very amiable fellow."

Jane Storey was a beloved secretary at Sherrod Elementary School in Palmer. She was also a devoted Iditarod volunteer. She was one of a growing number of hundreds of volunteers that were needed to keep this race running smoothly. She started as a volunteer at the Nancy Lake Restart in 1980, working with teams and crowd control. The number of mushers entering the race that year had almost doubled in seven years. Each year her volunteer job description grew. Jane always was very organized, great with names, accurate and precise in her work, and always willing to help out in any way. In 1989 she was a checker at Rainy Pass. She even sang the national anthem at the Iditarod restart one year. "Fortunately, the dogs joined in and the crowd carried the song, so my voice was drowned out," she remembered with a giggle.

"We had mini-courses at Sherrod," remembered Jane. She taught a mini-class on the Iditarod Race. "I took the kids out to Joe's lot to see the dogs and talk to Joe." He loved doing this. "The kids also made little tripods for the tables for the Iditarod banquets." These miniature replicas of the Iditarod Trail markers made everyone smile who attended the banquets.

Then in 1991 Julie Grizzle asked Jane to be the announcer at the Restart. "Please, we don't have anyone to announce." Jane couldn't say no. After the mushers were headed to Nome, Joanne Potts, who also started out as a volunteer and became hooked, said to Jane, "You're going to do this again. You and I are going to learn how to pronounce all their names."

This is how the Iditarod grew into the race of today—volunteers. Lots and lots of volunteers! Pilots, veterinarians, and ham operators volunteered. People from all over the country flocked to be checkers, dog handlers, phone operators, cooks, crowd controllers, the list goes on and on. In 1985 there were over 1,000 volunteers and in 2011 there were around 1,600 volunteers. The Iditarod could not be run without these avid Iditarod fans who give their time, energy, expertise, money, and equipment so freely.

By 1990 Joe's Knik Kennels was billed as the largest sled dog kennels in the world. Every year Joe was leasing teams to mushers from around the world. He sold dogs. He gave away dogs. He bred dogs. The Iditarod was Joe and Vi's life.

In 1993 something wonderful happened. Joe was invited to the XVII Winter Olympics in Lillehammer, Norway. This was a dream come true. There had been demonstration sprint races before, but never a long-distant race in the Olympics. The race would be 300-kilometers. Unfortunately, Joe could not take his own dogs. There was a rule that the dogs would have to be in quarantine for six months before they could race, so Joe would have to lease a team.

"I had to lease a team from Taisto Thorneus of Sweden," stated Joe. And racing those dogs turned into one mighty adventure.

Nan Elliot, a reporter for the *Anchorage Daily News,* went with Joe to Norway. "Nan Elliot was my photographer. I couldn't have made all the connections without Nan," said Joe with a grateful nod. "She knew how to travel."

They flew to Norway first, then headed up to Sweden. "Clear up to Lapland," Joe said. There he trained with Thorneus' dogs and learned, or tried to learn, some basic Swedish dog commands.

"The dogs were terrible fighters. I didn't learn enough Swedish to really be able to control 'em," said Joe.

One word Nan wrote in her article for the *Anchorage Daily News* was *go-po-go-po-ya-ya-ya.* The words were a real challenge and communicating with the dogs was really tough. On the way back from a training run in frustration Joe hollered, "Yum, yum, scoogie," to the dogs. Then he grinned.

"Well," he told Nan later, "the dogs don't seem to understand my Swedish, so I thought I'd try a little Pennsylvania Dutch on 'em. It means 'hurry up'."

But that didn't help either.

"I even wrote it on my gloves, but as quick as I would get in a bind, I would holler gee or haw."

After four days they drove back down to Lillehammer. Joe, wearing Bib #3, was one of the top eight honored mushers and the only American musher to start from the Olympic medals area. The other "fifty or so" mushers were leaving from a big field near the Olympic ski jump. Joe had twelve powerful fighting dogs in his team. His thought must have taken him back to those first Greenland fighters he got from the 10th Rescue over four decades earlier.

When the mushers left the stadium they had to make two right-hand turns. Nan reported Joe as saying, "You know the dogs are kind of like a semi-truck—the back end doesn't necessarily follow the front end. You don't dare use the brake on a sharp turn."

The first two musher's out, Roger Legaard, who had placed tenth in the '83 Iditarod, and Sven Engholm, a European champion, were bent way over their sleds as they headed out, but not Joe. "Then here comes Joe," reported Nan, "standing up all the way—just like a king."

"I managed to stay upright," said Joe, but I felt like I was in a high-speed vehicle with no steering wheel."

Explaining what happened next, Joe said, "The trail crossed the road at right angles." And here was the first problem. The route out of town was supposed to be marked, but something wasn't in place at one of the corners. Joe was following Legaard right down the icy road into downtown Lillehammer, missing the trail out of town.

"Cars were screamin' past you and you're right in the middle with a dog team. Sleds were bouncin' off of cars. We about got killed," Joe said in disbelief as he remembered that horrific ride. And they weren't the only ones making the wrong turn. Joe said he saw lots more mushers. In fact, three years after the race, Joe met a musher from Norway who raced in Lillehammer. The Norwegian musher said, "We were all ending up in town." In fact, he wound up downtown twice.

"I had a terrible fight right downtown," Joe continued. "I ain't seen a dog-fight like that in twenty years, but that probably saved my life." Word got back to the Olympic Committee of the fiasco and they got the mushers and their dogs out of downtown Lillehammer safely.

Nan wrote, "He agreed to join fifteen other mushers in the shorter version. After dropping the fighters—Pernod, Oesten, and Kurt—from his team, Redington started in honorary #1 position, was off again, doing what he does best."

But Joe's dogs were still not very cooperative. Then they staged a sit-down. It was all Joe and another musher, Erik Sundin, could do to coax the dogs to the next checkpoint. "I never had a dog sit down on me in my whole life," said Joe.

But he continued finishing third.

"They gave me a bowl for going down into Lillehammer and survivin'. I was seventy-seven years old and joined five other young Alaskans in their early twenties. Three were downhill skiers and two were cross-country skiers."

This was perhaps one of the most unusual races Joe had ever been in, but one he was very proud to be in because he represented Alaska and the United States of America. And he also had more great stories he could tell.

Nan also recorded this in her article about Joe. "There is not a musher in Scandinavia who does not know the name of Joe Redington and the Iditarod," said Thorneus, the former Swedish champion. "They are impressed that he started the race and that he still races at his age.

"Eric Sundin said, 'He is a living legend.'"

In April of that same year, Joe came up with a new idea for a race—a relay race over the 1925 Serum Run route. "Joe had it all written down in his little book," said Joyce Garrison. Joyce had met Joe in 1992 in Nome, where she was a volunteer cook for the Iditarod pilots, ham operators, and other volunteers. When Joyce got home after the race she said, "My daughter, Melissa, wanted to do the Junior Iditarod. We had six dogs, but needed ten. So we leased four dogs from Joe."

They had a cabin about a mile from Knik Kennels, so in the summer

"Joe was full of inspiration and always taught that there could be no limits to what you could do in life," said Melissa Garrison.

Melissa loved working in Joe's kennel and saw how much Joe loved his dogs, especially Luna. She learned "the bond between musher and dog cannot be changed by anything, even time." *Photo by Joyce Garrison*

Commemorative Serum Relay Race
HC 30 Box 5460
Wasilla, Alaska 99654

This is a Village race to be run by the Village. It has so much history and should be dedicated to the 1925 run from Nenana to Nome;—The greatest mushers ever. Lets show the World we still have good mushers and fast dogs.

and lets get all the Tots shots by two. I have faith in you, and proud to be working with you.

yours Truly,

Joe Redington Sr.

This is the letter Joe wrote to all the villages along the Commemorative Serum Relay Race route. Note Joe's handwriting. He never let his writing get sloppy and he only had a sixth grade education. For seventy-eight years he practiced doing the best he could in all that he did, even in his handwriting.

Joyce Garrison and Joe during the Commemorative
Serum Relay Race. All the villages celebrated
his birthday when he arrived. He turned 78 on
February 1, 1995. *Photo by Joyce Garrison*

Melissa paid for the lease of Joe's dogs by working in Joe's dog lot. "She had the best to learn from!" said her mom. Melissa ended up racing in three Junior Iditarod races.

On one of Joyce's visits to Knik Kennels, she and Joe got to talking about this new race. "Joe had an old bus in the back of his dog lot," she said, "and we sat at the table on this bus and figured out how to put on this race."

The relay race would commemorate the life-saving 1925 Diphtheria Serum Run to Nome on its seventieth anniversary by staging a four-musher team relay race along the same route, starting in Nenana. Each musher would hand over the team's race bib to the next member in the team and continue down the trail to Nome. It was to bring attention to that epic race against death and would be held for all Alaskans to remember.

Joyce was working in Anchorage at the Alaska Native Hospital and suggested that they do something for children. At the time a very low percentage of children below the age of two were immunized in Alaska. This race could

The Ladies of Harley, a part of the Harley Group, donated money for four insulated boxes to carry the serum each team would carry to Nome. From left to right with their road names are: Sherry Wales "The Purple Haze", not known, Diana Parks "The Princess", Stefanie Coppock "Jaz", Liz Tate "Lizard", one of Joe's ever-present puppies, Joe Redington Sr., Patti Bogan, "Peppermint Patty" standing by her bike. *Photo by Joyce Garrison*

Joe Redington with Edgar Nollner, the last surviving musher of the original mushers who carried the serum to Nome in 1925.

"Joe wanted something light, water resistant and warm," said Vi. "He had someone help with his design, then Joe sent the three sizes of boots to Timberline to see if they could make them. They took Joe's idea, changed it a little, and sold their own version of the Redington boot. The air force uses them in their survival gear. Joe also designed his own gloves with no thumbs. Gloves were worn inside. The thumb had the warmth of the other fingers, instead of always freezing up and becoming useless."

Joe with Luna and a former handler, Duke Lambert, standing by a sign for Redington Boots.

promote immunization for all children under the age of two. She contacted the Indian Health Service/Public Health Service and they were willing to get involved. Joyce said, "This was a race to vaccinate."

They contacted people all along the route of the serum run. "It's just going to be down-to-earth mushing with no big expenses," said Joe. "There was no purse, just trophies and a look back into history."

"Iditarod has gotten so big, the villagers no longer can afford the costs necessary to compete," lamented Joe. "The race will be no big expense. It will cost fifty dollars to enter." Then he added, "It costs $30,000 to run the Iditarod." Joe and Joyce got young and old alike to help in the race as volunteers, and joined a statewide "Shots for Tots" program. Each village had a goal to have 100 percent immunization of all children up to the age of two. And that meant they needed to educate each of the villages' clinic nurses and the whole community at each checkpoint. If the village achieved their goal, the health clinics received some gift that they needed such as baby scales or thermometers. All these prizes were donated.

Dr. Tom Porter, a pediatrician at the Alaska Native Hospital, spread the

Sponsors came to Joe to
promote their products.

Santa arrived at the Northway Mall in Anchorage
pulled by Joe's team of Alaskan huskies.

Joe standing in his dog truck painted with all his sponsors.

word with his Harley friends that this idea needed some support and that got the Ladies of Harley involved. They had fundraisers and raised enough money to purchase four specially-made insulated boxes for the serum that each team would carry to Nome. They also commissioned Gretta Duyck of Nenana to bead four moose skin bibs, one for each team.

"I love the Iditarod," said Patti Bogan, one of the Ladies of Harley. "Everyone thought the world of Joe. How could you not like Joe Redington. He's a dog person. And we're dog lovers, too. We adopt pets from people who don't want them any more."

The 1925 Diphtheria Race to Nome and this 1995 Commemorative Serum Relay Race both run to a humanitarian heartbeat. By the time the mushers got to Nome there was 100 percent immunization at every checkpoint.

Today this 768-mile race from Nenana to Nome is now called the Norman Vaughan Serum '25 Run in honor of Vaughan's many accomplishments. Vaughan continued what Joe started—to commemorate an event that saved human lives and will continue to promote ways to save lives through immunization of the young children in our state.

Joe's year was highlighted when he received the Alaskan of the Year Award

Joe with a replica doll of Joe made by Judy Bowers.

in 1995 for all that he did in preserving sled dog racing and the Alaskan huskies, his diligence to bring recognition and preservation to the Iditarod Trail, and now his idea to continue to get the villages involved in healthy activities like sled dog racing and to protect the lives of the children in Alaska now and in the future by educating them about ways to overcome the different health issues they face in their lives, as well as remembering the twenty courageous men and their hardy huskies who raced across Alaska to save the lives of the men, women, and children in Nome in 1925.

This is a picture of Joe at the starting
line in Anchorage for the Silver
Anniversary of the Iditarod. He
would have pictures taken and then
get copies or have postcards made
and sign them to give to people
as souvenirs and to promote the
Iditarod Race. *Photo by Jim Brown*

CHAPTER 34

Iditarod Silver

So a health to the man on trail this night; may his grub hold out; may his dogs keep their legs; may his matches never miss fire … good luck go with him.

JACK LONDON

A very special honor was bestowed on Joe Redington Sr., the Father of the Iditarod. The Iditarod Trail Committee Board voted to have Joe wear Bib #1 for the 1997 race to Nome. This was the silver anniversary of the Iditarod Race and for the first time ever, a musher who was actually running in the race would also be recognized as the Honorary Musher. Everyone recognized Joe's immense contribution to this race, for quite simply, there would have been no race had it not been for his vision, his perseverance through some very tough times, and his determination that there was always a solution for every problem. Joe was going to lead all the mushers down the Fourth Avenue chute wearing Bib #1. He couldn't have been prouder and yet he was quite humbled, too, by the honor. One wonders if he wasn't thinking back to the first race when Leonhard Seppala went out as the first Honorary Musher.

February 1, 1997, Joe turned eighty years old. And now, a month later, he and Vi were in downtown Anchorage getting ready to start the twenty-fifth running of the Iditarod Race to Nome. Joe's team was raring to go.

Luna, the best of the best and his most wonderful and gentle friend and leader, would not be joining him this year. "Luna died just before this year's

Iditarod," said Joe sadly. "He'd been to Nome ten times. I had him in the lead when I passed everyone up in 1988. I ran him in the Alpirod in Europe twice and two Beargrease races in Minnesota. Terrific dog, but he got old." Luna lived to be seventeen years old and was sorely missed.

This year Ruby and Billie were leading Joe to Nome.

Joe, with friendly, heartfelt patience talked to folks and children alike and signed his classy and handsomely bold signature on any piece of paper that was put before him. He always remembered what his dad taught him as a boy—your signature is a representation of who you are, so make sure you write it the best way possible.

The next second Joe was tending the dogs until someone else wanted to stop and chat or get his signature.

In this race, Joe would have Jerry Hickman, an Iditarider, riding in his sled as he left town. Iditariders bid to ride with a musher as part of the fund-raising for the Race.

Then it was time for the race to begin.

"Five-four-three-two-one. Go!" the Iditarod fans called out.

And it was a go for Joe. Ruby and Billie leaped forward at Joe's command and the team was off.

The forget-me-not sky smiled above the snow-covered streets teeming with crowds of excited Iditarod fans. The early spring temperature was a warm twenty-two degrees. All of the huskies in the fifty-three teams racing this year were barking with joy and leaping forward in their harnesses, just bubbling over with eagerness to get on the trail and run—run for the absolute joy of running. After all, running is what these huskies were made to do.

Raymie left Anchorage in thirty-ninth place. He was part of a trio of mushers who ran in the very first Iditarod back in 1973. A lot of changes had occurred in the last quarter of a century. Raymie was joined in this distinguished group by Dan Seavey and Ken Chase.

Cheering spectators lined the streets in Anchorage, all the way along the trail to Eagle River, waving and encouraging each musher as they passed. In Eagle River volunteers were serving moose stew and cornbread to onlookers and mushers alike. The dogs were then loaded into their trucks and driven to Willow for the restart. There wasn't enough snow in Wasilla that year, so they had to move the restart farther north.

Out on the lake at Willow, Joe was talking to well-wishers again right up to the countdown. Then Joe and his team were called to the chute.

Jane Storey led the Iditarod fans in the countdown, "Five-four-three-two-one."

"Mush," Joe commanded in his low, soft voice to his team of sixteen huskies. Ruby and Billie heard the command and pulled forward in their harnesses with a very eager team following. Down the rope-lined chute with cheering fans wishing him a safe journey and waving back, he headed across the lake and into the woods on the other side.

Before long, Willow was left behind and the wide open spaces and quiet solitude of Alaska that Joe and his dogs loved so much were all that there was around them.

The first night out on the trail, father and son camped together near Joe Delia's home on the Skwentna River. The thermometer on the back of Joe's sled read minus fifteen degrees. Cold, but not too cold. Joe took his easy-pulling, purple plastic sled over to where his dog food and straw were stacked, and piled them on the sled. These plastic sleds sure made hauling stuff easy. When the chores were done, he crawled into his sleeping bag, relaxed, and looked up.

The sky was filled with stars. Gazing through the dancing, pale green northern lights was a uniquely wonderful sight. Hale-Bopp, a comet the same age as our sun, was streaking ever so slowly across the wintry Alaska sky. Not until the year 4,358 would Hale-Bopp be seen by viewers again from earth. What a heavenly night.

Meanwhile, Raymie's wife, Barb, had a surprise for them. She had never been to Skwentna. "I got a call from Mike Koskovich. He was part of the Iditarod Air Force, but he didn't fly in '97." The Iditarod Air Force is a group of courageous volunteer pilots who have always flown supplies, dogs, people, whatever is needed along the trail, to support the Iditarod Race.

Barb continued, "He knew I always wanted to fly along the trail. He said to get ready and meet him at Knik Lake." So that is just what Barb did and she took two friends with her. She had a great time surprising Raymie and then they went to find Joe.

"What are you doin' here?" Joe asked with a warm grin. This was a special surprise for him, too.

They visited awhile, then everyone went to get some sleep.

After a short rest Joe woke up in the middle of the night. Raymie had already left. Their dogs loved running in the dark peaceful hours of night. Now it was time for Joe to get with it and set his outfit in order. He gave his team a snack then began packing his sled. When his sled bag was full, there was still gear on the snow to be stored somewhere. But where? This seemed to be a perennial problem for Joe. Over all these years he still had not figured out how to slim down his racing outfit. Being prepared for any circumstance was so embedded in his very being, that parting with that extra tarp or bag of food just wasn't possible.

"I've been known to have more stuff on the Iditarod than anybody. If anybody needed anythin', just go see Joe Redington. He's got it. I cannot get down to where I don't have somethin' to survive with."

There were times when his bag just wouldn't zip up all the way and this was no exception. He did a bit of rearranging, pressed down with his knee to squish his gear, and tried the zipper again. No luck. He couldn't get a good grip on the zipper. So he dug into one of his many pockets, grabbed his needle-nosed pliers, and pulled the stubborn zipper closed or as close as it could get to closing. He couldn't find his bungee cords, so he used a banner from the front of his sled to secure his load. He would figure out how to zip the bag later. Next, he harnessed the dogs, and they were off into the silence of the night.

Joe caught up with Raymie farther up the trail.

"We had a lot of fun in the race," Raymie said. "We'd pull over and have a steak."

Joe dug in his bag to find his omelet pan, put a steak on each side, and cook them up a good meal on his Coleman stove. Mr. Prime Beef sponsored Joe, so he had some great steaks to eat out on the trail. Then the two of them visited over a cup of tea or hot cocoa.

Over the years the Iditarod Race had transformed considerably. The cold, storms, hazards, and extreme beauty remained the same. There was still that wonderful sense of competition that racing brought to each musher. "But," Joe said, "I miss the campfires and the visiting we always used to have along the trail."

The conditions of the trail had definitely improved over the years. In places it was like a highway through the wilderness. The improvements in equipment, dog care and training, the advances in communications and technical support, and checkpoints fully prepared to meet the needs of all the mushers had led to much faster races. All these things were good, but Joe missed those earlier, more slow-paced races, even if they did require a musher to use his or her woodsman wilderness survival skills more often and tax their endurance levels to the max.

But for now, he and Raymie were just going to enjoy themselves and their dogs and this beautiful country. By the time they got through Rainy Pass, they decided they would take their 24-hour layover in Nikolai.

After traveling through the Farewell Burn area, Joe arrived in Nikolai and was handed a big box of Alaska Silk pies. A former sponsor had sent them out on the trail especially for Joe. And Joe loved sweets. He piled it on top of his sled and had Ruby lead them to the outskirts of the village where all the Iditarod mushers were to rest their teams.

In 1992 a new rule had been made. All the mushers had one designated area at each checkpoint where they must tie up their teams. And there were certain buildings where they could sleep, if they chose to do so. They were not to stay in the villagers' homes any longer. This was a big change for Joe and other longtime Iditarod mushers. They loved staying with their friends at their homes. But Joe could understand the need for such changes.

In Nikolai, Joe and Raymie were greeted by old friends. Joe loved getting caught up on what they were doing. One friend had just come back from an unsuccessful buffalo hunt. But that was okay. There was always tomorrow. Now it was time for friends to visit.

A bison herd roamed through this area. They were introduced in Delta Junction in 1928 and then transplanted in 1965 to the Farewell area. They were not only a source of food, but they could be a bit of a problem to mushers as they went through. These bison could be cantankerous, so everyone kept their eyes open and were very cautious. A section of the Iditarod runs through what they call Buffalo Tunnels, where stunted spruce surrounds the trail.

Raymie related an encounter he had with one bison. "A buffalo ran right beside me for a quarter of a mile. It was big and powerful. But it wouldn't come near the dogs. The big, old bull was like a bulldozer. Then it ran up a hill where there were some more of them on top. I ain't never seen any others, but I seen lots of poop and tracks."

As they were talking, Joe pulled out one of those deliciously rich Silk pies. He and Raymie invited their friends to join them up at the school gym for some dessert. There was lots of visiting and laughter and kids were running in and out of the gym. Joe set in to telling some of his famous stories that everyone looked forward to hearing about, some of the pickles he found himself in, and the great adventures he had lived through. The time flew by and everyone had a great visit.

But the race must go on, so Joe and Raymie headed back outside to prepare for the rest of the race. This year the Iditarod went the southern route through Iditarod, Shageluk, Anvik, Grayling, Eagle Island, and Kaltag where the trail heads west over the Kaltag Portage Trail to Unalakleet.

This middle section of the race took its toll on Joe. He had a rough fall near Iditarod hurting his back, so he traveled a little more slowly down the trail. He took longer rests at each checkpoint. Joe said his team had not been used for racing the past few years, as he had started a new business venture offering the "Ultimate Iditarod Tour" to a small group of people who wanted to mush dogs.

This new idea came after the 1992 race. "Lots of people would love to see the trail, but they don't want to race and they don't want to go by snowmachine. They like the history of the dog teams. I thought it was a good idea and I knew it would work." It was called Joe Redington's Iditarod Challenge. For a hefty price, he gave people who wanted to mush dogs along the Iditarod Trail, but didn't have the expertise or weren't able to do it on their own, a guided tour. He took six teams to Nome and provided everything they needed—gear, dog handlers, a cook, and a team of dogs for each client. They traveled fifty or sixty miles a day, took their time, and just enjoyed this wonderful experience with an Alaskan team of huskies as their mode of transportation. Dave Olson had been with Joe locating the original trail in the early 1970s. Now he was the support chief, the one in charge of making ready the campsites, food, breaking trail if necessary, and helping with any other needs the clients may have.

Before the tour began, each musher was introduced to his or her team of Alaskan huskies. Next, his clients quickly learned how Joe taught—the old fashioned way. By doing. Joe's instructions were quite general. He didn't give the specifics. Those were learned firsthand by each client as they headed out on the trail. They all faced some challenges. And they all came back having learned a lot and having even more questions. After a few days, they were ready to head up the Iditarod Trail to Nome. They left Knik two days after the Iditarod Race began. Their trip was slow, adventurous, one they would never, ever forget as long as they lived, and they all made it to Nome. Even though Joe said later, "A lot of people doubted we'd make it."

Much of Joe's life seems to have been about disproving what people thought.

And now here he was, eighty years old, and still racing the Iditarod. He knew Raymie was up ahead and he knew his favorite part of the trail was not much farther up the Yukon River. His spirits started to perk up.

Leaving Kaltag, he crossed a frozen swamp with the Nulato Hills in the background. The weather was good. "It's just plain old beauty," Joe said "Everything is gentle." The snow-covered rolling hills gave him such a warm sense of peace. The next ninety miles into Unalakleet cleansed his soul.

Barb, meanwhile, was flown to Unalakleet by Koskovich. It was a five hour trip from Knik to Unalakleet. "Mike pointed out places along the way. We landed on the ocean and I stayed with my cousin. I saw Raymie and then flew out to Vance's cabin." The cabin was ten miles up the Unalakleet River and Barb went there to wait for Joe.

Snowmachines and sled carried loads of food and gear for Joe Redington's Iditarod Challenge. The clients' sled dog teams followed.

"I was watching a large herd of caribou out the cabin window. They were walking slowly up river. Then they started trotting back. I said, 'There must be a dog team.'" And a short time later, there was a dog team.

Joe got a second surprise. Barb was waiting for him with a big smile. Her visit was a big boost to his morale. Then he was off to his old stomping ground and the village that was a second home to him.

He joined a longtime friend for a steak dinner and had a good visit. Then he left to go tend to his dogs and get some rest. The weather was great. The sun was shining, the wind forgot to blow, and the temperature was sixteen degrees. Perfect. And it was supposed to stay this way for a few days. Joe tossed each dog a frozen fish, which was like giving a child a popsicle on a summer's day. They loved it. Then it was time for a nap. Joe stayed in Unalakleet until the next day, giving everyone a nice rest before the push into Nome.

The wind decided to hold back its fury of previous years and present Joe with a final gift out of Unalakleet—a good fast trail, warm sunshine, and pure beauty. He was in forty-second place. He didn't like being so close to the end of the pack. He'd never been there before and he didn't want to start now. It was about time to pick up the pace.

Exercising like this, running and training puppies, helped keep eighty-year-old Joe fit. The puppies are trying to catch Joe while getting used to wearing a harness and pulling a little weight. *Photo by Jeff Schultz*

He arrived in Shaktoolik an hour and a half earlier than anyone expected. An old friend, Marlin Sookiayak, was surprised and very pleased. He told a reporter from the *Anchorage Daily News*, Frank Gerjevik, that Joe "got me started mushing again after 29 years." A few years earlier Joe came through with the Iditarod Challenge mushers and left him with one of his dogs. Gerjevik reported, "Sookiayak said that Shaktoolik, where dog mushing was fading, now had seven mushers. 'I give him [Joe Redington] all the credit for that.'" Joe left the village with a very satisfied smile on his face.

Joe Redington Sr., Father of the Iditarod, and his team of Alaskan huskies flew across Norton Sound into Koyuk. Leaving Koyuk to Elim he passed through summer fishing camps with many drying racks standing ready for the next season. At Elim Joe took his team out onto the Bering Sea ice passing tall, rocky bluffs. A villager on a snowmachine hauling wood waved as he passed by. The weather was ideal. Joe was feeling great. He had forty-six miles to travel to get to White Mountain. That's when some weather began to settle into the Topkok Hills. By the time Joe got there it was pretty fierce, but Ruby and Billie kept the team on the trail and heading through the storm. At White Mountain he took his mandatory eight-hour layover and then was off to the finish line.

Joe smiled to see the old derelict Swanberg gold dredge still planted firmly on the coast right outside of Nome, and behind it the old White Alice early warning site. Lots of memories. Joe was enjoying this immensely. Then Ruby and Billie led the team off the Bering Sea, up the seawall, into the town of Nome.

The ride down Front Street to the Burled Arch was wonderful.

Just before Joe arrived, Joanne Potts did something very special. She sprinkled red Kool-Aide on the snow at the finish line, a reminder to Joe of the very first Iditarod Race.

Vi, dressed in her warm parka and favorite purple hat, was there waiting with Raymie, Barb, and Ryan, their son, to welcome Joe, along with oh so many of his friends!

Raymie pulled Joe's team aside to let the next musher coming into town pass through the chute. Herbie Nayokpuk was there. "I'm glad you made it," he said putting an arm around his good friend.

Dan Seavey came in fifteen minutes ahead of Joe and he was there greeting Joe. Seavey told Frank Gerjevik, "We crashed and banged, and boomed through the night."

"I don't feel eighty," smiled Joe. He had no aches and pains now, just happiness. "I was hopin' to do better. But I'm well satisfied." Joe said to Gerjevik. "It's a hard race even for a twenty year old."

Joe finished the race in 13 days, 4 hours, 18 minutes, and 57 seconds—his third-fastest time. Out of the fifty-three Iditarod mushers who entered the race, Joe finished in thirty-sixth place and Raymie came in twenty-fifth place winning a trip to Hawaii, because it was the 25th Anniversary of the Iditarod. (Joe's first race in 1974 took him 23 days, 10 hours, 15 minutes, and 57 seconds, coming in eleventh place.)

Then Joe looked around him at his family with love. They followed his dream and raced in the Iditarod and now his two grandson's, Ray Jr. and Ryan, would be the third generation of Redington's to race along the historic Iditarod Trail. Life couldn't be more grand!

Vi with her great-granddaughter, Raynee, spending
time at Vi's pride and joy, the Knik Museum. In
the background is the sled that Joe repaired
with a snowshoe on his McKinley expedition.

CHAPTER 35

He's on the Trail

I do the very best I know how—the very best I can;
and I mean to keep on doing so until the end.

ABRAHAM LINCOLN

Right after Thanksgiving in 1997 Joyce Garrison was listening to the news on TV and heard that Joe Redington Sr. had been diagnosed with cancer. He was trying to prepare for the next Iditarod, but he couldn't because he was so sick. Vi took him to the hospital, where they found out what was wrong. Joyce went over to see him right away.

"We talked again the next day," Joyce said. "We sat down and I said I might be able to be of some help to you. I said I'd be with him through the whole cancer journey, if he didn't give up. We were together every day after that."

But she added telling Joe, "If I ever tell you to drink, you have to drink it. And he would drink, so he wouldn't get dehydrated. He was a good patient. First he had chemotherapy, then surgery twice, and then more chemo. He never complained." Joyce was with Joe for the next year and a half.

Vi drove Joe to his many doctor appointments. She was always right by his side with food, medication, and always her loving support.

Joe was teaching Joyce how to care for the dogs. Every time they came in from working with the dogs, Vi had coffee and snacks ready. "Vi was very gracious and very supportive of Joe," remembered Joyce fondly.

Burt Bomhoff speaking to a crowd of people at the Iditarod Volunteer Picnic that turned into Joe's Celebration of Life.

Iditarod Headquarters the day of the picnic for volunteers and the day everyone remembered and shared stories about Joe Redington Sr., Father of the Iditarod.

The Iditarod Air Force flying over head in tribute to Joe Redington Sr.

Many of Joe and Vi's friends stopped by to visit. Benoni Nelson, a longtime friend and director of the Knik Museum, often visited after she closed the museum. Benoni and Vi had a great time remembering their work on the Iditarod Annual with Dorothy Page. She called Vi, Dorothy, and herself "the girls." They had many fun times together.

"Vi was always caring for her men," said Benoni. This time was no different. "She was giving, conscientious, kind, and feisty at times."

Sitting with Joe and Vi, Benoni would say, "Let's talk story." And they started telling all sorts of stories and laughed and remembered wonderful times to be grateful for. They knew laughter and gratitude were so important in times of difficulty. They changed a person's outlook and brought a healing peacefulness to mind and body.

In the summer of 1998 Joe was told he was cancer-free. Everyone was so grateful. In July Vi and Benoni celebrated their birthdays together, as they had done so many times before. "Yaa hoo!" cheered Benoni. This was a birthday to celebrate.

And Joe? Well, Joe was being Joe. He started his training again, of course. There was another race to run and he was going to be fit and ready for it. He

Joe's headstone at the Wasilla Cemetery. Note the three special objects on the grave representing what meant so much to Joe— the American flag, Iditarod Trail marker, and a dog collar.

Iditarod Race Headquarters with a sign showing where visitors can take a ride with Raymie's Iditarod sled dog team.

Standing by the bronze statue of Joe Redington Sr. are two grandsons that are continuing the Redington legacy by racing in the Iditarod Race: Ryan on the left and Ray Jr. on the right. Raymie, their father stands with them.

walked five miles a day. Joyce was with him. Then they went on twenty mile runs with the dogs.

"Joe had twelve dogs and I had ten," said Joyce. "We went out running dogs at night at ten o'clock when no one was out on the trail. I was scared to death, but then I enjoyed it."

Joyce was taking care of the dogs and Joe was teaching her everything he knew. "He was always schooling me on what I needed to do and how to do it. I was in the best shape of my life."

"We went on a couple of camping trips," remembered Joyce. "We went to Flat Horn Lake. He hadn't been back there in thirty years."

He was out cutting down trees with a chainsaw, so they could build a fire in the woodstove. In the middle of the night Joyce was awakened.

"Joyce, you've got to get outside!" Joe said with some urgency.

The stovepipe had fallen and the whole cabin was filled with smoke.

"We were standing outside in the snow with our longjohns on, because the cabin was too smoky," Joyce laughed.

That winter, when he was preparing for the Knik 200, the cancer came back. Raymie called his brothers. Joee came down from Manley and stayed with his dad. On good days Joe and Joee would sit out in the dog lot and tell stories about his dogs.

Friends were coming over in a steady stream to visit with Joe and reminisce and tell wonderful stories. Rick Swenson, five-time winner of the Iditarod, spent several hours reminiscing wild and wonderful tales along the Iditarod.

Norman Vaughan came to visit. Raymie recalled their conversation, "Joe, when you get to heaven, I want you to start looking for dogs for me, because it won't be long before I'll be there with you, too." They both laughed. Then Raymie added later, "I know Dad got him some pretty good dogs."

Joyce sat quietly nearby. "Listening to their stories was incredible."

Love surrounded this pioneer Alaskan.

On June 24, 1999, with his family surrounding him, Joe closed his eyes on eighty-two full years of incredible experiences and a Redington legacy to be proud of.

A small circle of family and friends brought Joe to the cemetery in Wasilla. Joe told Joee, "I want to be buried in my sled." And that's what happened. Lavon Barve, Burt Bomhoff, Stan Hooley, Jeff Schultz, Bob Sept, and Jim Wood carried Joe in his sled bag and his special Tim White sled. They lowered the sled into the earth, covered it with protective covering, and Lavon Barve sang one last song to Joe.

That afternoon at the Iditarod Race Headquarters was the Iditarod Volunteer picnic for all the Iditarod volunteers, but even more came. This became a celebration of life for Joe. For three hours people were telling stories about Joe. That afternoon brought laughter and tears.

Lavon Barve, who ran his dogs in fourteen Iditarod races and was a printer of many issues of the Iditarod Annual, said, "No Joe Redington Sr., no Iditarod. Joe Sr. was the one who started it, stayed with it, made it happen, and made it a success and a reality. His personality and strong will was the reason."

All over the Valley and the state people were paying tribute to Joe in some way. Around Alaska the flag was flown at half mast. Businesses closed with signs that said: *Closed for Joe Redington* or *We'll Miss You, Joe*. People driving the roads saw these signs and remembered. A family in Big Lake sitting on their porch looked up and saw the Iditarod Air Force fly across the sky in tribute to Joe. They, too, remembered Joe.

Everyone felt the presence of their friend Joe Redington Sr.—trailblazer, pioneer, champion of the Alaskan huskies, and Father of the Iditarod, the Last Great Race on Earth.

Joe mushed his dogs over 200,000 miles, that's eight times around the world. Today the first place trophy for the Iditarod Race to Nome depicts a model of this great musher and his dog, Feets.

To this day, at every Iditarod Trail Committee meeting when roll call is taken, Joe's name is called and the secretary, Joanne Potts says, "Joe's absence is excused. He's on the trail."

Almost seven years later his devoted wife, Vi, joined Joe out on the trail.

Glossary

belay—to hold or stop a climber from descending too rapidly using a rope.

D.E.W. Line—Distant Early Warning system that ran across the top of Alaska generally along the 69th Parallel North. It was a series of radar sites built between 1954 and 1957 as a line of early warning communication defense running across the top of Alaska and Canada to detect any Soviet bombers that would fly over the U.S. and Canada during the Cold War.

C-rations—meals developed primarily as combat rations before World War II and used by the military. They contained three meals each for eight men. There were three meat units and three bread units per man per day. They had cans of meat and vegetable stew, franks and beans, ham, eggs, and potatoes, pork and rice, biscuits, candy-coated peanuts and raisins, caramels, jam, powdered coffee.

carabiner—an oval, metal snap link used to attach to a ropes and other things.

cheechako—from two Indian words that mean to become new, someone new to the country or a greenhorn.

Civil Air Patrol (CAP)—the civilian auxiliary of the United States Air Force. These volunteers provide emergency assistance and fly on search and rescue missions, as well as provide disaster relief assistance.

Cold War—a time of political and military tension between the Soviet Union and the powers of the Western World, mainly the United States after World War II (1947-1991).

couloir—a mountain gully, especially a gully filled with snow.

crampons—metal cleats; claw-like metal attachment fastened to boots to prevent slipping when walking on ice.

Come Gee!—180 degree turn to the right.

Come Haw!—180 degree turn to the left.

Cook Inlet—a small bay extending inland from the Gulf of Alaska. It was named after Captain James Cook, the great circumnavigator from England. He was searching for the Northwest Passage in 1778. On his ship was the world famous navigator William Bligh. It was William Bligh that discovered Fire Island, right off shore from Anchorage and explored Knik Arm and Cook Inlet. They learned that they had not found the long searched for Northwest Passage.

FAA—Federal Aviation Agency.

Gee!—musher's command to turn right.

grizzly—a brown bear. The term grizzly is used for brown bear found inland and in northern habitat. They are the largest omnivore in North America and the males weigh between 500 and 900 pounds. They have been know to run thirty miles an hour.

ham operator—an amateur radio operator.

Haw!—musher's command to turn left.

Hike! All right! Mush! Let's Go!—all commands to go.

jumars—part of rock climbing gear. A device used to assist climbing a rope. It slides up a rope open, then closes metal teeth into rope allowing climber to pull himself up to that point.

layering—In cold and unpredictable weather many layers of clothes are worn trapping heat between the layers for more warmth.

Mount McKinley—the tallest mountain in North America at 20,320 feet in elevation. The mountain is also called Denali, which means "The High One." The first ascent was in 1913 by Hudson Stuck. It was recently recalibrated and a foot in height was added to the height since Joe climbed it in 1979.

Mount Spurr—Mount Spurr is the second tallest active volcano in Alaska standing 11,067 feet. The earth's surface sitting under the Gulf of Alaska is continuously and ever so slowly slipping under the southern coastline of Alaska where there is a fault line in the earth's crust. It is part of what is called the "Ring of Fire" which surrounds much of the Pacific Ocean. Many earthquakes rock the region and about fifty-seven active volcanoes are found along this fault line. Mount Spurr sits right smack on top of it. Every so often it decides to belch out puffs of steam and ash filling the crystal clear Alaska air with its tiny particles of ash.

overflow—found on lakes, rivers, and streams where near-freezing water has seeped upward from beneath the ice to rest on the surface often covered with snow.

sastrugi—hard-packed, sharp, irregular ridges of snow formed by wind erosion. The ridges are parallel to the prevailing wind. They are very common on McKinley and range in size from ripples to over eighteen inches in height.

scratched from the race—when a musher drops out of the race because of some difficulty.

Seppala, Leonhard—Leonhard Seppala was a Norwegian who came to Nome, Alaska, in 1900 during the gold rush. He married Constance, a young woman who loved sled dog racing. He was asked to train fifteen Siberian huskies as a gift to be given Roald Amundsen on his expedition to the North Pole. But World War I broke out stopping all plans and the huskies were given to Seppala. He became known as one of the greatest sled dog mushers in Alaska both as a sled dog freighter and as a champion sled dog racer winning three All-Alaska Sweepstakes races in Nome. Because of his dog mushing skills, he and his lead dog, Togo, were key to getting the diphtheria serum to Nome in 1925 in about five and a half days. They raced through a fierce Arctic blizzard along the Norton Sound from Nome to Shaktoolik and back to Golovin covering 261 miles. Togo was the true hero of this life saving event. It has been estimated that Seppala traveled over 200,000 miles with his dog teams.

snafu—this is a military euphemism meaning 'situation normal all fouled up'.

snub line—strong rope attached to the gang line and drags behind the sled. Used to tie off the sled securely when the team is stopped or the snow hook can't be used in icy conditions.

sourdough——experienced old timer, man or woman, in Alaska. They got their name because they would often be found carrying a lump of sourdough in their pocket, so they could always have a starter for bread or pancakes.

States—a term used for the contiguous, lower forty-eight states in the United States before Alaska became a state and still used today.

10th Rescue—the original rescue unit of mostly Alaskans was established by the Air Force, June 14, 1942. During World War II they saw action in the Aleutian Island Campaign as a boat rescue operation. It was deactivated March 8, 1946, and expanded to the 10th Air Rescue Squadron at Elmendorf Air, November 14, 1952, and was expanded into the 10th Air Rescue Group and then deactivated January 8, 1958. Joe always referred to this group as 10th Rescue.

tides—the tides in upper Cook Inlet reach forty feet. The highest tides in the world are in the Bay of Fundy and are forty-five feet. The average tide around the world is two and a half feet.

tug line—a rope attached to the gang line and to the harness of the dog. It needs to be taunt if dog is pulling.

water glass—A term used for sodium silicate. It was used in the early 1900's to preserve eggs up to nine months. Water glass was mixed in water and the egg was dipped into the water sealing the egg. The water glass kept bacteria out and water in the egg.

White Alice Communications System—This was a system of telecommunications and connected Aircraft Control and Warning sites used by the Air Force during the Cold War. This system linked communication sites across Alaska before satellite communications was developed. This system connected Air Force sites in Alaska like the D.E.W. Line, the Distance Early Warning Line system, the Aircraft Control and Warning System, and was even used for some civilian phone calls. Granite Mountain was one site that was in operation from 1957 to 1976.

Whoa!—command to stop.

wind chill—the wind chill factor is how the air feels on exposed skin when the wind is blowing. The wind blows off the bodies protective heat layer and the faster the wind blows the faster the exposed skin cools. The wind chill temperature is lower than the actual air temperature.

Index